WITHOUT OFFENSE

THE ART OF GIVING
AND RECEIVING CRITICISM

OTHER PRODUCTS
BY DR. JOHN L. LUND:

The Myth We Call Perfection

For All Eternity

Expressions of Love

How to Hug a Teenage Porcupine

Bringing Love Home

Discovering the Lands of the Book of Mormon

WITHOUT OFFENSE

THE ART OF GIVING
AND RECEIVING CRITICISM

DR. JOHN L. LUND

Covenant Communications, Inc.

Cover image © 2004 Photodisc Collection/GettyImages

Cover design copyrighted 2004 by Covenant Communications, Inc.

Published by Covenant Communications, Inc.
American Fork, Utah

Copyright © 2004 by John L. Lund
All rights reserved. No part of this book may be reproduced in any format or in any medium without the written permission of the publisher, Covenant Communications, Inc., P.O. Box 416, American Fork, UT 84003. The views expressed herein are the responsibility of the author and do not necessarily represent the position of Covenant Communications, Inc.

Printed in the United States of America
First Printing: August 2004

12   10 9 8 7 6

ISBN 13: 978-1-59156-608-8
ISBN 10: 1-59156-608-8

To Bonnie—
my friend, companion, and wife

For the cooperation of the entire team at the Church's Copyrights and Permissions Office I remain indebted. This, however, is not an official Church publication. The views herein expressed are my responsibility. Many of the stories, however much they approximate reality, are fictional with the intent to teach.

CONTENTS

CHAPTER 1

CALLED TO LOVE

I was eleven months old the day Pearl Harbor was attacked. With many others, my father joined the navy to redress the wrong of the "day that will live in infamy." My mother joined the workforce, as many women did, to support the troops and to run the factories. She became a telephone operator. Many days she would work twelve hours.

As an only child, I was cared for by my Indian grandmother. Her name was Emma. She was born on the Chehalis Indian Reservation. It was this wonderful woman who changed my diapers, washed me, fed me, and sang Indian lullabies to me when I cried. It was her golden brown, oval face I would see all day long until my mother came home. She called me "Jon-né," a variation of the name John, which I shared with my father and his father. She would say, "O Jon-né, it good to see [you]." Her words were choppy; her love was not. She was always glad to see her grandson. I was her first.

All during those war years I remember my mother and grandmother saying, "When the war is over, your father will come home." I was six when I remember seeing my father for the first time. He was dressed in his navy blues with bell-bottom trousers and a collar with three white lines that went over his shoulders. He was wearing a white cap and spit-polished black shoes.

Because there was a shortage of houses for all the returning servicemen, my father, mother, and I lived in my Indian grandmother's house in Tumwater, Washington. My father spent a year remodeling our future home. When he finished, we left Grandma Em's for our new home in Lacey.

About that same time, I became aware that not everyone had an Indian grandma, and I started to feel embarrassed by her. I noticed that people made fun of the way she talked. My schoolmates would even mock me and call me "Tonto." To top it off, my grandmother had divorced my grandfather, and she drank firewater. (I told my children in later years that to be kissed by Grandma was an "intoxicating" experience.) Regrettably, I became judgmental and unloving.

My Indian grandmother really was a wonderful person. My mother said she never heard her criticize or speak ill of anyone, not ever. Frequently my father would say, "Your grandmother misses you, son. She asks for you all the time. Let's go over and see her." But I judged her unworthy of my love. The five-mile trips between our place in Lacey and Grandma's in Tumwater became fewer and fewer. I stayed away. I was always "too busy" with my friends. I made excuses, and finally Dad stopped asking.

* * *

"Judge not unrighteously, that ye be not judged: but judge righteous judgment" (JST, Matt. 7:2). These are the words the Savior spoke to His disciples in the Sermon on the Mount. Later He would teach, "Love one another; as I have loved you" (John 13:34). He gave the first of these commandments to those in a position to judge; the second was given to all His disciples. In the Church of Jesus Christ, there are just two job descriptions for disciples. One is to "love and judge." The other is simply to "love." Those with the job of loving and judging hold stewardship positions that come with keys. Judgment keys are strictly regulated. Jesus is the Judge of the living and of the dead, and He is a jealous God. This means He wants only those whom He empowers to exercise judgment keys. The rest of us are called only to love, not to judge those who aren't in our stewardship. This doesn't mean we can't use common sense and make wise choices. It means we need to be careful not to judge our fellow beings as being unworthy of our love and fellowship.

King Benjamin warned against withholding love and succor because of self-righteous judgmentalism. "Perhaps thou shalt say: The man has brought upon himself his misery; therefore I will stay my hand, and will not give unto him. . . . O man, whosoever doeth this the same hath great cause to repent . . . and hath no interest in the kingdom of God" (Mosiah 4:17–18). God is the only one who knows the thoughts and intents of the heart (D&C 6:16). Through the spiritual gift of discernment, those so authorized may share God's insight (Ex. 20:5; Acts 10:42; Alma 18:20–35). John testified that even Heavenly Father judges no man but has "committed all judgment unto the Son" (John 5:22). Those judgment keys belong to only those whom Jesus Christ, the head of the Church, appoints. He has called and appointed judges to govern and excommunicate if necessary. The keys to do so are given to General Authorities, stake presidents, and bishops. In fact, bishops are often referred to as "judges in Israel." These priesthood leaders are those who are called to "love and judge." All other members of the Church are called upon to "love" and to give loving fellowship.

In addition to the leadership of the Church, others are given stewardships to judge. In the family, parents—and only parents—are called to love and judge their own children with righteousness. All others in the family—siblings, grandparents, aunts, and uncles—may have opinions or advice, but these people are called only to love, not to judge. It is in this family setting that we learn how to relate to the rest of the world in terms of loving and judging.

Judging outside our stewardship is part of a larger problem of negativity in our society. President Gordon B. Hinckley said,

> There is a terrible ailment of pessimism in the land. It's almost endemic. We're constantly fed a steady and sour diet of character assassination, fault finding, evil-speaking one of another. . . . The tragedy is that this spirit of negativism seems to prevail throughout the country. . . .
>
> This spirit has infected the atmosphere on university campuses and the workplace. . . . The snide remark, the sarcastic jibe, the cutting down of associates—these too often are the essence of our conversation. In our home, wives weep and children finally give up under the barrage of criticism leveled by husbands and fathers. Criticism is the forerunner of divorce, the cultivator of rebellion,

sometimes a catalyst that leads to failure. Even in the Church it sows the seed of inactivity and, finally, in many cases, apostasy.

I come this evening with a plea that we stop seeking out the storms and enjoy more fully the sunlight. I'm suggesting that we accentuate the positive. I'm asking that we look a little deeper for the good, that we still our voices of insult and sarcasm, that we more generously compliment virtue and effort.

I'm not asking that all criticism be silent. . . . I am not suggesting that our conversation be all honey. . . . What I am suggesting and asking is that we turn from the negativism that so permeates our society and look for the remarkable good in the land and times in which we live; that we speak of one another's virtues more than we speak of one another's faults; that optimism replaces pessimism. (Fireside, BYU Marriott Center, 6 March 1994)

* * *

When I was eighteen, I prepared to leave home to attend Brigham Young University. I remember my father saying something about Grandma Em's heart. Under duress, I went to see this loving and caring woman. When she saw me her whole countenance changed. "O, Jon-né, come, give hug." After a forever hug and an "intoxicating" kiss, we sat and talked about my life. "Before [you] go, I give [you a] blessing." She took hold of both my hands and looked deep into my soul. Then she said ten things that I should have written down, but didn't. I remember they all started with, "May [you] always . . ." They had to do with the wind, the fire, the water, and the earth. I recall only the first one: "May [you] always walk with love in [your] heart."

I left for BYU; two weeks later I received word she had died of a heart attack. Later, after a mission to Mexico, I returned home, went to college, married, and became interested in doing research in my family history. I wasn't sure if Grandpa, who was a full-blooded Swede, wanted to be sealed to her or not. But I determined they could work it out with God. My wife, Bonnie, acted as proxy for my grandmother, and I for my namesake grandfather.

What followed was a sacred experience wherein I knew they had accepted this work. I was dumbfounded. How could it be? She drank, she had had a child out of wedlock, her life was not exemplary. A scripture came to my mind: "And also his blood atoneth for the sins of those who have fallen by the transgression of Adam, who have died not knowing the will of God concerning them, or who have ignorantly sinned" (Mosiah 3:11). I wept that I had been so judgmental of a grandmother who had always loved her Jon-né.

By this time, my father had died in an auto accident, and Grandma Em was solely survived by a younger sister, Aunt Mildred, or "Millie." I traveled halfway across the state of Washington to talk to Millie. She was old and very wrinkled. Her eyes were bad. When she saw me, she thought I was my father, who was called "Johnnie Jump Up" after a local flower. When I explained who I was, she said, "Oh, Jon-né!" It was as if I heard the voice of my grandmother again. We talked for hours. Finally, I took both of her hands in mine, just like my grandmother did with me when I was eighteen. I said, "Millie, you have to tell the truth about my grandmother." She paused a long time and finally told me the whole story.

My Indian grandmother had been violated on the reservation when she was fourteen years old. It was a traumatic experience in itself. However, the consequences were overwhelming to a child-woman. She was rejected by both her people on the reservation and those who lived outside. She was very young, pregnant, rejected, and alone. She kept the baby. She started to drink and never fully recovered.

I could hardly see through my tears as I drove to the cemetery. At Grandma Em's grave I knelt and asked her to forgive me for having been so critical and judgmental of her. I have prayed many times for God to forgive me for the greater sin. She was guilty of drinking alcohol; I was guilty of denying her an association with a grandson who should have been loving and appreciative. I also denied myself the association with a loving, nonjudgmental Indian grandmother. Her every deed and act was loving. The words of her Indian blessing haunt me to this day: "May you always walk with love in your heart."

If I could go back, I would stop by her house once a week and give her a big hug and a kiss. I would ask her if I could run an errand for her or take her somewhere. If her lawn needed to be mowed, I would just do it. But I can't. I can't go back, even though I stand on the same quiet earth. I'm confident she and the Lord have forgiven me, but it is still difficult to forgive myself for being judgmental, critical, and unloving. As a grandson, I was never called to judge. I was called to love, and I failed.

This experience has engraved itself upon my heart. I have tried to value all my relationships with family and friends and leave judgment with Jesus and with those who are called to "love and judge." As for me, I am simply called to love.

There is appropriate and inappropriate judgment. A righteous judgment is one that is made within our stewardship and in a manner approved of by the Lord. Do not mislead yourself; when someone is criticizing, he or she is being a judge. Only those people in their appropriate stewardship positions are justified in the use of reproof. All other relationships and criticisms require the permission of the one being reproved before the criticism can be shared.

This book is about applying gospel principles to the ways we deal with criticism. Ultimately, the way we give and receive criticism reflects our discipleship to the Savior, who showed us not only what we are to do, but also the "way" we are to do it. He declared, "I am the way, the truth, and the life" (John 14:6). Thus, discipleship is twofold. First, it is doing what He has asked us to do. Second, it is doing it in an appropriate manner.

Assignments for Chapter 1

1. Make a list of people you may have neglected who need your love.

2. Write a letter or make a phone call to each of them and tell him or her of your love.

CHAPTER 2

LIVING A HIGHER LAW:
AVOIDING INAPPROPRIATE CRITICISM

There is no such thing as constructive criticism. To construct is to build, to edify, or to put together. To criticize is to tear down, to find fault, to condemn. These two words describe two separate and opposite processes, like going up or going down. It is not possible to go both up and down at the same time. The thought of criticism being constructive is absurd. It makes as much sense as saying someone is a wise fool.

However, the phrase "constructive criticism" is used constantly in our society. We may think that if we say negative things in a way that sounds nice, there is nothing wrong with criticism. We can easily see, though, that the worldly approach to criticism hasn't improved society. It is only when we seek to live a higher law of love that we can better understand others and our relationships and avoid inappropriate criticism.

THE WORLD'S VIEW OF CRITICISM

New knowledge, even when it is based on tried and true principles, rarely improves human behavior. When we have been told something loud enough or long enough we tend to believe it, even in the face of overwhelming facts and evidence to the contrary (see D&C 93:39). For years the medical profession practiced bleeding their patients. By strong oral and religious tradition, it was believed that all sickness was in the blood. Even people with secular education could not be disabused of the idea. After all, it was taught at Harvard, Oxford, and the Sorbonne. It seemed perfectly logical to doctors and professors that if the blood of a person was impure and the cause of sickness, then draining off as much blood as they could would give the patient a better chance of survival.

Who knows the untold millions who died of bloodletting? Perhaps their doctors thought, "Oh well, maybe if a little more blood had been let, the patient would have lived." Similarly, who knows the untold millions whose self-worth has died from the critical "bloodletting" of well-meaning people? Maybe those well-intended people thought, "Just a little more criticism, and their self-worth will improve and their behavior change."

Imagine living at a time when most of the doctors, teachers, rulers, and the mass populous believed in bloodletting, and someone discovered they were in error. What happens to people who make statements that run counter to popular folk belief? They are punished and rejected. How well were Copernicus, Kepler, and Galileo received when they announced that the earth revolved around the sun and not the sun around the earth? They feared for their lives. It doesn't matter that they were correct. They went against tradition and religion. Traditions die hard. For hundreds of years people believed the earth was flat. They continued believing that even after the earth was proven to be round. Most people would chuckle at this. How could any sane, rational, intelligent human being continue to maintain some obviously ludicrous notion in the light of all the evidence to the contrary? So it is with constructive criticism. In our society, the educated, the rulers, and the masses generally believe and practice "constructive criticism." It approximates a religious tenet of faith. It is as difficult in our time to convince someone that there is no such thing as constructive criticism as it was to convince former societies that the earth revolved around the sun and was not flat and that bloodletting was ineffective.

But criticism in and of itself never builds anything positive. It never has and it never will. The process of construction is separate from the process of demolition. There are companies that deal exclusively with demolition of buildings. Other companies specialize in building construction. Then there are companies that do remodeling, which involves aspects of both processes. Remodeling is a tricky business. The remodeler must ensure that the basic integrity of the structure remains intact. The part to be remodeled is carefully dismantled. The wrecking crew is cautious to demolish only that part of the building that is to be replaced. Tearing down requires a different approach than does the construction phase. The process is either tearing down or building up. They cannot be done at the same time. Understandably, a demolition crew showing up to tear down a structure that was scheduled only to be remodeled would have a lawsuit on their hands. When we, as well meaning people, share "constructive criticism," we are sending in the wrecking crew.

That most people use the phrase "constructive criticism" in their vocabulary is a testimony of their misunderstanding of the two processes involved. It is also evidence of the difficulty of changing firmly entrenched traditions. Except for its redundancy, "destructive criticism" is a more accurate phrase to describe criticism, which is a tearing down process. "Positive reinforcement" best describes the constructive process, which is an edifying one. Criticism does not reinforce a positive behavior; it describes a negative one. Constructive criticism is a myth in the worst case and a misnomer at best.

Those who emphatically defend criticism as "constructive" tend to idealize it. They see it as a right, a moral imperative, a positive thing, and a responsible behavior. Their legacy is a trail of devastation. If they could only step back and view the consequences of their acts of destruction. If only they would objectively measure the practical effects of criticism, they would conclude that the cure was worse than the illness. Though it may be done in ignorance, the real tragedy is the damage done to the self-worth of those they criticized. Before doctors washed and sterilized their hands, many people died of infections carried by them from patient to patient. As well-meaning as they might have been, compassionate and self-sacrificing though their efforts were, the consequences were deadly. Like those doctors, well-meaning people continue to kill self-worth, believing they are doing a good thing. They have failed to understand there is no such thing as constructive criticism.

The Criticism Myth

The irony of ironies is that many people criticize in order to change behavior. They truly believe that describing unacceptable behavior will make it go away. Criticism, especially uninvited, unauthorized, improper criticism, only antagonizes, alienates, and creates hostility toward the giver of criticism. Many self-righteous givers of criticism feel divinely appointed and comfort themselves by knowing they and God are on the same side. So they tilt at the windmill as if this critical quest were some holy mission and they must expect rejection from others as the price they must pay for being "right" as the emissary of truth. Tragically, it is self-delusion. If criticism worked in changing behavior, there would already exist a perfect utopian society. There are things that change human behavior. However, describing behavior in critical terms, nagging, complaining, or preaching through critical words and deeds does not change it.

Whether the criticism is delivered verbally or nonverbally, the person being criticized will most often reject the person who is doing the criticizing instead of changing behavior. Criticism is a poor motivator. Change occurs when the motivation for change comes from within. Most criticism comes from the outside. Trying to change people is just like trying to teach a pig to sing. There is an old saying around the farm: "Don't waste your time trying to teach a pig how to sing. First of all, it doesn't work, and secondly, it irritates the pig." Even properly communicated criticism can "irritate the pig." Improperly given criticism may not only irritate the pig but turn it into a raging boar.

Coaches who exert the most profound positive effects upon their athletes are the ones who believe in their players, who genuinely care about them and accept them and inspire them to greatness. Those coaches who use fear, intimidation, ridicule, criticism, sarcasm, and other belittling ploys seldom inspire anything but resentment and hostility. Sincere praise and acceptance inspire behavioral change. Great coaches know that the talent, ability, and capacity lie within the player. Getting the athlete to believe in himself or herself is the key, because the motivation to become his or her best is the highest form of motivation.

Once an athlete is convinced that the coach wants more than just to win games, the athlete can accept properly given criticism that focuses on improved performance. The coaches with the best winning records have one thing in common. They love to see their athletes overcome adversity and become their best. The player who feels he or she is just a pawn in the coach's eyes plays the game to avoid ridicule but not to become his or her best.

Criticism may achieve a degree of control and conformity. But control and conformity are not change, and the critic deludes himself if he believes otherwise. Often criticism will result in a double standard wherein the criticized party lives one standard in the presence of the critic and abides his own standard when away and on his own. A sponge, for example, can be made to conform to whatever outside pressure is exerted upon it. Yet, as soon as the pressure is released, the sponge will assume its previous shape. Control is not change. So it is with the pressure of criticism. A critical person may be able to temporarily impose conformity, but as soon as he leaves, the person reverts to previous behavior.

For centuries, tyrants have controlled the masses through fear, threats, and criticism. What they also created were underground movements against themselves. Of course, there will always be opposition, even to a benevolent king. But should our enemies be those of our own house and heart? Enemies may arise from the outside, yes, but why would any of us want to create enemies of our friends, family, or coworkers by being a controller of others through constant criticism? Some people change in spite of criticism, but not because of it. Forced conformity is a shallow victory and a poor substitute for cheerful conformity rendered from a willing heart.

Criticism not only is ineffective, but may well be counterproductive because it weakens a person's self-worth as well as his confidence. Criticism, invited or not, lessens the probability for real change. One of the true dangers of listening to criticism day in and day out is that those so treated come to believe they are not worthwhile, they can do nothing right, and they may become hyper-self-critical. Soon, there won't be a need for anyone else to criticize them, for they will do it themselves. Self-criticism becomes self-fulfilled prophecy, and all of the evidence brought by others is now joined by all the evidence one amasses against oneself. And self-worth plummets.

It has been noted that grandparents get along better with their grandchildren than with their own children. This has led to a humorous saying: "Grandparents and grandchildren are natural allies, because they share a common enemy." Interestingly, most grandparents focus on loving their grandchildren and not on changing them or criticizing them. This change in expectation on the part of the grandparents makes them less frustrated and more capable of loving. The result is that grandparents are more effective at creating an environment conducive to change with their grandchildren than they were with their own children. One wise grandpa observed, "I just love 'em, I don't try to change 'em. There are plenty of folks out there who will try to change 'em, but there aren't very many of us who will just love 'em." The message: the world's "antidote" to improper behavior isn't what will build the best relationships. Perhaps there is another answer.

Good Intentions

I mentioned earlier that some demolition is involved in a remodeling project. Likewise, there is a time and a place for criticism. There are issues and behaviors which need to be corrected. Yet if criticism is so toxic, how could its use ever be appropriate? Think of criticism as a tiny vial of vaccine. Applied as a small dose in a specific area, it will immunize and thereby strengthen the person. If too great an amount is administered, it will inflict the very illness it was intended to prevent. Administered appropriately, it produces positive results; administered inappropriately, it kills.

There was a farmer in Idaho who sued his well-meaning neighbor for the misuse of a deadly chemical herbicide. It seemed that his neighbor had sprayed both sides of a long, private road common to both farms with an herbicide to kill all of the weeds growing there. In his desire to destroy the weeds, he failed to consider the side effects of the wind. As a result, thousands and thousands of dollars' worth of damage was done to the cash crops growing in the fields. The wind had carried the deadly herbicide far beyond its intended application. The judge assigned to the case disregarded the good intentions and focused on the destruction he had caused. The well-meaning neighbor paid a great price for his ignorance.

So it is with criticism. Well-intended critics need to be very cautious. Criticism intended for a specific application often has side effects that outweigh the assumed benefits. Our attempts to remove the faults or negative behaviors of others may result in the destruction of their self-worth, motivation, and positive outlook on life.

We tend to apply criticism generally when only specific criticism is appropriate. Some think that criticism is like a sword. Though a sword is a weapon of war, they think it can also be used for helpful purposes, such as harvesting grain or chopping wood. But when all is said and done, a sword is a weapon. Its primary purpose is to maim, injure, and destroy. A surgeon would be mocked if he came to the operating room with a sword instead of a scalpel. Criticism is often used as a sword when it ought to be used as a scalpel. Exactness and great care are required by qualified hands if the operation is to be successful.

Parasitism or Symbiosis

Relationships, like the human body, have a life of their own. They can die or they can be wonderfully healthy. A relationship is a connection between two people. The best relationships are those where each person helps the other become his or her best self. It is instructive to think of a relationship as having a shared existence, a mini-ecosystem of its own.

Parasitism is a term used in biology to refer to the association of two living organisms in which one organism feeds on the body of another, usually at the expense of the host. It may or may not kill the host, but it always weakens it. Parasites usually can't survive independently. Some human relationships are composed of one and sometimes two parasites that stay together for fear they will not survive alone. When both are parasites, they consume one another.

The opposite is true of a symbiotic relationship. Symbiosis is the association of two living organisms that exist for the benefit of each other. Most lichens, which are composed of an alga and a fungus, are examples of symbiosis; the alga provides the food, and the fungus provides the water and protection. In this association, or relationship, neither is harmed, and both benefit. It is truly a mutual improvement association. Relationships, whether husband–wife, parent–child, employer–employee, brother–sister, or friend–friend, have a life of their own. The whole is equal to the sum of its parts. A relationship will never be greater than the part that each of us contributes to make it successful. When both parties are committed to a mutual benefit that helps each to become his or her highest and best, a symbiotic relationship exists. This is the ideal. Anything less will ultimately turn one or the other into a well-meaning parasite.

A normal relationship infected with criticism will begin to consume itself. Is criticism so much a part of our behavior that it can't be eliminated? Is it too late to heal any of our relationships harmed by it? Criticism gnaws at the sinews of any relationship with its destructive effects until it leaves the relationship lifeless or miserable. It creates deep wounds and makes enemies of one-time friends, coworkers, and family. So many have lived so long with intense criticism they cannot imagine a relationship without it. They were seriously criticized as children. Why should marriage be any different? Why should our own parenting be any different? Why should any relationship we have with friends, coworkers, or family be free of what has become a way of life? It shouldn't be that way; and fortunately, we can improve our relationships with others. The Lord has taught us better ways to build our relationships.

A HIGHER LAW

Criticism can be appropriate if you remember three things. One, in most cases, only those with stewardship positions should correct those under their care. Two, criticism by people in nonstewardship positions should be inspired. And three, those corrections should be carefully and lovingly meted out and then followed by large doses of love and support. These ideas are part of a higher law of criticism, which will be discussed more thoroughly throughout this chapter and the rest of the book. These principles help us to overcome frustration in relationships, to seek to motivate change in righteous ways, and ultimately to respect others as the Savior would have us do.

Overcoming Frustration from Unmet Expectations

Building and maintaining an ideal relationship is difficult and can be frustrating. Learning to deal with this frustration in a Christlike manner is essential. We can start by trying to understand the reasons for frustration in relationships. All frustration comes from unmet expectations. There is no such thing as a frustration that is not tied to an expectation. Sometimes the relationship between an expectation and a frustration is obvious, like expecting a raise in pay at work and not receiving it. But some of us set ourselves up for frustration by creating unrealistic or unreasonable expectations. For example, one might think, "If you really love me, you will be able to read my mind and know how I am feeling." This is both unrealistic and unreasonable. However, because the expectation cannot be met, the person will be frustrated.

Frustration is a normal first response to an unmet expectation. The issue is what happens to the frustration. There is an entire range of human emotions we can choose from in reacting to frustration, including resentment, hate, anger, disappointment, resignation, despair, depression, determination, desire for mediation, relief, and love. Frustration is a first reaction. Choosing an emotion is a second reaction. Choosing a behavior is a third reaction based on the emotion we choose. Often, the time it takes to go from frustration to acting out is a millisecond. As demonstrated in the examples below, the process seems almost automatic. But these reactions involve choices. Practice and habit entrench negative behaviors as well as positive behaviors.

Reactions to Unmet Expectations

		Reaction 1	Reaction 2	Reaction 3
EXPECTATION	SITUATION →	THOUGHT →	FEELING →	ACTION
Clean house	Mess	Lazy people	Resentment	Criticism
Perfect driver	Traffic ticket	Unfair cop	Irritation	Sighing
Kind words	Insult	Hurt	Sorrow	Prayer
Happy marriage	Divorce	Disbelief	Resignation	Withdrawal
Good grades	Failed class	Bad teacher	Hostility	Yelling

Thought is the father of the deed. Thoughts generate feelings, and feelings generate behavior. Nearly all behavior is learned and will vary by family tradition. But what if we trained ourselves so that our first reaction to an unmet expectation was to have a brief conversation with God, a prayer in which we thank Him or ask for strength, patience, and the courage to act appropriately?

Through prayer and determination we can learn to act and react differently to unmet expectations. It is possible to teach an old dog new tricks if the rewards are great enough. Developing a positive, spiritual attitude and thinking in loving ways is a great reward. However, becoming our best self and being an influence for good in the lives of our loved ones is an even greater reward. It is possible to have love and discipleship to Jesus as the motivating first reaction. It is possible to have, as a second reaction, empathy and compassion. As the third reaction, it is possible to apply the teachings of Christ—to obey a higher law.

Jesus introduced such a higher law in the Sermon on the Mount: "But I say unto you, Love your enemies, bless them that curse you, do good to them that hate you, and pray for them which despitefully use you, and persecute you; that ye may be the children of your Father which is in heaven" (Matt. 5:44–45). This is the Savior's relationship advice to us.

In a telestial society, returning good for evil is considered weakness, foolishness, and something at which to scoff. Among the intellectuals it is considered "Pollyanna-ish," unrealistic, and a utopian dream. For the disciples of Jesus, the higher law is a lifelong quest to "always have his Spirit to be with them" (D&C 20:77). Our relationship with Him improves, but so does every other relationship in our lives. We come to see life as He sees it and understand others as He does.

Beverly Changes Her Perspective

Beverly knew that dinnertime was always a disaster with a two-year-old, a four-year-old, and a six-year-old. Tonight her mother-in-law was coming for dinner, and Beverly could feel the tension rising within her as the time approached six o'clock. She was short-tempered with the children and upset at her husband for inviting his critical mother for dinner. She was confident that the pot roast would be adequate, but she was concerned about the children and their behavior at the dinner table. Envisioning anything between three little angels politely sitting at the dinner table and a screaming food fight, she had "awfulized" the evening before it even began.

Beverly's expectations were off the chart. She was literally sick in her stomach by 5:30 P.M., and then she realized it wasn't worth it. She was becoming more and more angry at her mother-in-law, and she wasn't even there yet. Beverly stopped and asked God to help her not be held hostage by her fear of her mother-in-law's criticisms anymore. She felt strengthened in her prayer and determined that kids were kids and her mother-in-law would just have to like it or lump it. Either way, Beverly was going to be fine and civil and kind toward her mother-in-law.

The kids behaved as usual, and there were only two glasses of milk that got dumped on the floor, instead of three or four. The two-year-old did manage to get the carrots in both his hair and that of his four-year-old sister. The six-year-old was sent away twice for teasing his sister, but all in all it was a fairly typical dinner experience. The mother-in-law did make several suggestions about child rearing, but they went in and out of Beverly's mind, and she was not upset. Once she changed her expectations to please the Lord and herself, she eliminated her frustrations.

We cannot live a higher law without a spiritual perspective to guide us. In the gospel, there is an eternal perspective which speaks of faith and hope and of doing what we can do with the tools we are given. One of the greatest tools we have is asking in prayer for the companionship of the Spirit. The highest law cannot be lived without the strength of the Holy Ghost. The Lord has made it very clear: "Pray always, and I will pour out my Spirit upon you, and great shall be your blessing" (D&C 19:38).

To seriously embrace the power of the gospel requires that prayer become an attitude, not just an event. This was the intent of the teaching of Jesus that "men ought always to pray, and not to faint" (Luke 18:1). At another time, after much praying, the Lord commanded His disciples to stop praying and yet to carry the attitude of prayer in their hearts (see 3 Ne. 20:1).

Many of us pray only in a crisis. We wait until there is a problem and then we call on God. And then He can count on not hearing from us until the next crisis. Some of us actually believe we are imposing upon God if we pray too often. This is not the case. Remember, it is an evil spirit that teaches a man not to pray (see 2 Ne. 32:8–9).

With only a short time to spend with His disciples on the American continent, Jesus spent much of it praying with them and for them and for their children. Then He gave them this admonition:

> Behold, verily, verily, I say unto you, ye must watch and pray always lest ye enter into temptation; for Satan desireth to have you, that he may sift you as wheat. Therefore ye must always pray unto the Father in my name; and whatsoever ye shall ask the Father in my name, which is right, believing that ye shall receive, behold it shall be given unto you. Pray in your families unto the Father, always in my name, that your wives and your children may be blessed. (3 Ne. 18:18–21)

This is what is meant by having a prayer in our hearts always. We will discuss the important role of prayer in a later chapter. For now, suffice it to say that prayer helps in changing our expectations to focus on pleasing God and loving our fellow beings. The focus should not be on pleasing man or on changing others. By changing our focus, we can respond to frustrating situations and trials with love and compassion instead of criticism.

Another aspect of living this higher law is to turn away from the negative behaviors that could impede positive relationships. If we habitually respond critically to life's unmet expectations, we need to ask the Lord's forgiveness and pray for His help to change. Repentance is usually thought of as cessation from sin. The word *repent* is actually Greek in origin and means to "change the mind" or, quite literally, to "think differently." The Hebrew equivalent means to "turn away." True repentance involves turning away from the natural selfish man and thinking with an eternal perspective.

One woman was heard to say, "I'll be happy when everyone I love does everything I want them to do, the way I want it done." This woman's expectations are setting herself and all of her loved ones up for certain frustration. She is also setting herself up to be frustrated with God, because if God doesn't give her what she wants, why pray? In this single statement, she transfers her power *not* to be frustrated to all the members of her family or to God. Chances are she will not feel loved by God or the family, when in reality she is loved by both. Her family may avoid her (though God never will). It is painful to be avoided by the very ones she professes to love. But her family doesn't want to be around someone they feel they are constantly disappointing. Nor do they want to be around someone who is constantly criticizing them. What a sad, sad life this woman is having. In the end, reality will teach her that too many expectations will rob her and her loved ones of a better relationship. The only hope for this woman is to change her expectations and to humbly approach God in sincere prayer and ask to be directed by the Spirit. With the Lord's help she can alter her behavior and love the people around her instead of judging them.

When critical people are asked why they are criticizing, they frequently respond, "Because the person being criticized was wrong, and so I wanted to correct his or her behavior, answer, issue, or statement." That is the way the critics look at the situation, but their way is not the best (or Christlike) way. We usually criticize because someone is not measuring up to *our* expectations, and we are frustrated. We want other people to do what *we* want them to do, what we think is right and proper. Therefore, when others are not performing to our expectations, we lash out, nag, gripe, complain, murmur, cry, swear, and verbally attack them. Another response to unmet expectations is to sulk, pout, withdraw, and give our loved ones the silent treatment.

Ironically, while the critics' lips drip with verbal venom, their hearts are hoping that someone will love them, care for them, respect them, accept them, appreciate them, want to be with them, and, yes, even overlook their weaknesses.

There are more productive ways of communicating frustration, and they work. Criticism doesn't remove frustration; it only describes the behavior causing the frustration. Frequently, criticism feeds its own fire, and what started out to be a contained burn becomes a massive forest fire burning out of control. It's a description, not a cure. If we do not find appropriate ways of communicating our frustration, we will eventually and invariably increase our critical natures and destroy our own effectiveness as communicators. Less effective communication means that our frustrations will increase until we explode into anger or tears of resentment. We may implode into sulky, silent oblivion, where despair dwells and everyone gives us a wide berth. It need not be. There is a way to properly express our frustrations and to do so in such a manner that both the giver and receiver are edified. As we come to better understand others and our role in their lives, we can better see how love—the Lord's antidote to frustration—will improve our relationships and help us be less critical. We will better live this higher law of love when we develop such understanding and respect for others.

Motivating Change

Recognizing how difficult it is to change ourselves, we see how impossible it would be to force others to change. As we come to see how we and others are motivated, however, we can better assist change in a positive way, rather than resorting to critical behavior. After an entire semester of graduate-level study in a class on motivation, we learned that people are motivated by fear, by reward, and by love. Fear is a short-term motivation that goes away once the threat disappears. Fear can create temporary control and conformity, but not permanent change.

Rewards are much more effective and long lasting as motivators. Short-term rewards, long-term rewards, and intermittent rewards keep people focused on goals. (Rewards are not bribes, however. A bribe is by definition illegal and immoral.) Heavenly Father has promised a reward of heaven and eternal life for those who endure to the end of their mortal lives and learn to love God and their fellow beings. In the Doctrine and Covenants we find the Lord's promise: "How oft have I called upon you by the mouth of my servants, . . . and by mine own voice, . . . and by the voice of glory and honor and the riches of eternal life" (D&C 43:25). To abide with loved ones in the presence of God is a life-changing incentive.

But without question, love is the greatest motivator of them all. Love of country, love of family, and love of God will continue to inspire men and women to lay down their lives. The power of love can inspire us to eliminate all inappropriate critical messages. As Christ understood this power of love, it is no wonder that He gave this higher law: "A new commandment I give unto you, that ye love one another; as I have loved you, that ye also love one another. By this shall all men know that ye are my disciples, if ye have love one to another" (John 13:34–35).

Uninspired and inappropriate criticism kills love. Criticism is toxic to love and must be shared only under the direction of the Holy Ghost. There can be no exceptions, but there must be room for forgiveness. In understanding motivation, there are two very important questions that need to be addressed. First, "How do we learn?" and second, "What are my limits in effecting change in another?"

How We Learn

By understanding how people learn, we can save an enormous amount of time and frustration by not expecting people to learn in ways that won't work. Uninvited criticism will not change behavior. It is a waste of time, and it "irritates the pig." The basic ways we learn are by observation, by instruction, and by experience.

Learning from observation. For sighted people, this type of learning occurs as we process what we see with our eyes. We see how things respond to natural or man-made laws and thereby understand our world. This type of learning also includes learning from the examples of others. By watching the examples of others and by mirroring those behaviors, we bring the behaviors into our life experiences. The old adage "Monkey see, monkey do" reinforces the importance of proper role models. It is true that "what we do speaks so loudly that others cannot hear what we say." Observation, example, and role models are primary ways of learning.

Learning by instruction. If learning by observation is an eye experience, learning by instruction is fundamentally an ear experience. It requires an open mind and a willing heart. Sometimes people will ask, "Isn't criticism a form of instruction?" The answer depends upon the open mind and listening heart of the receiver. Criticism that does not respect the "space" of the receiver is rarely instructive and most often counterproductive. Invited criticism, properly given, may be instruction. Uninvited criticism seldom is.

The basic truth is that we can only teach to the level of willingness of the listener. If the listeners are unwilling to learn, we will not be instructing them, but preaching to them. It will be a lecture. Without their minds being willing and prepared, the information we give as parents, bosses, Church leaders, or friends will not qualify as learning by instruction.

Consider the example of Jim and his wife. For twenty years, Jim's wife has nagged him about throwing his dirty clothes in a pile in the bedroom. It's not important to Jim. It doesn't matter. He has heard the same message for twenty years. He doesn't lack the knowledge; he knows how to pick up his clothes. He just doesn't understand the value of picking up after himself.

Hearing is only learning if the listener is open to change and willing to do so because life will be better. Jim's wife could try punishment, withholding love, or any number of threats and coercions. They probably have been tried and didn't work either. Jim's wife could come to him and say, "What could I do for you that would make it worthwhile for you to pick up your clothes and put them in a clothes hamper in the laundry room?" Now she is dealing with the real issue of Jim's motivation. Negotiating for change will work. Ill-given criticism as a motivator of change is a waste of time.

Learning by experience. This is learning by feeling, by touching, by bumping into boundaries and learning our limitations. It also includes learning by trial and error and by the suffering we endure from natural consequences. This is learning at the school of hard knocks. Some of us who will not learn by observation or by instruction are left to learn by the tough lessons of life. A young child may be told to watch out for the corner of the table or else she may hit her head and it will hurt. The child may even watch another bump his head, and only after two or three knots on her own head does she learn for herself to watch out for the corner of the table. The following story illustrates learning by experience.

The Spoiled Son

The story is told of a wealthy man who wanted to teach his spoiled and irresponsible son the value of money before dying and leaving his estate in the hands of his son to squander away. One day, the father called the son into his den and told the son to go out and earn five hundred dollars and bring it back to him, or he would cut him out of the will. The troubled young man went to his mother with this tale of woe. The mother counseled him to wait for a month, dress up in work clothes, and give his father five hundred dollars that she would provide.

The time passed, and the son met his father in the den. He was wearing work clothes and gave to his father the money his mother had given him. The father promptly took it, walked over to the fireplace, which had a cozy fire burning in it, threw the five hundred dollars into the flames, and said to the son, "This is not your money. You did not earn it by the sweat of your brow. Now, go out and earn five hundred dollars and bring it to me, or I will cut you out of my will."

The young man returned to his mother and complained about the failed ploy. "This time, wait a month, cover your face and clothes with some dirt, and be sure your father sees you leave for work every day. Then sneak back to the house, and I will give you another five hundred dollars to take to him in a month." The time passed, and the son met the father in the den. Once again, the father took the money and threw it into the fire and said to his son, "You must earn this money yourself."

Totally bewildered and frustrated, the young man went to his mother and asked how the father knew that he had not earned the money. They concluded that the father must have spies watching them, and therefore there would be no way out except for the son to get an honest job and earn the five hundred as the father had directed. So it was that the son went forth and found employment and worked hard in the heat of the day, and after a month he met a third time with his father and gave him the five hundred dollars he had earned. The father took the money and threw it into the fire. Immediately, the son jumped to the fire and began to pull out his hard-earned money. "Yes," said the father, "this is money you have earned."

Some people can learn by observation, and some can learn by instruction, but there are some people who will learn certain lessons only by the things they suffer (see D&C 105:6). Most lessons are best learned by natural consequences instead of artificially imposed ones, such as criticism (notice that it is not one of the basic methods of learning and instruction).

Understanding Our Stewardships

Knowing how people are motivated and learn is only part of living the higher law. We must also recognize our role in the learning and changing process. What our role is in that process has everything to do with stewardships. Using the paradigm of the family, we could say that all stewardships fall into one of three categories: parent–child, brother–sister, or child–parent. In other words, we are either a parent, a sibling, or a child.

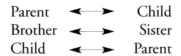

Many times we change hats and play all three of these roles in a short period of time. While serving as a bishop, I was in a meeting with other bishops discussing regional welfare needs. My relationship to them was brother to brother. The stake president called me out of that meeting for a short consultation. My relationship to him was son to father. On the way back to the bishops' meeting, a ward member stopped me to share a concern. My relationship to the ward member was that of father to child. In a matter of minutes I had played all three roles.

The relationship of an employee and his or her boss would be child to parent. Coworkers would be brother to sister. All those who are in authority over a person would be in a parent role. Those for whom one has no responsibility would be at a level of brother–sister. The husband–wife relationship is a brother–sister stewardship, where both parties are equals.

Continuing to use this model, let's pursue the question, "What gives us the right to criticize?" Is there a right, an inherent privilege, a just prerogative for parents to criticize children? Yes, when done properly. Is there a right for children to criticize parents? Under certain conditions, when inspired by the Holy Spirit, the answer is yes. Is there a right for a brother to criticize another brother? Possibly. There are circumstances when the Holy Ghost might inspire criticism, such as in the case of reconciling with an offended brother. However, none of us has a blank check to criticize.

Those of us in the parent role probably have the most latitude in criticizing our children, but even here it is not an unconditional freedom. Those in brother–sister or child–parent roles would have less leeway and more narrowly defined parameters for giving Spirit-directed criticism. For further clarification, let's discuss a couple of these relationships in depth.

Spouses. Husbands and wives have a brother–sister relationship. They are equals, and that is the way the Lord would have it. The Apostle Paul admonished, "Nevertheless neither is the man without the woman, neither the woman without the man, in the Lord" (1 Cor. 11:11). There seem to be but few who understand it that way. Unfortunately, many husbands take the role of "father" toward their wives and think they are not equals. Such a man treats his wife as if she were a child and tells her what she "should," "needs," and "ought" to do, or say, or be. He feels free to criticize and somehow feels as though marriage gives him that "right." In all brother–sister/husband–wife relationships, that which gives us a "right" to criticize is the *permission* of the one being criticized.

In all fairness, there are many women who parent their spouses. They assume a "mother" role over their husbands without the slightest regard for coequality. They tell their mates what they "should," "need," and "ought" to do, or say, or dress, or be. This is a major violation of the gospel principle of stewardship. When either husbands or wives assume that marriage gives them the right to be disrespectful or to act as a parent to their spouse, they are wrong and are exercising unrighteous dominion. It is the opinion of most professionals that a major contributor to divorce is inappropriate criticism. Furthermore, it sets a terrible example for their children, who will likely grow up to perpetuate these same behaviors.

Parent–Child. A few verses of counsel in Ephesians apply to the parent–child relationship.

> Children, obey your parents in the Lord: for this is right. Honour
> thy father and mother; (which is the first commandment with

promise;) that it may be well with thee, and thou mayest live long
on the earth. And, ye fathers, provoke not your children to wrath:
but bring them up in the nurture and admonition of the Lord.
(Eph. 6:1–4)

A parent should lovingly raise his or her children, reproving them
only when necessary. Children should honor their parents, accepting
the reproof in the manner in which it was given. There is a way to
criticize and to do it effectively. Appealing to our position as a parent,
breadwinner, homemaker, spouse, or boss is not the effective way.
Claiming to be right, or to be bigger, or to be smarter, or to be faster
does not qualify us to criticize. Loving someone or caring deeply does
not give a right to correct. We must remember that only in the most
desperate, life-threatening, extreme circumstances should we offer
uninvited criticism without receiving first the permission of the Holy
Ghost *and* the one being criticized.

To daily find ourselves criticizing our loved ones, employees, and
friends is to assume an ego of god-sized proportion. Where is the
child that needs a constant diet of criticism? Where are the employees
of whom it can honestly be said they need daily criticism to be
productive? Criticism is a cancer that will kill love or sap its strength
as certainly as any parasite attacking its host's body.

When people (including children) say they are not being treated
right, they almost always mean they do not feel respected or valued
because of the critical things said to them. Choosing to respect all
persons and their right to their own opinions, attitudes, and space
used to be called courtesy and regard. If we are part of a relationship
where courtesy, regard, and respect have been lost in a maze of
unkind words, then we need to repent and again enthrone words like
"please" and "thank you."

The Role of Respect

Once we understand our role in the lives of others, the final part
to living the higher law is respect. Respect is a gift. It says more about
us as the giver than the receiver. Respect is given to others because we
as the givers of respect are good people. To treat each person with

respect is a higher law. Those who continue to live the law of an-eye-for-an-eye will soon find the blind leading the blind. Those who believe that respect must be "earned" will eventually discover that no one can be respected. The reason for this is the lack of absolute standards for evaluating who deserves to be respected. Ultimately, even self-respect will disappear if the standard is "perfection or nothing."

One of the great messages from the play *Pygmalion,* and later the movie *My Fair Lady,* was how people respond when treated with respect. What is it about that movie that lifts the human heart? Why do tears come into our eyes as someone triumphs over a difficult background? What is it about the human spirit that calls us to a higher and better self? Why do we cheer when common people act in an uncommon manner and rise to the occasion, such that a hero is born? Another great story that shows just how life changing the simple gift of respect can be is the tale of Don Quixote.

The Possible Dream

In the play *Man of La Mancha,* Don Quixote possesses an impossible dream. He sees the world through rose-colored glasses. He treats people with respect and sees in them a higher and better self. Surrounded by the mirrors of reality which bespeak of filth and wretchedness and of man's lowest nature, he encounters a barmaid known by many men. Her name is Aldonza, literally a "dunce," a slow-minded dullard. Don Quixote refuses to call the barmaid "the dumb one." Instead, he calls her Dulcinea, or the "sweet one."

"No," Aldonza responds. This is a case of mistaken identity. She has been confused with someone else. She is, in her own eyes, a dumb one, a dunce. And as long as self-perception is reinforced by those around her, she continues to act the wench. She concludes he is nothing but a crazy old man, deluded by his impossible dream. But Don Quixote refuses to see her in any other light. There, in the darkened heart of Aldonza, he sees sweetness.

So it is that Don Quixote, undaunted by the jeers of others, continues to see the best in Aldonza. He treats her with respect and is mocked and scorned for it. Even Aldonza at first mocks the old fool. However, as time passes and as with unrelenting respect he treats her as "a fair lady," she cannot resist enjoying, if only for a moment, what it feels like to be respected by someone, even a crazy old fool. Her reality rejected all rights to be respected, as judged by everyone. Ah, but his reality was to respect her. He chose to respect her independent of others, independent of her own self-esteem, and independent of all circumstances. His respect for her was a gift.

Then a marvelous transformation occurs. Aldonza becomes Dulcinea. Self-respect is born because Don Quixote gifts her respect. She likes how it has made her feel inside. It feels better than anything else.

At the very end of his life, Don Quixote questions for a moment if he has just been a fool after all. His friends assure him that he has not been a fool. He dies firm in the faith of his "possible dream." As Dulcinea leaves the deathbed of Don Quixote, a former acquaintance calls out to her, "Aldonza, Aldonza." Her eyes flash. She fixes her gaze upon the suppliant and announces with conviction that her name is Dulcinea.

Some will discount the entire notion of respect being given as a gift. Yet Jesus taught us to respect all men and women because that is what a good and righteous person should do regardless of whether others have earned it.

The Savior and Respect. The Savior gifted respect to all people. He is man's great Exemplar of living this higher law. He cared not for gender, social status, or race. There are many occasions in the Bible when Jesus gifted respect to people who might not have been considered "worthy" by others.

Of the Samaritan woman at Jacob's well, Jesus asked for a drink of water. The Samaritans were hated by the Jews as a mixed race of apostates with a heathen core. The Samaritan woman was surprised that Jesus would even speak to her. She seemed doubly shocked that He would ask her for a favor. She said, "How is it that thou, being a Jew, askest drink of me, which am a woman of Samaria? for the Jews have no dealings with the Samaritans" (John 4:9).

Later in the conversation, He addressed her as "woman," which was a title of respect (John 4:21). He addressed her as such even though He knew she had been divorced five times and the man with whom she was now living was not her husband. Did such a moral vagrant deserve to be treated with respect? Apparently, the Savior thought so.

Jesus followed this pattern of gifting respect to the woman who was taken in adultery. After the scribes and Pharisees dropped the stones they had planned to throw at the woman, Jesus was left alone with her. Notice how His love and respect is manifest in a gentle correction to repent, rather than harsh criticism:

> When Jesus had lifted up himself, and saw none but the woman, he said unto her, Woman, where are those thine accusers? Hath no man condemned thee? She said, No man, Lord. And Jesus said unto her, Neither do I condemn thee: go, and sin no more. (John 8:10–11)

In all relationships, whether parent, sibling, or child, people we love deserve to be treated with respect as sons and daughters of God. Respect is a standard of excellence in each relationship to which we are a party.

Common Consent and Criticism. Part of respect is the noble principle of common consent. It is a key to a healthy human relationship. When we make common consent part of our relationships, we send a message that we respect the space, the time, the privacy of another. Amos, a wonderful Jewish prophet, posed a question: "Can two walk together, except they be agreed?" (Amos 3:3). Will we be open to criticism if we don't agree to hear it? It's not likely.

Those seeking to criticize must gain the consent of the person they wish to reprove. By treating people with respect and by asking for and receiving permission to criticize, we have achieved common consent. This sense of oneness and agreement is the unity Jesus prayed for in behalf of His disciples (see John 17:20–23). How do we approach a brother with whom we need to reconcile? How do we leave our gift at the altar and make amends (see Matt. 5:23–24)? It requires humility to ask for forgiveness. It requires courage to let go of an issue which destroys unity.

The intent is clearly that two people walk a common path. The moment one party becomes insecure and fearful and wants to exercise any degree of compulsion upon the other, the journey of true common consent is over. The principle of unity is a characteristic of a Zion community and of a Zion relationship. Inappropriate criticism does not achieve unity.

RECOGNIZING AND AVOIDING
INAPPROPRIATE CRITICISM

Often we believe we are living this higher law of love and respect without recognizing that we are still being critical. Before closing this chapter, let's clarify what things are included in critical behaviors. These behaviors range from the obvious, such as sarcasm and being contrary, to the more difficult to detect, such as telling the "truth." All are inappropriate forms of criticism we must strive to avoid.

Sarcasm

This is the act of making fun of a person in a clever way. The word originally came from the Greek *sarkazein,* meaning, literally, "to strip the flesh."

People justify the use of sarcasm because it is infused with humor. The one being sarcastic can always claim humor as his or her objective, while removing a strip of flesh from the one lashed by the tongue of the critic. For example, a husband might say, "I like your hair, dear. I wonder how it would look if you combed it." It's a funny line. Everyone laughs. Even the one who is the target of the joke may laugh, but inside, where self-worth abides, she bleeds a little and feels less worthy as a human being. Sarcastic words demean and belittle. They are meant to injure. Thomas Carlyle, the famous Scottish essayist, stated quite accurately, "Sarcasm, I now see to be, in general, the language of the Devil."

Analysis, Appraisal, Evaluation

Because these terms are primarily logical and not emotionally based, they frequently seem justified. Objects can be evaluated, and ideas can be and ought to be subjected to the scientific method. Performance can be measured, and productivity can be evaluated and appraised. But when analysis, appraisal, and evaluation are applied to people, they become subtle forms of criticism. Masking criticism in this way is no less devastating to the one being judged. Because the criticism has been intellectualized, it appears more "constructive," more palatable, and less harmful. Not so. People are human beings with basic emotional needs of acceptance, love, belonging, and appreciation. The most self-actualized person on earth, if subjected to a consistent diet of criticism, will eventually retreat to a fantasy world of books, TV, or sports; become a hermit; or fall apart emotionally.

Questions

Many people feel that if their criticism is placed in the form of a question, it is not really criticism, but only a question. But the "didn't you?" "haven't you?" "aren't you?" questions have an implied criticism within the asking because the assumption is that they "should have." Does this mean that we can never ask a question? No. It means we must become aware that many of our questions are implied criticisms and therefore destructive.

Direction Giving

"I wasn't being critical, I was just giving them directions." When we are always giving directions to a loved one or an employee, especially uninvited opinions or uninvited directions, it is interpreted as a lack of confidence by the one who is receiving the directions. "Do this, do that, don't do it that way, watch out for that car, turn left, pick that up, put that down . . ." ad nauseam.

Be aware that direction giving can be a form of criticism because it assumes the person is not capable and needs the critic's special knowledge. It is our nature to want to please. Children want to impress their parents with their newfound knowledge and skills. Employees like to impress a boss with newfound ways of improving production performance. Excessive direction giving stifles creativity. It sends a message of incompetence to the receiver. For example, a small child is just learning how to tie his shoes.

"No, no, you are doing it all wrong. Do it this way!"

The tone of voice is critical, and the directions are saying, "You are incompetent."

Some psychologists suggest that those who are always giving directions are themselves quite insecure. The constant giver of directions may want to feel needed. "I declare, I just don't know what goes on here when I'm not around to keep this place together. I don't think you could find your head if it weren't attached to your neck."

In giving directions, the same principle of respect applies when invading the space of any person or relationship. First, ask for permission. Genuinely petition.

"Honey, would you like me to show you how to tie that shoe? I remember how frustrated I used to get when I was your age when my fingers didn't do what my brain wanted them to do."

"No, I want to do it myself."

"Okay, but if ever you need some help, let me know."

If we as direction givers are not careful, we will develop dependency-centered children or employees. They will feel incapable of doing anything. Also they will fear that whatever they do will be wrong. Therefore, they show no initiative, no creative efforts. Now we, as the direction givers, have created our own nightmare. More and more of the decisions have to be made by us. People are always coming to us to have us tie their shoes, since we are the only ones who really know how to do it right. Now, as direction givers, we can complain that nothing gets done unless we are there to tell everybody what to do. If we are in this pickle and want to get out of it, we must stop giving uninvited directions. "I'm sure you can figure it out; and by the way, whatever you come up with will be fine." If it's really not fine, then don't offer it, but begin to let go and foster independent behavior. "Come up with a couple of options, Dave, and bring them back to me."

Being Contrary

Some of us don't realize that contrariness is a form of criticism. One form of contrariness is also the practice of correcting facts. For example, one person will be telling a story, making a statement, or relating an incident. The one "being contrary" will jump in uninvited to tell the truth of what happened, to correct an error, or to set things straight. Contrariness may also manifest itself as taking the opposite side of an issue for the sake of argument. Both kinds of contrariness are intimidation, a kind of emotional arm-twisting. Being contrary is rude, insensitive, and a violation of the space and relationship of the speaking person. But the contrary person feels justified in displaying this lack of respect because he is "right." He or she is just "being honest." It is purely and simply a form of criticism. It is argumentative, frequently arrogant, imprudent, distracting, and very, very unattractive.

Since contrariness is so widespread and can be difficult to perceive in ourselves, let us examine this form of criticism in a few scenarios. First, let's observe Mike and Jane. Mike and Jane are talking to each other. Mike is remembering how they first met. The feelings Mike is experiencing are warm and loving toward Jane.

"I remember when I first saw you after graduating from high school."

"No," said Jane, "you first met me at a dance in high school."

"Anyway," said Mike, "the first time I saw you that summer, you were sitting on the fender of my best friend's car. I thought how lucky he was to have such a pretty girl sitting . . ."

"It wasn't your best friend's car; it belonged to his dad. And I wasn't sitting on the fender; I was in the front seat."

Whatever good feelings Mike had for Jane are now gone. He is angry with her. She, on the other hand, feels totally justified and wonders why he can't be honest in telling the story. She is blinded by "contrariness." After all, she was only setting the record straight, telling the truth. He shouldn't be so sensitive. He is only angry because she caught him in a lie. "I wish he would not exaggerate. It is so embarrassing when he tells these stories and gets all the facts mixed up." So goes the reasoning of Jane. However, contrariness is contradiction and an invasion of the right of the speaking party to relate his or her own first-person experience. Jane should have asked for permission to "set the story straight."

Most of the time, it is unwise and inappropriate to be contrary. It is especially rude to interfere between two others involved in an ongoing dialogue, even if one is a part of a conversation. Contrariness is counterproductive to a healthy verbal interaction. Most people afflicted with contrariness have a "debate mentality" and see their interruption as being intellectually honest, open, and forthright. In other words, they see their contrariness as a strength and are often puzzled as to why others don't see it the same way.

One time a man raised his hand during one of my lectures and asked, "What am I supposed to do when I hear somebody lie or misrepresent a story I know to be different?" He went on to say, "If I just sit there and say nothing, am I not agreeing with what is being said? Isn't my silence tantamount to approval?"

These were great questions and observations. This is how I responded to his genuine concerns. I told him that the best response is to wait until you are alone with the person relating the story and then express your concern. If you truly feel you cannot wait to correct the story, ask for permission to interrupt and wait for approval before you speak. Failure to do so shows disrespect, and because you have openly challenged someone in front of others, the predicted outcome is a hostile attitude on the part of the speaker. At best you will be perceived as rude and insensitive, and at worst as arrogant and self-righteous.

When you do speak, allow for someone else to perceive the same situation differently. You could say, "It always amazes me how people can experience the same situation and come away with a different point of view. If anyone is interested, I would be happy to share my version of the story after the two of you are finished." Don't be surprised if no one wants to hear your version. After all, you weren't invited into the conversation. However, unless it is vital or truly important, it would be better to say nothing. It would serve your best interest to model the principle of respect for the right of another to see things differently rather than to project a "know-it-all" attitude.

Another form of contrariness is taking the opposite view or the opposing side. These people see themselves as defending the underdog or bringing balance to an issue. For some, it is a way of thinking and an extremely difficult bad habit to break. Consider the story of Tom and Kathy. Tom is expressing his frustration at his work and how unappreciative his boss is, when Kathy begins to defend Tom's boss by pointing out the pressure he must feel by having all the responsibility.

Kathy is being contrary. She is trying to make the situation better by arguing with Tom about his feelings. What Tom really wants is understanding, but what he gets from Kathy is, "You should be grateful you have a job."

Contrary people defend and try to explain an opposite view when the real issue is the right of someone to express his or her frustration. The situation of Tom complaining to Kathy calls for understanding and not for solutions.

Ideally, contrary thoughts are best written down. They are best reserved for a later, private moment. And of course, permission to express the contrary thought should be sought for first. Disregard for this counsel will lead the people who are afflicted with contrariness to stumble blindly through life. They will feel as though they are wonderful communicators. In reality, they are passed over for advancements or promotions because they are perceived as brash and lacking in sensitivity. Many contrary people are gifted, talented, bright, capable, and superior in performance. Therefore, contrariness becomes a liability, not a virtue or asset. Although they may be right—and certainly are in their own eyes—they are not as useful to the company, organization, or relationship as they might have been. Instead of abandoning the behavior, they abandon the job, or the marriage, or the relationship. They move on with the same self-defeating behavior to inflict it upon the next job, the next relationship, until it too crumbles under the weight of contrariness.

"Truth" as Criticism

"I'm not being critical. I'm only telling the truth. I'm just being honest." There are many who use this form of criticism. In the name of truth, they brutalize others. The critic hides smugly behind the truth, regardless of its consequences. Some people feel that because something is true, they are justified in printing it in the newspapers or saying it. Unfortunately, they do not understand that there is a higher and nobler principle than truth: it is to edify. The Lord has said, "And that which does not edify is not of God, and is darkness" (D&C 50:23).

You could yell "fire" in a crowded theater, and there might only be a fire in a wastebasket. It is true. You could expose young children to every detail of sexual perversion known. It is true. But we need to take a more careful approach. We don't try to hide the truth from truth seekers, but we need to consider whether they are prepared to receive the truth. Many truths should only be shared according to the preparation of the recipient (see Alma 12:9–11). In the Doctrine and Covenants we read: "For they cannot bear meat now, but milk they must receive; wherefore, they must not know these things, lest they perish" (19:22).

It is well established that overcoming weaknesses, bad habits, and inappropriate behavior are best accomplished by building up the self-worth and self-confidence of the individual. Sincere praise for productive effort and positive reinforcement are the basis of modifying behavior. Blasting someone with his or her faults, even though what is said is true, is nonproductive and certainly not edifying. It is true that in the heat of anger or frustration, one might say truthful things in order to hurt or make another feel bad.

Wisdom and common sense require that criticism be used sparingly. We should criticize so seldom that when we do, we will be heard. The frequently critical person is tuned out before the message is delivered. Nor is it justified to criticize in the name of being honest. The so-called open, honest relationship, where both members feel free to express their concerns, often provides a forum for the more critical partner. Maybe the fundamental question that ought to be asked is not, "Is it honest?" but, rather, "Is it edifying?" Will it ultimately be uplifting? Will it be good for the individual and the relationship? If a criticism does not qualify under the latter, it should not be spoken at all. Maybe grandma was right when she said, "If you can't say something nice, don't say anything at all!" This rule applies to self-criticism as well.

Self-Criticism

Many people are their own worst critics. Their self-worth is so low they have a difficult time receiving love from others. Frequently they lack a certain kind of graciousness; this lack causes them to reject sincere compliments from others. When we don't accept ourselves, it is very hard to believe that others can accept us. However, other people enjoy fishing for compliments by being self-critical. The hope is that others will come to their emotional rescue. This type of self-effacing is a ploy to receive acceptance. Consider the following dialogue:

"Did you make that dress?"

"Oh, yes, but it's just something I threw together. It's not very good at all."

"No, no, I really like it. I think it's beautiful. I wish I were that creative."

There is a role for reflection, self-evaluation, and personal improvement. However, this is best accomplished alone or when we are counseling with a friend or professional. Most self-criticism is disingenuous. It is a self-defeating behavior, a bad habit, and a poor attempt at humility. Many times it is an effort to protect ourselves before someone else has a chance to tear us down. All of these scenarios are emotionally unhealthy. There is appropriate self-criticism which has as its goal to become one's highest and best self. But it is a false humility to deface oneself in front of others. Personal, private soul searching and reflection upon becoming a better self is the kind of self-evaluation which may lead to improvement. In an appropriate environment, confessing one's faults may be appropriate (see James 5:16). Making comments like, "I'm so dumb," "I never do anything right," or "I can't believe how stupid I am," is not productive. If someone gives you a compliment, just say thank you and practice being gracious as well as not being self-critical.

THE TWENTY-FOUR-HOUR CHALLENGE

Usually, when I am presenting this material in a seminar and reach this point, people begin to feel they can't say or do anything. They've learned all about criticism and the higher law but don't quite know what to do with it all. They imagine they have done just about everything wrong. They feel there is no hope for them. They are convinced they have made a mess out of everything. Many would just as soon take another assignment other than mother or father, wife or husband, sister or brother, boss, friend, and so on. It is a bit overwhelming. It is easy to get discouraged and even depressed. However, there is hope.

For example, most people are unaware that their chances for increased health begin immediately when they stop smoking. Their health doesn't change when they think about not smoking anymore.

It doesn't change when they make a commitment not to smoke. Their health improves only when they *actually stop* smoking. So it is with criticism. Try it out; you'll probably find that you're a happier person.

For a period of twenty-four consecutive hours, refrain from criticizing anything or anyone, even yourself. It isn't as easy as it sounds, nor is it as difficult. When you "slip," you must start your twenty-four hours over again. One man moaned, "It will be the Millennium before I get this assignment right."

Unless it is a life-or-death situation or the job absolutely requires a critical review, abstain from all forms of criticism. This includes sarcasm, uninvited opinions, analysis, appraisals, evaluations, insights, questions, direction giving, and contrariness. There are a few people whose employment requires them to be critical—for example, building inspectors, supervisors, and quality control people. People in these special cases are exempt as long as they are on the job. But the criticism must relate directly to the work. And lastly, even if the criticism is justified, ask for and receive permission to criticize.

The majority of people do not succeed in their first attempt. Do not be too discouraged if you have to start over again thirty or forty times. Remember, do not criticize yourself, spouse, children, parents, coworkers, the boss, the government, or dumb drivers.

Warning! There are some traditionally hard times at which you will be prone to criticize. These include times when you are tired, hungry, driving, or under a time constraint. Getting the kids to bed may push parents over the line. So be forewarned.

You may ask, "What if a critical thought enters my mind, but I don't say it aloud? Does it count against the twenty-four hours?" If a critical thought enters your mind and you get rid of the thought in a moment, then it does not count and you do not have to start your twenty-four hours over. If, on the other hand, you let that critical thought stay in your mind and you develop it into a full production with quadraphonic sound and vista vision, then you must start your twenty-four hours over again.

One lady who asked this question after a seminar looked puzzled for a moment, glanced up at her husband who was standing by her side, and said, "Okay, I'll try to go for twenty-four hours without criticizing or dwelling upon a critical thought." Then, pointing to her husband, she said, "But he will never make it!" There was a pause. "Oh dear," she said, "I will have to start my twenty-four hours over again, won't I?"

Her husband did not verbally respond. However, he frowned at her, and a slight sneer formed at the edge of his mouth. He also pointed his finger at her in a mocking manner. This, of course, was nonverbal criticism. I pointed out to him that nonverbal criticism was also a reason for him to start his twenty-four hours over again.

The two of them walked off, muttering, "This is going to be harder than we thought."

"Yes," I said. "Overcoming a lifetime of habit is hard."

In one study involving more than eight hundred people, after three days, only twenty people had been able to go for a period of twenty-four hours without criticizing. They were even permitted to count sleeping time as a part of the twenty-four hours! The responses from those who made it were interesting.

"It was easy," said one woman. "My husband and son were out of town."

One man in the group observed, "I was so criticized as a child that I decided I would not be a critical adult."

One man suggested that we form an organization called "C.A.," or Critiholics Anonymous, and hold weekly meetings.

One mother reported that after she had gone twenty-four hours, her teenage daughter, who was unaware of her mother's efforts, asked if she was feeling okay.

Because criticism is the accepted mode of communication in our culture, it is difficult to refrain from criticizing. Most people have been raised in a critical environment. Many have been taught to be critical and analytical and to subject people and things to the scientific method. Some have difficulty speaking a single sentence without criticizing or being sarcastic. We shouldn't be too hard on ourselves if we don't succeed in a week. This is a difficult assignment.

Why Should I Try?

Seeking to live this higher law is worth the effort. These are the results you should experience by abstaining from criticism and seeking to live the Lord's higher law:

- Increase awareness of the critical nature of society
- Become aware of your own compulsion to criticize
- Experience the power of self-mastery

There are several answers to the question, "Why should I try to stop criticizing?" Here are some of the more important ones:

- To lay the foundation for love instead of rejection
- To increase the number of positive interactions
- To be more emotionally safe as a person
- To be more effective in communicating
- To reduce unnecessary conflict
- To enjoy greater peace and harmony in all relationships
- To have the Holy Ghost as a companion

Assignments for Chapter 2

1. The first assignment is to ask a loved one how he or she would like to be approached when you have a criticism to give that you believe would make him or her a better person or improve the relationship.

2. The second assignment is to give your spouse or child a way to approach you with a criticism he or she believes will make you a better person or improve the relationship.

3. Be gracious and just say "thank you" when someone pays you a compliment.

4. Take the Twenty-Four-Hour Challenge.

CHAPTER 3

"THE GREATEST REVELATION
THAT GOD HAS EVER GIVEN TO MAN"

Mastering the *art* of giving and receiving criticism in the Lord's own way endows you with a new power. It is the power to love, to nurture, and to inspire. Imagine children, friends, and loved ones feeling confident in your love. They come seeking your counsel because there is trust. They truly believe their eternal best interest is vouchsafed in you. When you master the *art* of giving and receiving criticism, you enter into a new zone of safety. Loved ones are attracted to safe people and are willing to receive counsel from them and follow it. They will seek for your blessings and for your approval. This is not a pipe dream. It is the reality of those who have experienced love and have sought the Lord's counsel in their relationships. They have learned to live the higher laws. It is through principles of righteousness that these people have learned to live together in love.

EXPERIENCING LOVE

This power to love, nurture, and inspire must be experienced in order to be fully appreciated. Otherwise, it is like trying to describe the taste of salt to someone who has never tasted it.

"Does it taste bitter?"

"No."

"Does it taste sweet?"

"No, it tastes salty."

How does anyone describe the exhilaration of achieving a lifelong goal, or seeing the beauty of a sunset at sea, or witnessing the miracle of childbirth to one who has never experienced it? The view from the top of the mountain is made sweeter by the difficulty of the climb. It is not easy to climb the mountain. But the experience is worthwhile. Our quest at controlling the tongue is a similar experience—difficult but worthwhile.

Mastering the art of giving and receiving criticism is learning to be in control of the words you speak and speaking them in a kindly way. Controlling the tongue may be the single greatest step toward self-mastery and discipleship to Christ. The rewards include a greater love for all, and that love will be returned. It will come without compulsory means.

Contrast the picture of loved ones seeking your counsel with that of loved ones avoiding you. For most of us, giving criticism is not about finding fault. It is about changing a behavior in a loved one. The fundamental desire of our hearts is to be helpful. Even as a messenger of reproof it is our intent to help the individual improve. Armed with a pure motive and with good intentions, we are baffled at how poorly our critical insights are received. What most of us as critics lack are what can be called "approaching skills." We simply blurt out our criticism because of our own frustrations. But what is worse is that most critics do not feel the need to improve approaching skills. Rather, we feel that the receiver of criticism should be able to take it. After all, if the criticism is true and in the best interest of the one being criticized, why can't he or she just thicken his or her skin and take it? However, disregarding the feelings of others by blurting out criticisms is not what Jesus would have us do.

When Jesus said, "I am the way," He was teaching us the manner in which we should journey through mortality on our way to our eternal home. How we approach another, how we treat each other, and even how we criticize is a part of that eternal journey.

A BETTER WAY: THE GREATEST REVELATION

Jesus came to show us a better way to deal with each other. The natural man is selfish. He is "an enemy to God" (Mosiah 3:19). In order to be "a friend of God" (see Isa. 41:8; D&C 93:45) and not an enemy, we must learn how to be in the world and not of the world. We must associate with others, but not treat them in the world's acceptable form of selfish critique. In striving to do things the Lord's way, we declare our intent of discipleship. But discipleship is not only learning what the Master wants; it is learning *how* He wants it done.

As for *how* the Lord wants us to treat others, He has given us ample instruction, expressed most clearly, perhaps, to Joseph Smith in Doctrine and Covenants section 121. The Prophet received this revelation while he was incarcerated at Liberty Jail. The revelation details how relationships are to be governed, and the characteristics of a good disciple are set forth.

These precepts contained within section 121 are so important that President David O. McKay stated that it was "the greatest revelation that God has ever given to man" (quoted in Alvin R. Dyer, "Stand Up and Be Counted," *BYU Speeches,* 20 March 1963, 9). President Heber J. Grant agreed. He said, "I am thankful that even when the Prophet Joseph and others were in Liberty Jail one of the greatest of all the great revelations that have come to this people was given to him" (James R. Clark, *Messages of the First Presidency,* 5:302).

These superlative expressions cause us to ponder the meaning of what these men of God saw in this revelation. Certainly it deserves a very thorough examination. In it are hidden keys of knowledge which unlock the doors of how we are to approach each other. Because verses 34 through 46 are so instructive, I've decided to quote them in their entirety.

> Behold, there are many called, but few are chosen. And why are they not chosen?

> Because their hearts are set so much upon the things of this world, and aspire to the honors of men, that they do not learn this one lesson—

> That the rights of the priesthood are inseparably connected with the powers of heaven, and that the powers of heaven cannot be controlled nor handled only upon the principles of righteousness.

> That they may be conferred upon us, it is true; but when we undertake to cover our sins, or to gratify our pride, our vain

ambition, or to exercise control or dominion or compulsion upon the souls of the children of men, in any degree of unrighteousness, behold, the heavens withdraw themselves; the Spirit of the Lord is grieved; and when it is withdrawn, Amen to the priesthood or the authority of that man.

Behold, ere he is aware, he is left unto himself, to kick against the pricks, to persecute the saints, and to fight against God.

We have learned by sad experience that it is the nature and disposition of almost all men, as soon as they get a little authority, as they suppose, they will immediately begin to exercise unrighteous dominion.

Hence many are called, but few are chosen.

No power or influence can or ought to be maintained by virtue of the priesthood, only by *persuasion,* by *long-suffering,* by *gentleness* and *meekness,* and by *love unfeigned;*

By kindness, and pure knowledge, which shall greatly enlarge the soul without hypocrisy, and without guile—

Reproving betimes with sharpness, when moved upon by the Holy Ghost; and then showing forth afterwards an increase of love toward him whom thou hast reproved, lest he esteem thee to be his enemy;

That he may know that thy faithfulness is stronger than the cords of death.

Let thy bowels also be full of charity towards all men, and to the household of faith, and let virtue garnish thy thoughts unceasingly; then shall thy confidence wax strong in the presence of God; and the doctrine of the priesthood shall distil upon thy soul as the dews from heaven.

The Holy Ghost shall be thy constant companion, and thy scepter an unchanging scepter of righteousness and truth; and thy dominion shall be an everlasting dominion, and without compulsory means it shall flow unto thee forever and ever. (D&C 121:34–46; italics added)

The focus of these verses is empowering love by reproving in a Christlike way. One of the most Christlike men that ever walked the earth, President David O. McKay, gave precious insight into this revelation.

"Reproving betimes with sharpness when moved upon by the Holy Ghost . . ."—that limiting clause is very significant. "Reproving betimes with sharpness," not because of selfishness, not because of any personal antipathy, not because of personality, but "when moved upon by the Holy Ghost; and then showing forth afterwards an increase of love toward him whom thou hast reproved, lest he esteem thee to be his enemy" (D&C 121:43). You search through pedagogies, theories of teachings in vain, and find no passage that will compare with that in governing people. (Conference Report, April 1962, 93)

Is it possible the reason President David O. McKay so appreciated these verses is because they are a divine blueprint for loving? Hidden within this "greatest revelation" that God has ever given to man is the way to become Christlike and a partaker of Christ's divine nature. It is a way—maybe the only way—to escape the corruption of the world and overcome the "natural man."

Elder Neal A. Maxwell viewed this passage as instruction for living a higher law than the world sets forth.

Thus at the very time he [Joseph Smith] was suffering telestial abuse and oppression from secular authorities ranging from judges to jailers, Joseph was instructed on the completely opposite manner, the celestial way, in which the Lord's priesthood leaders are to lead! . . .

Obviously this supernal spiritual style of leadership as thus set
forth could not be sustained for long by anyone who was casual
in his commitment or who was not making significant spiritual
strides in developing the attributes of Jesus. (Neal A. Maxwell,
But for a Small Moment, 10)

What Elder Maxwell calls the "attributes of Jesus" are those principles of righteousness that we seek to develop. A serious disciple
would seek to become like the Master. He or she would want to learn:

- The skill of persuasion (see 2 Ne. 33:4; Ether 8:26;
  Moro. 7:13–18).
- The trait of long-suffering (see 1 Pet. 2:19–21; Alma
  42:30; Morm. 2:12).
- The characteristics of gentleness and meekness (see 2
  Cor. 10:1; Gal. 5:22).
- The mystery of love unfeigned (see 1 Ne. 11:22).
- The strength in kindness (see JST, Joel 2:13–14;
  Jonah 4:2; 2 Cor. 6:6).
- The power of pure knowledge (see Hosea 6:6; Luke
  11:52; Alma 32:28).
- The art of reproving while maintaining the Spirit
  (see D&C 11:21; 42:14; 46:7).
- The courage to show forth an increase of love after
  reproof (see Gal. 6:1).

I refer to these here not only as attributes of Christ, but as
approaching skills of love. They are "approaching" because they are the
skills we need not only to approach one another, but ultimately to
approach the Lord with purity. The challenge is to apply each of these
without compulsory means, without hypocrisy, and without dishon-
esty. Living these principles of righteousness gives us the ability to
"reprove betimes with sharpness" and do it so as not to offend the
Holy Ghost. "Reproving betimes with sharpness when moved upon by
the Holy Ghost" requires all nine of the aforementioned traits. The
"showing forth afterwards an increase of love" is an extension of love
unfeigned (not faked nor pretended) and requires additional effort.

When men and women, fathers and mothers, husbands and wives, brothers and sisters act in harmony with these principles, they enjoy a greater outpouring of the Holy Spirit. When men and women operate with the principles of righteousness, love will flow without compulsory means. Kingdoms built by force can only be maintained by force. Relationships that are built upon love can be sustained by love. We'll now take a closer look at each of these principles and skills, as well as recognizing and avoiding their worldly counterparts.

Principles of Righteousness: The Approaching Skills

APPROACHING SKILL	WORLDLY COUNTERPART
Persuasion comes from the Latin word *persuadere; per* means "thoroughly," and *suadere* means "advise." Persuasion means to thoroughly advise. It is to invite and to entice (see Moro. 7:13–17). Persuasion offered in love is to lovingly and knowledgably instruct.	The opposite of persuasion done in love is compulsion, force, coercion, nagging, and intimidation, all of which may include yelling, cursing, swearing, and name-calling. It's purpose is to belittle or to humiliate. These are all forms of unrighteous dominion.
Long-suffering requires restraint. It means to be patient and to wait for the right opportunity to teach or share. The focus is on the loved one and his or her willingness to receive counsel.	Instead of being long-suffering, impetuous critics are impatient, quick-tempered, and short-fused. They focus on their frustration, and they act before they consider the consequences.
Gentleness means sensitivity of disposition, tenderness, meekness, and refinement of manner. It means treating people with respect, being "soft-tongued"—well-spoken, amiable, and courteous (see Prov. 25:15).	The opposite of gentleness is harshness. It means acting in an autocratic, domineering, oppressive, and heavy-handed manner. It is to bully, demand, and override. It is to be inflexible and "sharp-tongued" (see Ps. 57:4).

Meekness reflects a submissive, humble, and mild attitude. It means to remain well composed, tranquil, peaceful, and not easily offended.

An attitude opposite of meekness is prideful, haughty, arrogant, puffed up, disdaining, high-handed, stiff-necked, egocentric, self-righteous, and unapproachable.

Love unfeigned means an unpretended love, not faked, nor phony, nor counterfeit. It is genuine, sincere, heartfelt, honest, and true. It is forthright and reflective of love which focuses on the best interest of the loved one. It is a love which "is stronger than the cords of death" (D&C 121:43–44). It is real, candid, and unvarnished. It is a love to be trusted.

Feigned love is a lie. It is counterfeit, manipulative, dishonest, untrue, false, and faked for selfish purposes.

Kindness speaks of benevolence. It means to treat people with respect, consideration, tolerance, and generosity. The focus is on "how" we treat others. It is sympathy and tenderness; it is friendliness, comfort, and graciousness.

Unkind people are inconsiderate of the feelings of others. They are hurtful, insensitive, harmful, brash, discounting, denigrating, and imprudent.

Pure knowledge is spiritual knowledge. It means truth, which is a knowledge of things as they were, are now, and are to come (see D&C 93:24). This is Spirit-discerned information that gives us confidence to act. It is intelligence, light, and truth.

The opposite of pure knowledge is ignorance or incomplete knowledge. It is acting without the facts, failing to see the big picture, flying off the handle, or overreacting. It is assuming, presumptuous, and extremely judgmental.

Reproving betimes with sharpness when moved upon by the Holy Ghost means to deliver the message early on, being very precise and exact. It is to preserve the self-worth and separate the issue or behavior from the worth of the soul. It is to conduct oneself in such a way that the Holy Ghost abides with us the entire time.

Inappropriate reproving includes uninvited, unauthorized, and improperly given criticism. It disregards the ability and willingness of the recipient to receive criticism. It is an unrighteous dominion without respect for the criticized. It is based on frustration, not edification.

An increase of love is a greater outpouring of love so that the one criticized is absolutely assured of the love of the critic.

Not showing forth an increase of love is picking up where one's relationship left off after a criticism and licking our wounds. Rather than an increase of love, there is a regression and a cautious exploration to return the relationship to normal.

When an individual is able to reprove or criticize without losing the Spirit, he or she is partaking of the divine nature, the attributes of Jesus, and becoming truly Christlike. The individual is acting on principles of righteousness, or using these approaching skills. Unfortunately, it is very easy—some may say even natural—to do the opposite of the principles of righteousness.

The natural man, being selfish and shortsighted, sees only the flaw to be changed and the wrong to be righted. The worth of the soul and the preparation of the one to be criticized are lost in the demand for justice. The natural man is spiritually immature and substitutes his own perceptions for the prompting of the Spirit. Therefore, to combat this natural man, we must maintain the Spirit in our lives. The Holy Ghost always teaches us to prepare ourselves and the individual to be criticized. The Holy Ghost has been described as the mind of God. The Lord's plan requires all to act in the eternal best interest of others as prompted by the Spirit. This is His work and glory (see Moses 1:39). Those who work against the eternal best interest of others are working against God (see Luke 16:13). While our actions are not always based on conscious decisions (often we revert to automatic, natural reactions), we are still pitting our will against God's when we fail to live the higher law after we've learned it.

So it is that many people are called to love in this way, but few are chosen because their hearts are set upon riches, honors of men, and the selfish things of a perishing world, as discussed in section 121. They do not learn this one overwhelming lesson: the powers of heaven are completely bound and inseparably connected with these nine principles of righteousness known as persuasion, long-suffering, gentleness, meekness, love unfeigned, kindness, pure knowledge, reproof, and an increase of love, given with the Spirit. If a person attempts to call upon the powers of heaven with any degree of unrighteousness (such as pride, domination, or anything related to them) he or she will find the Holy Ghost withdrawing. A grieved Holy Ghost will stand away from the person and watch him or her fight against God's ways of doing things. The withdrawn Spirit (see D&C 19:20) will stand as a silent witness if we try to carry out the Lord's program in the devil's way or persist seeking happiness in unkind ways. For, as Samuel the Lamanite prophesied to the wicked Nephites: "Ye have sought all the days of your lives for that which ye could not obtain; and *ye have sought for happiness in doing iniquity,* which thing is contrary to the nature of that righteousness which is in our great and Eternal Head" (Hel. 13:38; italics added).

Until critics are willing to change, they will experience what Mormon called "the sorrowing of the damned" because God will not allow them to find happiness in unrighteous dominion, which is sin (Morm. 2:13). Though the world's response to frustration and methods of criticism may seem easier and require less discipline, those who adhere to such natural-man tendencies will find that life is actually much harder. Try as they might to find it otherwise, they will learn in the end that "wickedness never was happiness" (Alma 41:10). Unrighteous dominion is sin and a wicked way of trying to do the Lord's work. It has always been Satan's plan to disrespect the agency of men and women. Compulsion, coercion, and physical and emotional intimidation are Satan's tools (see Isa. 14:12–15; Rev. 12:3–9; D&C 29:36–37; Moses 4:1–4).

The irony for those who want to use an unrighteous means to compel righteousness is that they fought a war in heaven for the right of self-determination. They fought Lucifer himself for the privilege of maintaining their freedom of choice. Now they are either consciously or unconsciously using Satan's approach to force others to do what they want them to do through manipulative, demeaning, or otherwise inappropriate criticism. As soon as they receive a little power or a little authority, they resort to force. Sooner or later they will learn the futility of this pathway. Maybe it will take the loss of a runaway child, a divorce, the loss of earthly possessions, the loss of Church membership, or the loss of personal dignity and friends before they learn by the things they suffer.

Living Together in Love

There can only be two reasons why someone would not want to live this better, loving way—ignorance and pride. Ignorance and pride are the enemies of knowledge and humility. It need not be so. God has endowed every human heart with the predisposition to respond to love. It is not hard to love. It only becomes hard as we try to control another and the loved one resists change. Love turns quickly to frustration. Frustration turns into anger and criticism. Love becomes lost in frustration. The question is, how do we show love and yet give needed reproof without driving the wounded soul into the wilderness? How do we incorporate those necessary precepts from the "greatest revelation" that God has ever given to man? The answer is in the Lord's great revelation to man, Doctrine and Covenants 121, where the Lord teaches us how to live together in love.

Is it possible to live in a love-centered home? Yes, it is. There have been several groups of people who have lived the law of love. Enoch and his city, the people who were all converted unto the Lord in 4 Nephi, and other various individuals and groups have lived together in love. We see that this Zion-like life *can* happen. Rather than wondering if it's possible, the more pertinent questions may be, Do we as critics possess enough love to exercise the necessary patience? Are we critics willing to subdue our frustrations for a higher cause? It will require a perspective as wide as all eternity and yet grounded in the reality of here and now. Before we as critics vent our potentially damaging message, are we willing to humble ourselves in mighty prayer and call upon the Lord for spiritual guidance? And if our criticism is unnecessary or inappropriate, can we learn to take our frustrations to the Lord and only our love to others? This is what it means to live based in principles of righteousness and to approach the divine in our own nature.

Assignments for Chapter 3

1. Commit to memory the nine principles of righteousness: persuasion, long-suffering, gentleness, meekness, love unfeigned, kindness, pure knowledge, reproving with the Spirit, and showing forth after criticism an increase of love toward the one criticized.

2. Pick one principle a day to work on until you have cycled through all nine.

CHAPTER 4

THE SPIRITUAL GIFT OF CRITICISM

Up to this point we have discussed proper criticism as an art. Criticism can also be considered a gift of the Spirit in two different ways. Criticism can be a gift *from* the Spirit, and it can be a gift *of* the Spirit. First, criticism from the Lord (or chastisement) is a gift in helping us improve ourselves. Second, criticism, if it is done properly and effectively, must be given with the Spirit.

THE LORD CHASTENS THOSE HE LOVES

> Verily, thus saith the Lord unto you whom I love, and whom I love I also chasten that their sins may be forgiven, for with the chastisement I prepare a way for their deliverance in all things out of temptation, and I have loved you. (D&C 95:1)

As the Lord states here, criticism is not given as an end in itself but as preparation toward becoming a better self. When we are criticized by the Lord (or His appointed servants), we ought to remember that this criticism is given because He loves us. He wants us to become better so we can return to Him. If He did not care, He would leave us to ourselves, never correcting or strengthening. But He does counsel us out of pure love and genuine concern. So ought our criticism be given. There are stewardships wherein if one does not criticize one will be held accountable before God for inaction. Below are two examples from the scriptures.

The Prophet Samuel speaking of Eli:

> For I have told him that I will judge his house for ever for the iniquity which he knoweth; because his sons made themselves vile, and he restrained them not. (1 Sam. 3:13)

Nephi's brother Jacob:

> And we did magnify our office unto the Lord, taking upon us the responsibility, answering the sins of the people upon our own heads if we did not teach them the word of God with all diligence; wherefore, by laboring with our might their blood might not come upon our garments; otherwise their blood would come upon our garments, and we would not be found spotless at the last day. (Jacob 1:19)

This places criticism as a great burden upon the shoulders of parents, priesthood leaders, and authorized critics. It requires fortitude to face someone with kindness and to criticize him or her with a gentle spirit. As with all spiritual gifts, the ability to criticize and chasten as He would with His perfect love requires the Spirit. To rephrase Doctrine and Covenants 42:14: "The Spirit shall be given unto you by the prayer of faith; and if ye receive not the Spirit ye shall not [criticize]."

Those who have tried to give and receive criticism in the Lord's own way know it is a difficult task. However problematic it is to manage, however, those who would profess discipleship to Jesus Christ must continue to accept the responsibility of being a giver and receiver of criticism with the Spirit. But, remember, we are not alone. The very God of heaven is there to help. This assistance may come in the form of strength or a softening of one's own heart. A person is not excused nor released from this responsibility because of the "packaging" of another. In other words, a true believer in Christ is obligated to have the Spirit when criticism is being given or received, independent of the action or reaction of the other party. It requires great dependency upon the Lord.

Developing the art and skill of giving and receiving criticism in the Lord's own way is indeed a spiritual gift to be sought after and honed by heavenly guidance. It has more to do with having a positive approach than being a perfect person. Criticizing with the Spirit requires self-control, patience, and love. When these ingredients are present, the Spirit can bear witness to "the truth of all things" (Moro. 10:5). One of the truths to which the Holy Ghost can bear witness is appropriate criticism. He can help us know how to change when we receive criticism, or how to offer criticism lovingly. The goal we should set for either giving or receiving criticism is found in a revelation given to Joseph Smith: "Wherefore, he that preacheth and he that receiveth, understand one another, and both are edified and rejoice together" (D&C 50:22).

The Holy Ghost is the agent of change and the divine messenger to each of Heavenly Father's children. Among His several functions are to guide, to comfort, and to carry the message of truth to the hearts of men and women everywhere. It is a major part of the mission of the Holy Ghost to bear witness to the truth of all things. This includes changing the hearts of the children of God. Thus, criticism given in a proper way gives the Holy Spirit an opportunity to soften the heart of the receiver of criticism. "For when a man speaketh by the power of the Holy Ghost the power of the Holy Ghost carrieth it unto the hearts of the children of men" (2 Ne. 33:1). The following story shows how the Holy Ghost can soften even the most unlikely of persons.

Two Elders in Germany

Two missionaries were tracting in Germany. They knocked on the door and were greeted by a hostile man. He asked if they were Mormons. Immediately after the elders answered in the affirmative, he slugged one of the missionaries in the nose and knocked him to the ground. The elder stood up amid the curses of this man and managed to make a single statement: "This day you have struck a servant of the Lord who came to bring you a message."

A year and a half later, two more elders knocked on this man's door. They were obviously unaware of the greeting given to their predecessors. This time, however, the elders were invited in. The man was humble and contrite. He related his striking of one of the previous missionaries. He went on to add, "For more than a year and a half I have awakened every night in a cold sweat to the words, 'This day you have struck a servant of the Lord who came to bring you a message.'

"Please, please," he begged, "tell me your message." He was baptized and confirmed a member of the Church and, after another year and a half, traveled to the Salt Lake Temple to do his temple work. After a few inquiries he found out that the missionary he had struck was married and attending the University of Utah. He decided to pay him a visit.

This time it was the elder who opened the door. Not recognizing the man, he invited him in. When the man spoke English with a distinct German accent, the entire event returned to the elder's mind. At first he feared for his life. He believed the man had tracked him down—as indeed he had, but to thank him, not to hit him. Through his tears this humble, contrite man asked the former missionary to forgive him. He thanked the young man for telling him, "This day you have struck a servant of the Lord who came to bring you a message." They parted more than friends. They were brothers in the gospel. (A version of this story was told years ago by Antoine R. Ivins. This is the essence of the story to the best of my memory.)

The moral to the story is that the elder did what he was supposed to do in bearing a witness. It was the Holy Ghost who afflicted the man's mind for more than a year and a half and softened his heart. It is the mission of the Holy Spirit to change men's hearts. Proper criticism offered in love can be the catalyst for a person to become open to change, but true change, which leads a person to a better self, always comes from within. It is a conversion experience. It requires the support of the Holy Ghost, a vision of a better self, and belief in one's own worth to make the change.

Patience, Love, and Self-Control

Like the elder in the story, a critic who is filled with patience, love, and self-control can become a conduit for the Holy Ghost. It is the Spirit that will carry the critical message of change to the heart if the message is delivered in a proper manner. Inappropriate criticism has no chance of success because it offends the Spirit. It is an exercise in frustration and futility. Even if proper criticism is given, it may take years for the receiver to respond to the influence of the Holy Ghost—hence the need for patience.

If we are not possessed of self-control, patience, and love, the giving or receiving of criticism will have to wait until we are in control in order to be effective. When criticism is given or received by someone who is out of control, impatient, and resentful, poor reactions are predictable. So are the hostile outcomes. Even appropriate criticism runs a high risk of rejection. Spirit-directed criticism is not just "another way" of approaching criticism. It is the *only* way that has a real chance of succeeding. If there is a possibility for change, the difference between acceptance or rejection of a critical message may be the demeanor of the message bearer.

Giving and receiving criticism in the Lord's own way requires preparation. Because patience, self-control, and love are requisite principles, sincere disciples of Jesus will seek for these things. With mighty prayer and a genuine concern for the one to be criticized, the follower of the Lord will humble himself. In order to be an instrument in God's hands as an agent of change, he will yield to meekness. He will allow the Holy Ghost to carry the message to the heart of the receiver. The Spirit has always been associated with true conversion. Consider the powerful sermon of King Benjamin. In those early chapters of the book of Mosiah, he offers very strong guidance and correction to his people. Some could have taken offense that their king would try to tell them how to live. But they didn't. Why? Because of the king's humility, his obvious love for them, and his patient offering of correction and instruction. The result? Consider his people's response:

> And they all cried with one voice, saying: Yea, we believe all the words which thou hast spoken unto us; and also, we know of their surety and truth, because of the Spirit of the Lord Omnipotent, which has wrought a mighty change in us, or in our hearts, that we have no more disposition to do evil, but to do good continually. And we, ourselves, also, through the infinite goodness of God, and the manifestations of his Spirit, have great views of that which is to come; and were it expedient, we could prophesy of all things. (Mosiah 5:2–3)

The result was that these people accepted King Benjamin's sincere plea to improve and draw closer to God. His words did not change them, but his love did. His Spirit-guided counsel was received by the Spirit, and all were edified. Had he lashed out in rebuke, forcing the change, the results would likely not have been as deeply felt and long lasting.

We are not called to change the hearts of others. We are called to love God and to love our fellow beings. We are called to be examples of true believers in Christ. We are to model Christian ideals and pray for our loved ones and even our enemies. We are to invite, entice, encourage, inspire, and righteously persuade others to improve. We are to teach one another. However, we can only teach if the pupil is willing in his or her heart to receive the teaching.

On occasion we are justified in "reproving betimes with sharpness." The qualification is that we as critics are prompted by the Holy Ghost and not by our own frustration. When the Spirit is present and truly dwells in our heart, the greatest opportunity for change exists. Uninvited, unauthorized, and improper criticism will place the focus on the critic, not on the critic's message. To criticize in the Lord's own way requires the messenger to be Spirit-directed and Spirit-guided. When this occurs, we are possessed of the spiritual gift of criticism and are on the pathway to charity.

A TRUE CRITIC

In addition to guidance by the Spirit, a closer understanding of what it means to "reprove," or criticize, "betimes with sharpness" can help us be a critic in the best sense. Many of these words have a different connotation today than they did when section 121 was received in the early nineteenth century. Let's consider those earlier meanings. Noah Webster's 1828 *American Dictionary of the English Language* defined the words *criticise* [sic], *reproof, betimes,* and *sharpness:*

> *criticise:* to notice the beauties and blemishes
> *criticised:* examined and judged with regard to beauties and faults
> *criticism:* the art of judging with propriety of the beauties and faults

reproof: blame expressed to the face; censure for a fault, reprehension

betimes: seasonably; in a good season; before it is late [early on]

sharpness: keenness of an edge; . . . acuteness of intellect; the power of nice discernment; quickness of understanding

One hundred and seventy–plus years ago a true critic was one who could see the beauty as well as the blemish. Reproof had to be spoken to the face of the person being criticized and not behind his back. *Betimes* meant "when the time was right, in a good season, before it was too late." *Sharpness* meant to be acute of intellect and to demonstrate "niceness" when discerning another. To "reprove betimes with sharpness" was to censure another directly to his or her face at a proper time and season before it was too late and he or she was past feeling. It meant to be precise and exact in focusing on the behavior or issue being discussed. All of this should be done today with one caveat—the Holy Ghost must be present.

The prophet Isaiah could claim the spiritual gift of criticism: "The Lord God hath given me the tongue of the learned, that I should know how to speak a word in season to him that is weary" (Isa. 50:4). Being able to speak a "word in season," even the word of knowledge, or words of wisdom, or Spirit-directed criticism, is a spiritual gift (see D&C 46:17–18). The following insight about speaking a "word in season" is instructive: "Seek not to declare my word, but first seek to obtain my word, and then shall your tongue be loosed; then, if you desire, you shall have my Spirit and my word, yea, the power of God unto the convincing of men. But now hold your peace" (D&C 11:21–22).

There are times to "hold your peace." There is "a time to keep silence," but there is also "a time to speak" (Eccl. 3:7). A true critic knows these times. There are times when criticism is necessary. There are circumstances which require the courage to be appropriately critical. There are behaviors and issues that demand attention. There is a time, a place, and a season when criticism may be the forerunner for change and improvement. On those occasions, when the Spirit is present, it is possible for both the person who "giveth" and the person who "receiveth" to be edified. "And whoso receiveth not by the Spirit, cannot be benefited" (D&C 91:6).

Unfortunately, in the day-to-day world most people are moved upon to criticize by frustration instead of waiting to be moved upon by the Holy Ghost:

> Verily I say unto you, he that is ordained of me and sent forth to preach the word of truth by the Comforter, in the Spirit of truth, doth he preach [criticize] it by the Spirit of truth or some other way? And if it be by some other way it is not of God. And again, he that receiveth the word of truth, doth he receive it by the Spirit of truth or some other way? If it be some other way it is not of God. (D&C 50:17–20)

Giving and receiving criticism with the Spirit is difficult for both the giver and the receiver. It is hard for the giver of criticism not to be overcome with negative emotion, to become angry, to yell, or to package the criticism in such a way that the focus is on the messenger and not the message. It is equally hard for the receiver of criticism to focus on the content of what is being said and not to be sidetracked by defensive reactions, the tone of voice, the timing, or the demeanor of the critic.

In a class on communication skills at the University of Washington, Professor Robert Anderson made a very profound observation. He said that "the effective communicator keeps the focus on the message. Anything the communicator does to detract from the message makes him or her less effective and robs the message of its full power." If criticism is to be effective, the critic must be in control of his emotions; otherwise, the listener will focus on the emotional state of the critic and not on the message. Under ideal circumstances, the critic will ask for the permission of the one being criticized to meet at a time and place which will allow them to be alone. When such kindness and respect are present, they enhance the opportunity for the person being criticized to reflect upon the content of the message.

The more centered in Christ a person is, the easier it is to give and receive criticism, reproof, and chastisement. The more our ego is involved, the more difficult it is to give or receive criticism. The difficulty, however, does not excuse us from giving and receiving criticism in the Lord's own way. A true critic can maintain self-control, understanding the situation in full, knowing the proper time and place, and living to maintain the Spirit in his or her life to criticize properly.

Bridling Our Tongues

A critic who is true to the principles outlined in Doctrine and Covenants 121:43 will learn to bridle his or her tongue, both in offering and responding to criticism. Developing the self-mastery necessary to control the tongue requires years of practice and patience with self and others. A profound spiritual commitment to love as Jesus loved and to speak as Jesus spoke is a lifelong goal. James, the brother of Jesus, declared the following:

> If any man offend not in word, the same is a perfect man, and able also to bridle the whole body. Behold, we put bits in the horses' mouths, that they may obey us; and we turn about their whole body. Behold also the ships, which though they be so great, and are driven of fierce winds, yet are they turned about with a very small helm, whithersoever the governor listeth. Even so the tongue is a little member, and boasteth great things. Behold, how great a matter a little fire kindleth! And the tongue is a fire, a world of iniquity: so is the tongue among our members, that it defileth the whole body, and setteth on fire the course of nature; and it is set on fire of hell. For every kind of beasts, and of birds, and of serpents, and of things in the sea, is tamed, and hath been tamed of mankind: But the tongue can no man tame; it is an unruly evil, full of deadly poison. Therewith bless we God, even the Father; and therewith curse we men, which are made after the similitude of God. Out of the same mouth proceedeth blessing and cursing. My brethren, these things ought not so to be. Doth a fountain send forth at the same place sweet water and bitter? (James 3:2–11)

It appears that motive, the fountain of the heart, is at the core of whether we control our tongue or not. The natural man will continue to be a selfish man and to speak without the Holy Ghost. More profoundly, the Christian man or woman who does not learn to control his or her tongue will be an enemy to self and an enemy to the mission of Jesus Christ, which is to bring to pass the immortality and eternal life of all God's children (see Moses 1:39). Discipleship to Jesus has always involved controlling the parts of the human body and elevating them to the highest and best in self and others.

Would it not be considered blasphemy if we spoke to Jesus, or Heavenly Father, the way we criticize a friend or loved one? The LDS Bible Dictionary defines blasphemy as follows: "Generally denotes contemptuous speech concerning God, or concerning something that stands in a sacred relation toward God" (Bible Dictionary, "Blasphemy," 625).

What could be more precious to God than the soul of one of His little ones? It had been better that millstones were hung around the neck of the verbal abuser and he were cast into the sea rather than offend one of His little ones (see Matt. 18:6). What could stand in a more sacred relationship to God than His family? Verbal abuse is inflicting spiritual abuse because it attacks the worth of a soul. It is blasphemy. Uninvited, unauthorized, and improperly given criticism is a sin.

There is a way to package criticism so that the focus can be on the message and not the messenger. However, the messenger bears the burden of delivering an unwanted package. There is an aura of negativism associated with the best of criticisms. Piercing the negative darkness is only possible when the receiver of criticism is confirmed in the worth of his soul. Herein lies a key of knowledge. The art and skill of negative feedback requires the critic to ignore his or her own ego and keep the self-esteem of the receiver intact, all while discussing the issue or behavior in question. It is a task of great intricacy and requires a great deal of self-control to speak carefully and by the Spirit.

Separating ego from issue may be as challenging as developing the ability to communicate love. It demands that respect be shown to each child of God. It demands that we be Christlike. President Hugh B. Brown said that a "Christlike life is always a combination of earnest, personal conviction and generous regard for the other man's opinion. Dedication to and defense of truth never require or justify breaking the second commandment to love our fellow men" (Conference Report, October 1959, 108).

We cannot expect to possess the peace of Christ which surpasses all understanding unless we are willing to control our tongue, which can be either an instrument of peace or a weapon of anger. When our tongue becomes a weapon, it unleashes anger, and we say things we later regret.

Righteous Indignation versus Righteous Criticism

Similar to controlling the tongue, controlling one's emotions is essential for a critic to give criticism properly. Elder J. Golden Kimball said:

> Experience teaches me that when I have been angry, I am quite sure I did not have the Holy Ghost, and I was not in any proper condition to administer reproof. It took me quite a long while to learn that. When I became excited, fanatical, and over-zealous, I mistakenly thought it was the Spirit of the Lord, but have learned better, as the Holy Ghost does not operate that way. My testimony is that the internal fruits of the Holy Ghost are joy, peace, patience, longsuffering, and kindness. (Conference Report, April 1907, 81)

Under the guise of "righteous indignation," many justify their anger. They lack the humility of a J. Golden Kimball. They give themselves permission to be angry at a spouse, a parent, a child, or any person because the object of their anger was wrong, sinful, or hurtful. Once blame is fixed, they combine their anger with criticism and feel justified in being "out of the Spirit" because of the other person's actions. But one is never justified in acting without the Spirit.

Anger is a choice. It is a poor choice, because it transfers the focus from the message to the messenger. The scriptures do not support anger as a Christlike behavior. There are those who support anger as an appropriate Christian behavior under the guise of "righteous indignation." They use Jesus cleansing the temple to substantiate their view of righteous anger. The assumption that Jesus was angry while driving out the money changers is not reinforced in the scriptures. (The one time Jesus is identified with anger is in Mark 3:5. He reacts by healing the man with the withered hand. What a marvelous example to respond to anger by doing a good deed!) In the Bible, two key verses are used by the "righteous indignationist." They are Matthew 5:22 and Ephesians 4:26. The Joseph Smith Translation adds a valuable insight into the issue of anger. The following are these passages of the King James Version and Joseph Smith Translation combined. The words crossed out and italicized represent Joseph Smith's changes.

Matthew 5:22 (KJV and JST):

> But I say unto you, That whosoever is angry with his brother without a cause shall be in danger of the *his* judgment: and whosoever shall say to his brother, Raca, *or Rabcha,* shall be in danger of the council; but *and* whosoever shall say *to his brother,* Thou fool, shall be in danger of hell fire.

In Joseph Smith's translation of Matthew, the words "without a cause" are crossed out, implying that there is never any justification for us to be angry. There is no permission to excuse the Spirit and journey into the emotion of rage. Paul teaches in Ephesians this same doctrine. Note again how Joseph Smith rendered the translation.

Ephesians 4:26 (KJV and JST):

> Be ye angry, and sin not: *Can ye be angry, and not sin?* Let not the sun go down upon your wrath.

Rather than trying to justify anger, Joseph Smith's translation makes it clear that being in a state of anger will lead to sin. Paul goes on in this letter to the Ephesians to counsel:

> Let no corrupt communication proceed out of your mouth, but that which is good to the use of edifying, that it may minister

grace unto the hearers. And grieve not the holy Spirit of God, whereby ye are sealed unto the day of redemption. Let all bitterness, and wrath, and anger, and clamour, and evil speaking, be put away from you, with all malice: and be ye kind one to another, tenderhearted, forgiving one another, even as God for Christ's sake hath forgiven you. (Eph. 4:29–32)

To be hurt, disappointed, and even frustrated by the behaviors of others is understandable. But choosing to lose the Spirit, to be angry, and to be critical are not justifiable behaviors for a disciple of Jesus.

There is a difference between our anger and the Lord's. Whereas we may react sinfully as a result of our anger, the Lord's anger is the disappointment and grief of heart He feels when His disciples' behavior requires him to punish them (see Moses 7:26–40). Disobedience brings a loss of blessings. A loving Father in Heaven and His Son, Jesus Christ, do only those things which are in our eternal best interest: "He doeth not anything save it be for the benefit of the world; for he loveth the world, even that he layeth down his own life that he may draw all men unto him" (2 Ne. 26:24).

The scriptures frequently use the word *wrath* as well as the word *anger*. Neither of these words connotes a god yelling and screaming in a rage of emotion. God is patient, long-suffering, and merciful, but not indifferent. He cares.

PREPARING THE WAY

Of course, there are times when the Lord reproves His children. But in everything the Lord does, He is preparing a way for them to improve. "I prepare a way for their deliverance in all things" (D&C 95:1). God knows that His children will make mistakes. In all that God does in the great plan of deliverance, He is allowing His children to learn and preparing them to return to the kingdom of God.

Seldom do the purveyors of criticism in this world look toward the long-term best interest of those they criticize. Even fewer prepare a way for the one being criticized to improve. But this is part of living the Lord's higher law governing relationships. This is what motivates truly Christ-centered critics. If we are to follow God, we will always prepare a way for the criticized to improve and to have "hope." Criticism in the Lord's own way may lead to punishment. However, the punishment will be sufficient to teach the consequence and prepare a way for improvement, yet not deny hope. So much of mortal criticism now given is solely the punishment. It is a message of rejection with no hope of restored trust, love, or acceptance.

Hope for Mary

Mary, a sophomore in high school, was grounded by her father from using the car because of failing grades due to her unwillingness to turn in her homework. Her father sat on the edge of her bed about twenty minutes later and created hope.

"Would you like to know what you could do to earn the privilege to drive the car again?"

The daughter sighed, "Get straight A's, right?"

"No, not quite that," Dad said. "But if you will turn in all of your homework assignments this week, you can drive the car on a weekend night. If you turn in your homework for two weeks, you can take the car two days, and so on until your complete driving privilege is restored in seven weeks of turning in your homework. If you foul up and miss a week, we will have to go back and start over. By the way, I will be checking personally with your teachers each Friday. What do you say? Is it a deal or not?"

"Yeah, I guess so," Mary said, hiding the little smile of hope that crossed her face.

The authorized times, places, and circumstances for Spirit-directed criticism represent less than one-tenth of 1 percent of current practice. The remaining percentage is ill-timed, unauthorized, out of stewardship or out of control even within stewardship, unnecessary, and improperly given. It represents unrighteous dominion; fosters resentment, contention, and anger; and is ill-advised. The focus is seldom the best interest of the one being criticized; rather, it is the frustration of the critic and the disappointment he or she feels. Developing the art, skill, and the spiritual gift of giving and receiving criticism in the Lord's own way requires His help.

Assignments for Chapter 4

1. Keep track for one day on a 3 x 5 card the people you criticize and why.

2. Decide what specific steps you will take to keep the focus on the message the next time you feel the need to criticize.

3. Rate your work on the approaching skills discussed in the last chapter:

      a. Excellent
      b. Fair
      c. Poor
      d. Need major improvement

CHAPTER 5

WHY SHOULD I CHANGE?

Before we can even consider motivating anyone else to change, we ought to consider our own hearts and habits. Much of living the Lord's higher law of loving does not come naturally. It requires work and, yes, change to maintain the Spirit in our lives and to fulfill our stewardships in the Lord's way. Our salvation and that of those in our care depends on our ability to do things the way the Lord wants us to. As we come to understand why we need to change, we will realize that the only way to change is the Lord's way. Only then can we bring the influence of the Holy Ghost into our relationships to help others change for the better.

REASONS TO CHANGE

In a class on relationships and communication, a student asked the question, "Why should I change?" It is a legitimate question. She went on to explain that life wasn't all that bad as it was. Her relationships were satisfactory. She didn't particularly appreciate it when people were critical of her and it was obvious that others didn't like it when she was critical of them, but, "Hey, that's life." This was a sincere young lady who was content with her life and saw no need to change.

The question was thrown out to the entire class. "Why should a person be willing to learn how to give and receive criticism in the Lord's own way?"

The answers began to come back:

"Because it is right."

"It's a commandment."

"You are hurting other people by improper criticism."

"What you are doing now isn't effective."

After a little more pondering and meditation, the answers took a different direction:

"It will make you a more effective communicator."

"It will make you a more emotionally safe person."

"It will put you more in control of your life."

Even though the answers resembled sound bites and one-liners, they began to reveal an awareness of a better way. There was more to life than each was currently experiencing. The picture was not clear. The vision was not complete, but there was more and it was better. Finally, an older married student raised her hand and said,

"It will enable others to receive your love."

All the answers given were good reasons to change, but that was the purest, most Christlike motive. After all the answers were written on the board, the students were asked to expand upon their answers. Some of their comments and thoughts about the eight answers above are listed below.

1. It is right to learn to give and receive criticism in the Lord's own way. This answer was enough for some of the students. They didn't require additional motivation. They were willing to change their behavior on that premise alone. Other students admired the strength of character required to operate on that principle.

2. It is a commandment. The ability to give and receive criticism in a righteous way is a Christlike trait, and discipleship to Jesus requires obedience to His commandments.

3. We are hurting other people by improperly criticizing them. The students could empathize with people hurt by improper criticism because they themselves had been improperly criticized in their lives. This empathy led them to evoke the scripture: "Verily I say unto you, Inasmuch as ye have done it unto one of the least of these my brethren, ye have done it unto me" (Matt. 25:40). Compassion for others is a worthwhile motive and reveals a tender and sensitive heart.

4. Giving and receiving criticism improperly isn't effective. If it's not working, find another way. What is needed is a solution. Find some way that works and do it. Unfortunately, some people don't know when to let go, even when things are not working. For some students pragmatism was the only motivation they needed to move them toward criticizing in a proper way.

5. It will make us more effective communicators. Being a better self by improving effective communication skills seemed to drive this particular point of view. There is too much "hassle" in not being a productive and efficient communicator. It's not worth the misunderstandings, the hurt feelings, the arguments, and the host of negative spin-offs that accompany improperly given or received criticism. Inefficiency is a poor way to run a business or a human relationship.

6. It will make us more emotionally safe. Doing good and being an instrument in the Lord's hands provides a safe place emotionally for those that we love. A safe emotional harbor from the storms of life is a worthy goal.

7. It will put us more in control of our lives. There is great truth in this answer. It deals with self-mastery. Conquering anything that keeps a person from becoming his or her highest and best self is a noble undertaking. Giving ourselves permission to become angry and critical of another's behavior is yielding control of our lives. Choosing to direct the inner self to a higher and greater plane by refusing to improperly criticize is of more value than virtually any other conquest.

8. It will enable others to receive our love. All the students agreed that it is hard to feel love from a critic. The woman taken in adultery (see John 8:3–11) was not condemned by the Lord, even though He told her to sin no more. The woman (and the class of students) felt that Jesus separated His love for her from His disapproval of her behavior. Giving reproof in the Lord's way enabled the woman to feel

His concern for her well-being. This is a very important statement which includes one of the keys to God's happiness.

God's work and glory is to help each of us become our very best. Sometimes this involves criticism, but in a loving manner. When people enter into the work of helping others achieve their highest and best selves, they have enlisted in the service of their God (see Mosiah 2:16–17). In losing their mortal life in loving service to others, they secure for themselves immortality and eternal life.

The glorious news of the gospel of Jesus Christ is that man has the ability and capacity to love as God loves. It may be embryonic—it may be influenced by time and limited in mortality—but the genes to love as God loves are there within man. Men and women are the spirit sons and daughters of God (see D&C 76:24). The spark is struck from an eternal blaze. Jesus came to teach His mortal kin how to love and how to treat one another. He said, "A new commandment I give unto you, that ye love one another; as I have loved you, that ye also love one another. By this shall all men know that ye are my disciples, if ye have love one to another" (John 13:34–35). Why should we change? To love as He loves. It is the only way we can be worthy and help others to be worthy to return to Him.

THE ONLY SURE WAY

At some point in each person's journey in life or in death, he or she will have to confront Jesus. Eventually every knee will bow and every tongue confess that Jesus was right (see Philip. 2:10–11; D&C 76:110). This acknowledgment will be accompanied by the awareness there is no other way in which man can live in harmony with his fellow beings on earth or in heaven than by Jesus' way (see 2 Ne. 9:41; 25:29; Mosiah 3:17). The sooner this truth is learned, the less will be the hurt, heartache, and sorrow experienced by those who sought alternative ways.

President Howard W. Hunter proclaimed that Jesus was

> the great standard! The only sure way! The light and the life of the
> world! How grateful we should be that God sent his Only

Begotten Son to earth to do at least two things that no other person could have done. The first task Christ did as a perfect, sinless Son was to redeem all mankind from the Fall, providing an atonement for Adam's sin and for our own sins if we will accept and follow him. The second great thing he did was to set a perfect example of right living, of kindness and mercy and compassion, in order that all of the rest of mankind might know how to live, know how to improve, and know how to become more godlike.

Let us follow the Son of God in all ways and in all walks of life. Let us make him our exemplar and our guide. We should at every opportunity ask ourselves, "What would Jesus do?" and then be more courageous to act upon the answer. We must follow Christ, in the best sense of that word. We must be about his work as he was about his Father's. (*Ensign*, May 1994, 64)

How does a disciple of Jesus Christ develop the ability to overcome inappropriate criticism except by coming to Jesus? The way to conquer all spiritual weakness is to come unto Jesus. We can overcome a bad idea, trait, or thought by replacing it with a better one, just as Jesus replaced the older Mosaic laws with higher ones. Criticism given or received the right way, at a right time, and with a right spirit is a better idea. It is the only path that a true believer in Christ can follow.

For the baptized, confirmed member of The Church of Jesus Christ of Latter-day Saints, coming unto Jesus means receiving the Holy Ghost. It means to live in such a way that we may enjoy the companionship of the Spirit (see John 14:16–17, 26–27).

Now back to the original question, "Why should I change?" The answer is, "The Lord's way works." Inappropriate criticism does not. Yet, there is a greater reason to change. The Lord extends a precious promise to those who are willing to submit to His conditions: "I, the Lord, am bound when ye do what I say; but when ye do not what I say, ye have no promise" (D&C 82:10). As we come to love in the Lord's way, our criticism arises out of sincere concern for the welfare of the souls in our stewardship. The Lord has promised that through our faithfulness (1) our garments are cleansed of the sins of those in our stewardship (see Jacob 2:2) and, more importantly, (2) eventually those we've sought to help can return to God and be saved from their sins (see Enos 1:13–18).

Binding the Lord with Faithfulness

All those in stewardship positions, especially parents and spouses, can exercise more faith in God's plan of salvation. Fear of losing the souls of their children has led to desperate and unrighteous dominion on the part of parents. With God's love and the devil's way of doing things, they hope to save their children from eternal damnation. But it doesn't work that way. Only with God's way is there a promise that those who are faltering can come back.

Suffice it to say that unrighteous dominion, improper criticism, and coercion are not the Lord's way. Faithful parents can bind the Lord with a promise that in doing things His way, those in their stewardships will not be tied down in resentment but lifted by the Spirit. Even as the goodness of Jesus blesses the lives of those "less good," even so goodly parents can extract from God a promise for their children and their children's children to the third and fourth generations. Parents can save their children by strict obedience to the Lord's commandments. The scriptures are filled with many examples of the goodness of parents binding God to a promise. For example, Mosiah bound God to a promise for the safety of his sons among the Lamanites (see Mosiah 28:4–9). Enos 1:8, 10, 12, 15, 18 and Doctrine and Covenants 10:46–53 are but a few of many such promises. Joseph Smith stated, "When a seal is put upon the father and mother, it secures their posterity so they cannot be lost, but will be saved by virtue of their father and mother" (*Teachings of the Prophet Joseph Smith*, 321).

Imagine for a moment the power of faithful parents, friends, or loved ones who by their commitment bind God to a promise. The Lord said He wanted criticism given and received in the spirit of meekness and gentleness and with love unfeigned (see D&C 121:41–44). If you will do this, you will bind God to a promise of bringing the wayward back in His own due time. He will keep it. Heavenly Father has already prepared a way through the Atonement of Jesus Christ for the salvation of His children. Consider the words of Orson F. Whitney:

You parents of the wilful and the wayward! Don't give them up. Don't cast them off. They are not utterly lost. The Shepherd will find his sheep. They were his before they were yours—long before he entrusted them to your care; and *you cannot begin to love them as he loves them.* They have but strayed in ignorance from the Path of Right, and God is merciful to ignorance. Only the fulness of knowledge brings the fulness of accountability. Our Heavenly Father is far more merciful, infinitely more charitable, than even the best of his servants, and the Everlasting Gospel is mightier in power to save than our narrow finite minds can comprehend.

The Prophet Joseph Smith declared—and he never taught more comforting doctrine—that the eternal sealings of faithful parents and the divine promises made to them for valiant service in the Cause of Truth, would save not only themselves, but likewise their posterity. Though some of the sheep may wander, the eye of the Shepherd is upon them, and sooner or later they will feel the tentacles of Divine Providence reaching out after them and drawing them back to the fold. *Either in this life or the life to come, they will return.* They will have to pay their debt to justice; they will suffer for their sins; and may tread a thorny path; but if it leads them at last, like the penitent Prodigal, to a loving and forgiving father's heart and home, the painful experience will not have been in vain. Pray for your careless and disobedient children; hold on to them with your faith. Hope on, trust on, till you see the salvation of God.

Who are these straying sheep—these wayward sons and daughters? They are children of the Covenant, heirs to the promises, and have received, if baptized, the gift of the Holy Ghost, which makes manifest the things of God. Could all that go for naught? (Conference Report, April 1929, 110–11; italics added)

At this point, most of us are afraid to hope this promise could apply to us. We doubt our worthiness. We may feel it is perfection or nothing. But God doesn't expect us to be perfect at this overnight. He expects us to endure to the end, love our fellow beings, and have faith and hope in Christ (see 2 Ne. 31:15–16, 20–21; Mosiah 4:6–7). He expects us to keep loving and correcting, if necessary, in His way. If we do so, the Lord is bound by His promise.

We can take comfort in Jacob's words, "God will be merciful unto many; and our children shall be restored" (2 Ne. 10:2). And we can gain strength and increase our determination to be as righteous as we can be by reading the following from Brigham Young:

> I could say something encouraging to parents, if they would heed. Let the father and mother, who are members of this Church and kingdom, take a righteous course, and strive with all their might *never to do a wrong*, but to do good all their lives; if they have one child or one hundred children, *if they conduct themselves towards them as they should*, binding them to the Lord by their faith and prayers, I care not where those children go, they are bound up to their parents by an everlasting tie, and no power of earth or hell can separate them from their parents in eternity; they will return again to the fountain from whence they sprang. . . . I am sorry to hear Elders of Israel *use words, and manifest anger and impatience that are unbecoming.* (*Journal of Discourses,* 11:215–16; italics added)

Imagine, again, binding the Lord with a promise that would save our loved ones. What will you give in exchange for the souls of those you love? Most of us would give our lives, but will we restrain our tongues? Will we incorporate the following verses into our thoughts and actions?

> No power or influence can or ought to be maintained by virtue of the priesthood, only by persuasion, by long-suffering, by gentleness and meekness, and by love unfeigned; by kindness, and pure knowledge, which shall greatly enlarge the soul without hypocrisy, and without guile—reproving betimes with sharpness, when moved upon by the Holy Ghost; and then showing forth afterwards an increase of love toward him whom thou hast reproved, lest he esteem thee to be his enemy. (D&C 121:41–43)

God is waiting to be bound by the righteous walk and talk of His children. The question must be asked, "Will we reprove in the Lord's own way to save our loved ones?" And herein may lie the best answer to the question, "Why should I change?" In discipleship to Jesus, we may not only save our soul but also the soul of a loved one.

Assignments for Chapter 5

1. Write a letter to yourself and answer the question, "Why do I need to change?"

2. The Lamanite king said to God in humble and mighty prayer, "I will give away all my sins to know thee" (Alma 22:18). What are you willing to sacrifice in order to bind God to a promise to save your loved ones? Are you willing to let go of any and all evil speaking, criticism, and faultfinding that is not prompted by the Holy Ghost?

Note: The word *sacrifice* is a Latin word and comes from two words: *sacra,* meaning "holy," and *ficere,* a verb meaning "to make." A sacrifice is not something you give up. It is something you "make holy."

CHAPTER 6

ASSISTING CHANGE IN OTHERS

Now that we have prepared ourselves to give and receive criticism artfully, it is time to learn more details of how to do so. There are five steps we must take in order to give or receive criticism in the Lord's own way:

1. Assist change in others
2. Seek help in mighty prayer
3. Act out of love
4. Show an increase of love
5. Distinguish between appropriate and inappropriate criticism

This chapter will deal with the first step, and the next four with the remaining steps. Experience has taught that all five are necessary in order to maintain the strength required to sustain the giving and receiving of criticism in the Lord's own way. This chapter will discuss how and when we should help others to change.

As we learned in the last chapter, change is very difficult in our own lives. It is much more difficult to enforce in the lives of others. This is because everyone has agency. The words of the following hymn come to mind:

> Know this, that ev'ry soul is free
> To choose his life and what he'll be;
> For this eternal truth is giv'n:

That God will force no man to heav'n.
He'll call, persuade, direct aright,
And bless with wisdom, love, and light,
In nameless ways be good and kind,
But never force the human mind.
(*Hymns*, no. 240)

Imposing our criticism on others will not change them. Being right or having a position of authority is simply not sufficient to force our will upon another in any circumstance. Some have suggested, tongue in cheek, that a book needs to be written called *Free Agency and How to Enforce It*. Of course, the book has already been written by Lucifer, and it seems to have been a best seller. This is not our job. Our job is to follow God's example and "call, persuade, direct aright, . . . be good and kind" when called upon to do so.

As discussed previously, true change comes from within each person. God will not force His children back to Him. The reality is that we cannot change a friend or loved one unless the friend or loved one is willing to change. Is it hopeless? Is it vain? It is hopeless and vain if the methods for change are not consistent with the laws of heaven. It is vain and hopeless if our objectives and methods include force, coercion, abuse, and uninvited, unauthorized, and improperly given criticism. What hope is there to assist a loved one? Rather than stand by as an idle witness to the self-destruction of those we love, there is something we can do to properly assist change. Coming to recognize the proper way of assisting change teaches us the Lord's program for our involvement. We see our necessary role in the Lord's plan for bringing those in our stewardship home to Him.

ASSISTING CHANGE

Assisting change requires a conversion on the part of the would-be catalyst. It is a conversion to assist change in "the Lord's own way." There is a tremendous amount of good we can do in behalf of another to assist change. By definition, a catalyst facilitates a chemical reaction, speeding up the process of change. As parents, we want to speed up the process of change in the lives of our children. Therefore, we criticize them, hoping the truth of what we have to say will speed up a change. It doesn't; it brings frustration. And frustration brings more criticism. The negative downward spiral continues until we, or they, flee the relationship.

For an outside party to influence a friend or loved one to change requires a positive interaction and patience. The challenge faced by most of us as "want-to-be" agents of change is patience. What we face is a friend or loved one who doesn't want to change. The friend or loved one may even be belligerent about not changing. Typically, we, as the concerned friend or parent or spouse, match the intensity of resistance with desperate pleas and warnings. What ensues is a power struggle. Because of frustration, both parties are out of control, but for different reasons. The wayward is out of control because he or she wants the right to make a poor judgment decision. We want-to-be catalysts are out of control because of frustration, and launch into any number of horror stories which may indeed become reality. At some point after harsh and critical words have been exchanged and the frustration has reached its maximum, there is almost always a power play, a threat of eviction or abandonment. Neither party wants separation as the outcome, and both hope that the threat of leaving or being kicked out will bring about conformity or freedom. Often a truce is declared or negotiated by a third party. However, neither combatant has backed off from his or her position. The relationship is a time bomb waiting for the next battle. This predictable outcome may bring about apparent conformity. It is an illusion.

Control is not change. Conformity is not change. Forced submission and acquiescence are not change. As frustrated parents or friends who want to assist change, we wonder what more we can do. We try to save our wayward from the consequences of their poor judgment decisions. We want to rescue them from themselves. We bail them out of problem after problem, only to find that nothing has changed. Our loved ones are still on a course of self-destruction. We loan them money. We pay for programs to help them. We take them to counselors. It seems that every solution is defeated by the waywards' unwillingness to accept responsibility for making their life better. Nothing seems to work.

Sadly, most of us do not start out with the Lord's programs. Instead, we run the gauntlet of frustration and exhaust all of our personal options. As parents or friends, we try love and understanding. Our impatience and frustration reach the breaking point. We abandon love and understanding as one more failed attempt. We resort to improper criticism, force, coercion, punishment, and finally abandonment. Hurting and smarting, we give up. We emotionally withdraw to a safe distance and mourn the lost potential of what might have been.

This pattern is being played out daily in the lives of thousands. What a tragedy! What a waste of energy and personal effort! To properly assist change requires patience, but at least it works. Those of us who think we have tried the Lord's way with no result have been too impatient. When we do not receive the immediate answer we expected to our sincere prayers, our frustration with the wayward expands to include frustration with Heavenly Father. We conclude that if God isn't going to do what we want, when we want it, we will do it ourselves. So, trusting in the "arm of flesh," we press forward, believing that God has abandoned us. The truth is that we have abandoned our faith in God's ability to rescue our loved one. The following story illustrates how one woman did not really govern her relationship in the Lord's way, and the frustration this led to. Notice that everything wasn't made perfect in the relationship but that love and trust and reliance on the Lord were eventually restored.

Gifting Unconditional Love

Jill was a single mother of five children and worked full-time out of the home. Brenda, her sixteen-year-old, was her challenge. The other four children seemed to be on track. They were doing well in school and were active in the Church. Brenda was failing school because of her unexcused absences. The relationship had degenerated to where neither of them could be civil to each other. Brenda just wanted to have fun and be with friends and live in the moment. She resented her lack of freedom. Jill had become a screaming banshee owing to a psychological struggle with her daughter. This is where the counselor was brought in. Punishment only led to more rebellion. What Jill was doing wasn't working. She was doing the best she could, but it was not effective.

Brenda was dishonest, uncooperative, immoral, and now violent. A very basic contract was drawn up with minimal requirements.

In a private session with just the mother, the counselor reviewed her alternatives:

- Things could stay as they were.
- Things could get worse, and Brenda would be removed from the home.
- The mother could let go of imposing her will and seek to assist change.

One of the difficult issues Jill had to face was the feeling that she was rewarding Brenda for acting poorly. To show love to an abusive, lying, dishonest child went against Jill's basic values of respect and responsibility.

It was agreed that perfection or nothing would be unrealistic for either the mother or the daughter. There would be mistakes and setbacks. In order for Brenda to change, the mother would have to change her approach. It began by Jill stopping her constant messages of disapproval. Since Jill thought criticizing and carping were signs of responsible motherhood, it was difficult for her to keep her mouth shut. Jill was afraid Brenda would think she had won the power struggle. She was concerned that Brenda would become more difficult to manage. Only the fear of losing her daughter altogether motivated Jill to follow the counsel. She began by taking her frustrations to God and not to Brenda.

Brenda agreed to five minutes a night where her mother could give her negative feedback. The rest of the day, for twenty-three hours and fifty-five minutes, Brenda would not be criticized. The counselor recommended that Jill write down her criticisms in black and white where Brenda could see them without the mother's facial expression, body language, and tone of voice. This would allow Brenda to focus on the content. With a few major exceptions, their home began to be more peaceful. Finding ways to take her love to her daughter and her frustrations to God was getting easier for Jill. With absolutely no trust for her daughter, the mother began gifting unconditional acts of love, one each day.

Brenda turned seventeen and began attending an alternative high school. Jill had let go of nearly every expectation. She continued to do daily deeds of love. Brenda and her mother were talking, not yelling.

Brenda didn't lack knowledge of values; she lacked commitment to values. Brenda's selfish need for peer approval had caused her to trade away all values except the acceptance of her friends. Her guilty conscience made her angry with God, the Church, and her family. She was the black sheep, and she knew it. In a counseling session, Brenda confessed that she was a disappointment to her mother, but now she knew her mother loved her anyway. Brenda did not come back to the Church, but she participated in family prayer and in family activities. The relationship became better, but not perfect. It would not have come even to that point except for Jill's willingness to let go of forcing change and focus instead on daily expressions of love and assisting her daughter with only her positive choices.

Update on Jill and Brenda

Brenda is now twenty-two years old. She had a child out of wedlock and a failed marriage with a man other than the father of her child. She worked for a while as a waitress and decided she wanted to go back to school. She finished her GED and is attending a local community college. She hasn't missed a class, as she frequently did in high school, because the motivation to change her life has come from within.

Jill was tempted, as grandmothers are, to take over the raising of Brenda's baby daughter, but she wisely offered to tend the child while Brenda attended college and on other special occasions. At first Brenda did not act as a responsible mother and expected her mother to be a twenty-four-hour-a-day child-care center. When Jill refused to do that, there were threats of "never seeing her grandchild again," which lasted a couple of weeks until Brenda's other resources ran out. Later, when child protective services were called in by the father's family, Brenda changed her priorities. At long last, Brenda cares more about her life than others do. Brenda had an interview with her bishop recently and has decided that she would like to raise her daughter within the LDS Church.

Granted, there is a lot left to improve in this relationship, but it's heading in the right direction. It is better to be a foot from hell and walking away from it than it is to be ten miles away from hell and running into it.

Brenda's struggles are not over, but her life has improved significantly from that of the wild-eyed, rebellious sixteen-year-old she once was. Her life could be worse—much worse—except for the wise and measured behaviors of a mother who chose to take her frustrations about her daughter to the Lord and her love to her daughter. There would be less hurt, heartache, and sorrow in the world if all of us went directly into the "Lord's program" for changing the heart of a loved one.

THE LORD'S PROGRAM FOR CHANGE

Jill and Brenda's story shows us some of the key steps to the Lord's program for change—namely, taking frustrations to God in mighty prayer, taking love to the loved one, setting boundaries to protect yourself and to avoid becoming an enabler, being an example of the values you desire, sharing to the level of the loved one's willingness, and exercising faith and patience in God's divine intervention. Let's explore each of these further.

Take Frustrations to God in Mighty Prayer

One of the first things Jill had to learn to do in assisting change in her daughter was to take her frustrations to the Lord instead of Brenda. More will be said on mighty prayer in the next chapter. For now it is sufficient to understand that the powers of heaven can be activated for the good of our loved one by the prayer of faith. By taking our frustrations to God in mighty prayer, we spare the relationship from fruitless carping, emotional alienation, and lost rapport. We, as the friend or parent who wants to assist change, must be willing to change our approach. Often this desire comes only after we have learned, through the things we have suffered, that the alternatives to the Lord's approach don't work. Prayer works.

Take Love to the Loved One

Armed with a desire to properly assist change but filled with trepidation, we as fledgling disciples of Jesus Christ leave our frustrations with the Lord and commit to taking our love to our loved one. The Lord's program is to focus on the good in a person and build upon it. Truly, in the heart of the most wayward is a spark to be better. However tiny the spark, it can be fanned into fire by the love of another or the desire for a better self. God's long-suffering love for each of His children sets an example for all who believe in His Son. God's love reaches out to each of us through Christ.

> For God so loved the world, that he gave his only begotten Son, that whosoever believeth in him should not perish, but have everlasting life. For God sent not his Son into the world to condemn the world; but that the world through him might be saved. (John 3:16–17)

In the Lord's program, He calls us to reach out and fan the flame of His love. He invites us to assist in changing others by becoming agents of love. There is an eternal truth which says uninvited, unauthorized, and improper criticism will not generate love, nor change behavior. Love generates love. "We love him, because he first loved us" (1 Jn. 4:19). The wayward do not lack knowledge. They do not lack condemnation. They lack love.

A Mission to Love

As a counselor, I asked Marti to go one month without once criticizing her fifteen-year-old son. I challenged her to go to the Lord every time she felt upset or frustrated with her son. I explained to her that the Lord was anxious to soften his heart.

"Let God change your son. Let God have the burden. Lay the responsibility for change upon the altar. Become an agent of love. Every time you are tempted to vent your frustration to your son, go to God in prayer and ask for strength to love him. For one month do at least one loving thing a day for your son, but don't give one word of condemnation."

Marti asked me what she should do with her resentment. I said she should turn it into a loving behavior.

"For one month, Marti—just thirty days—don't give one criticism. If you fail, start your thirty days over. Think of this as the 'loving thing' to do.

"Imagine you have been called into the office of the prophet of God. He places his hands upon your head and gives you a mission call. For one month you are called to give only love and not one word of criticism. Would you do it, Marti? Would you follow the counsel? I know you would. You are a woman who loves the Lord. Pray about this counsel. Follow your heart, but not your frustration."

We met once a week for the next month. She reported how hard it was at first to break the old habit of criticizing. She did think of it as a mission. Marti found herself praying fifteen or twenty times a day. She said every time she felt frustrated she would go over and put her arms around her son and say, "I love you." He was hostile at first and very defensive. By the end of the third week he began to hug her back. During the fourth week, he came to his mother and cried. He just wanted to be held. Her words were words of love. "It has to be hard for you, son. I'm sorry you're hurting. I know you'll get through this. I love you and I'll always be here for you."

"Mom, I've made such a mess out of my life and I'm only fifteen years old. I've got to stop screwing up."

Marti continued praying and loving. For the first time she saw a ray of hope. She continued with her mission.

One day, after several years had passed, the phone rang, and I was invited to the missionary farewell of her son.

Agents of love must come to recognize that love, not inappropriate criticism, is the catalyst for change. Love will bless both the giver and the receiver. It will power the engine that propels the disciple to the necessary patience. We as the agents of love must seek for strength, courage, and perspective from God in mighty prayer. In turn, God will strengthen the disciple to give love to the wayward.

But from where does the wayward seek love? The answer is, "In all the wrong places." The wayward is desperate for acceptance and love. Desperate people accept desperate alternatives to their highest and best self. They set up barriers which block out their ability to receive the love of God. They discount themselves and even hate what they do or what they have allowed themselves to become. Therefore, love from self or for self is eliminated as a source. From where will the love come? It must come from you.

However, if you are in a critical mode and your frustration manifests itself in raging disappointment, you cease being an instrument in God's hands. You become a part of the problem and not part of the solution. You are neither an agent of love nor a catalyst for change. You must take your frustrations to God in mighty prayer and seek for the strength to nurture the one who is difficult to love. Charity for all begins with charity for one. It may be the very one that is the hardest for us to love. Love is a spiritual gift given of God to every man, woman, and child on earth. It is embryonic and needs to be nurtured. Love grows by loving. Consider the analogy:

> Living inside of me are two ravenous animals. One is an animal
> of fear and doubt. The other is an animal of love and faith.
> Which one will live? The answer is, the one I feed.

The more we feed our love, the more we have to give. The more we feed others our love, the more they feel it and respond to it. Through mighty prayer, studying the words of the scriptures and the words of the living prophets, giving loving service to others, and working in the Church to build the kingdom of God, we will build up our spiritual reserves to love another. By giving active missionary service or supporting the effort to proclaim the gospel, redeeming the dead, or magnifying our calling to "perfect the Saints," we will add to our spiritual reserves. Without reserves of love, we remain an empty well. Occasionally we are blessed with loved ones and friends whose gifts of love sustain us, so that we in turn can share our love with the wayward.

Eventually, however, each of us will have to tap into the waters of everlasting life, even Christ. Jesus becomes a source of "loving water," as well as living water, that springs up as an eternal fountain. When we as agents of love connect to Jesus as our primary source of approval, we free ourselves from codependency on the approval of those we love. We are then able to appreciate the love of others but not be dependent upon that love. Not being dependent, we are available to love free of the fear of rejection. We free ourselves in Christ of the expectation and of the need to be loved by them. What we cannot do is to free ourselves from the need to love and be loved.

The frustration of unrequited love is painful, but it need not be hopeless. God is not asking that we live without love. He is asking that we don't become so dependent upon the love of others that we do things that are contrary to their eternal best interest or our best interest out of fear of losing their love. Love of God and love of our fellow beings are the two great commandments (see Luke 10:27). There is a key of eternal power in loving God more than we love others. It is the power to love others without having to be loved in return. This is not easy. It was never intended to be. However, in order to live in the day-to-day reality, we have to learn to feast upon the words of Christ. These reminders of the love God has for us can make the lack of love from others more bearable.

Tolerable Misery

After Mona complained about her circumstances, which included an unappreciative spouse and children who were running with a bad crowd and getting into trouble with the law, I asked her about her testimony of Jesus. She proceeded to tell me that she had a testimony of the gospel and knew the Church was true and that Joseph Smith was a prophet of God. She believed in the Atonement, and yet she never felt worthy to pursue a relationship with Jesus. When I began to explain how a relationship with Jesus was developed through prayer and study of the scriptures, she interrupted with the following, "You're not going to tell me to study and pray, are you? I get so sick of these simple answers. I've tried praying more, and I don't understand the scriptures. I read a sentence and I don't even know what I have read."

I replied, "So, Mona, you don't really want a solution to your problems; you just want to complain about them. You are miserable and have learned to substitute sympathy from friends and others for the love and appreciation of your husband and children. You don't want to seek the reserve of love you could be receiving and giving. Things are not changing in your world; in fact, they are getting worse. You tolerate it because you cannot see any way out. You live in what I call 'tolerable misery.' It's bad—even rotten at times—but you tolerate your misery and reject solutions which appear difficult, because you prefer to stay a prisoner of 'tolerable misery' rather than to pay the price of work and effort required to free you."

Mona did not want to hear about the hard work and effort necessary to develop a relationship of love with the Godhead through heartfelt prayer and study of the scriptures. Frankly, I appealed to Mona to be diligent and humble. She refused to be either.

There are many Monas out there. They stay in tolerable misery and seek a life of sympathy. Mona actually believed that she had tried prayer and it didn't work for her. Studying the scriptures was too hard because she didn't understand them.

Jesus gave two parables about prayer in Luke 18:1–14. Diligence was the message of the tale of the importuning widow, and humility was the point of the story about the Pharisee and the publican. Mona lacked diligence and humility in her quest to make Jesus and the love of God the solution to her frustrated life. It is no easier to revisit an abandoned solution than it is to stick to a diet. How many of us keep looking for a solution to losing weight other than to eat properly and exercise? Where is the magic pill, the snake-oil elixir that we can just take and not have to worry about eating right and exercising?

Developing spiritual strength through diligence and humility with the prayer of faith and study of the words of God is a real solution that depends upon us alone. We come to love those that we know. We can come to know God through prayer and study of His words. Most of us have already filled our lives with an impossible schedule, and there is no time for study and meaningful prayer. Those that we love and want to love us aren't going to give us the time we need.

I met again with Mona after several more years. "I'm ready now," she said. "I'm sick and tired of being sick and tired. What do I need to do?"

Obviously, Mona had come to a point of frustration where tolerable misery was tolerable no more. I remember thinking of Alma teaching the poor among the Zoramites and noting how some of them were humble in whatever circumstance they we were in, while others were compelled to be humble by the things they chose to suffer (see Alma 32:12–25). Mona agreed to start out by taking an adult religion class and reading the Book of Mormon cover to cover, just to become familiar with the language of the scriptures. She also began a diligent quest for a better relationship with the Lord through prayer. She actually started to feel her prayers and not just say them. Mona is a work in progress. She is seriously looking to develop the ability to love by building up her spiritual strength through study and prayer. She is on the road to learning charity, the purest of love, even the pure love of Christ. Mona is on her way to becoming an agent of love.

This is also the ideal. Most live in a reality where the love of others is essential to their own feelings of worth. This is precisely why Mona and each of us need to develop the ability to love others without being held hostage by requiring their love of us before we can be loving. One does not have to be perfect in order to begin to love as Jesus loved.

For a period of time, loving the wayward may require that the parent, spouse, or friend not depend upon the love of those we appropriately criticized. The pain of our criticism may inhibit the one being criticized from doing anything but withdrawing. It may be that, short of perfect charity for all people (see 2 Ne. 33:7–9), we as the agents of love will have to depend upon the love of the Lord to sustain us. Remember, charity for all begins with charity for one. Usually, we marry our greatest challenge in life, or give birth to it! Often we are taught charity by bearing with a difficult-to-love member of the family. This allows us to grow line upon line in developing the spiritual gift of the pure love of Christ. We cannot be used as agents of love if we do not show forth loving behaviors. Without some semblance of charity or love, how can anyone serve as an instrument for good in the hands of God? We can't; we are "nothing" (see Moro. 7:46). We must go to the source of charity, even the Father, to obtain the needed strength. By following the Lord's plan, we as the agents of love become instruments in the hands of God.

Set Boundaries to Protect Yourself

In all our loving we must be careful, however, to keep the issues of love and trust separate. The principle of protecting ourselves from physical, emotional, or spiritual abuse should seem obvious. However, there are many well-meaning people who are confused by the two issues. It is as if love and trust were put into a blender and mixed together. The resultant effect is a hodgepodge of confusion wherein the victim of abuse is unable to discern between loving behavior and trusting behavior. Nevertheless, it is our responsibility to set limits on what we are willing to tolerate.

For example, if someone is yelling, cursing, or giving us uninvited, unauthorized, and inappropriate criticism, it would be appropriate to find a way to exit the immediate situation. One could say something like, "I'm leaving the room (or the house, or the car), because I do not give you permission to treat me in this manner. I am not leaving the relationship. I will be happy to talk about this when you are in emotional control. If you cannot handle a calm discussion of your concerns, please write them down and I will read them tonight."

One woman I counseled said, "If my husband spoke to me like that, I would hit him." She honestly felt she had a right to say whatever she wanted whenever and however she wanted. She was offended if her husband did not listen to her complain, nag, criticize, and even rage. She felt an entitlement. When I suggested that hitting her husband repeatedly constituted physical abuse, she scoffed and dismissed it as inconsequential.

If someone becomes physically abusive, call the police. To stay in a physically, emotionally, or spiritually abusive situation only gives permission to abusers; it does not assist change in them. It encourages them to continue and to escalate their abusive actions. Not only is it damaging to the relationship, but it fosters coercion, intimidation, and manipulative behaviors. It is understandable that children who are abused have a harder time as adults knowing where to draw the lines and establish boundaries. Once a person is aware that abuse should not be tolerated, there is no excuse to permit abusive behavior from friend, family, spouse, or child. Sometimes calling the police is the loving thing to do. As hard as it may be, sometimes those in a stewardship position may have to remove a toxic person from the situation or home involved.

Separating Love and Trust

Darla was a fourteen-year-old who was verbally abusive to her mother and father. She had learned that there were no limits on her abusive behaviors. Darla found power in abuse. She found more freedom to be with her friends, to have fun, to enjoy autonomy, and to live for the moment by being belligerent, arbitrary, and combative.

The parents, in the mistaken guise of love, had tolerated Darla's abuse. They thought it was the loving thing to do. They were fearful of her running away and being in a worse environment. They were concerned about her losing future opportunities. They were, in fact, being held hostage by fear, doubt, and a confused notion of love.

When a counselor outlined a strategy for dealing with Darla, the parents were horrified. What they failed to recognize was that they had already lost Darla. The strategy involved a declining list of options for Darla that made her responsible for her behavior. The declining list of options included Darla being placed in a home for troubled girls. The counselor explained that this final option was to send the message loudly and clearly that the parents would not tolerate abusive behavior.

There was room in the program for Darla to be forgiven and to earn trust by obeying a few simple rules. She was to be where she said she was going to be, doing what she said she would be doing. She was expected to be home at the mutually agreed-upon time or, if the agreement was violated, upon the arbitrary time imposed by the parents. Her freedom to function at school, at home, and with her friends was conditioned on her behavior. Each violation would add one week onto the time she would be permitted to obtain a driver's license. The parents were going to enforce the new rules completely. If Darla did not respond to the positive reinforcement program, the parents were to implement the consequences in three stages, the last stage being her exit from the home. By following through with their stated objectives, it was hoped that their credibility with Darla would be established.

The counselor warned the parents that unless their resolve was firm and unwavering, Darla would return to her old ways. Because of the past belligerence, the parents were told to expect that Darla would try escalating the conflict. The parents were to exit the room if Darla became verbally abusive or critical. They were to offer her another opportunity to communicate, following the rules of courtesy and respect. Under no conditions were they to allow her to take them out of control of what they would tolerate and not tolerate. They agreed they would help Darla with all of the positive moves she would make, but they would not "help her one inch to hell."

The parents also agreed to put her into a Christian girls' school near Orlando, Florida, for a minimum of six months if she failed to respond to their few, but reasonable, boundaries. The parents continued to do loving things on a daily basis for Darla. At the same time, they held firmly to their stated agenda. As the counselor predicted, Darla increased her belligerence and escalated the conflict. Soon Darla was looking at over a hundred violations. This meant she could not drive until she was eighteen. Quickly, Darla moved through each level of strategic retreats the parents had outlined. One day, unannounced to Darla, two huge Samoan security guards and a lady hired as a companion and driver entered Darla's room and hauled her off to a girls' "reform school." She was kicking, screaming, swearing, and cursing at her parents. "I'll never forgive you," she shouted. "I hate you! I hate you!" She yelled rape and tried to get someone to rescue her. She was no match for the Samoans.

The facility was escape-proof. There were four levels of freedom, and the girls could earn privileges by obedience. It usually took forty-five to sixty days before the girls realized this was real. Darla was told to make her bed. She refused; her bed was taken away and she was given a sleeping bag and a pillow. She was informed that if she faithfully rolled up her sleeping bag for a week, they would restore her bed. After a month Darla earned her bed back. She could write only to her parents, and all mail that arrived for her was sent back to her parents. Darla begged and pleaded with her parents to let her out. She promised obedience. She had learned her lesson and would be a new person. The parents wavered and called the counselor. The father wanted mercy, and the mother held firm. The counselor informed the parents that the real issue was their credibility. They had said six months, and they needed to stick to it or they would be right back where they started.

The parents agreed and prayed mightily for a true change of heart. They wrote to her and told her of their resolve. If she worked her way up to at least the third level, she would be released at six months. If not, she would be required to stay another six months. Darla was beginning to believe her parents for the first time in her young life. At six months Darla had achieved the fourth level of freedom, which permitted her to go with a group to an outside movie. Later she confessed that she thought she would run away while at the movie. What she didn't know was that the Samoans were guarding the exits. Had she run, she would have been returned to the first level and a sleeping bag and a six-month extension. She finished a year's worth of home-study high school in six months.

Her parents met with her at the end of the six months and informed her that if she returned to her old ways they would send her back. She believed them. A contract was drawn up with very specific behavioral objectives. The past was forgiven, and Darla would again be able to obtain her driver's license at sixteen. Violations would add one week beyond her sixteenth birthday for each infraction before she would be able to get her driver's license.

After the honeymoon period of a couple of months, Darla tested her parents again and found them absolutely committed to do what they said they would do. The parents continued to love Darla. Trust was a separate issue. Darla earned her license at sixteen years and one month because of a few infractions. She graduated from high school and attended a local community college. She married a returned missionary in the temple, with her parents shedding tears of joy the entire time. The parents ended up being instruments in the hands of the Lord because they set boundaries on an abusive relationship. Who better to love her to her highest and best self than her parents?

These parents learned the value of real boundaries and thus were able to properly assist change. They also recognized the need to be realistic in their expectations. Their "I trust you" plan was based on responsible behavior, not on perfection. These parents learned that the art of parenting was the art of gradually transferring responsibility for life from their shoulders to those of Darla as she demonstrated an ability to handle it. They found that the art of parenting is the art of letting go. It was not the skill of hanging on. By protecting themselves, establishing boundaries, and setting reasonable behavioral objectives, they now enjoy a loving daughter.

Be an Example of the Values You Desire

Praying, loving, and setting limits if necessary is not enough to effect change in others. We must model the behavior we expect of others. Again, this does not mean perfection or nothing. It means striving to do our best. This adds credibility to the message as well as the messenger. A false message would be, "Do as I say, not as I do." James advised all disciples to be "doers of the word, and not hearers only" (James 1:22). Jesus, the perfect example of all things righteous, said, "Wherefore, follow me, and *do the things which ye have seen me do*" (2 Ne. 31:12; italics added). The following story is a modern-day example of two men, a father and his son, who lived what they spoke.

Sekeli Sali Manu

This is the true-life story about a Samoan boy named Sekeli Sali Manu. He was born the tenth of eleven children in Western Samoa, on the island of Savaii. His father was the branch president and went through incredible persecution. Twice his father was stoned and left for dead. What the father said and how he lived were one and the same. He said there was always time to read the scriptures. While fishing in his outrigger canoe with his sons, the father would call them to the surface by pounding a rock against the canoe. While bobbing up and down with the undulating waves, seven Samoan boys saw their father take the scriptures out of a plastic wrapping. They listened to him read to them for twenty minutes a day.

When the father was dying, he gave a father's blessing to each of his sons and daughters in turn. Sekeli was not home. He was far across the island, working. A runner was sent to fetch him. The father stated to his wife, "I no die until I give my boy Sekeli a blessing." The frightened Sekeli entered the *fale* (an oval hut) out of breath and fearful that he was too late.

Sekeli knelt on the mats in front of his standing father. The father gave Sekeli a tremendous blessing and closed with these words: "Sekeli, you be the kind of father that I was." In a few minutes, the father passed away.

From seventeen to twenty-four years of age, Sekeli went on to serve almost six years as a building missionary for the Church and two more years as a regular missionary. He later served two additional missions for the Church. He died in his forties and left eight children with a loving wife, Connie. But he also left his testimony, sealed by his personal example.

As a man he was once asked, "Do you ever think of your father, Sekeli?"

He responded, "Every day of my life I hear the voice of my father saying to me, 'Sekeli, you be the kind of father that I was.'"

"When you die and see your father again, what will you say to him, Sekeli?"

"I will look him in the eye and say to him, 'Father, I was the kind of father that you was'" (personal history of Sekeli Manu as related to me personally while serving as the Olympia Washington Stake mission president).

The power of personal example seals the truth of our words (see D&C 135:3–5). We must set the example of exchanging anger for patience and replacing verbal abuse with respect. Kindness and gentleness must win over harshness and violence. Invitation, enticement, and persuasion must emerge in lieu of compulsion, intimidation, and domination. This is the only way we can share in another's experience to grow and change.

Share to the Level of the Loved One's Willingness to Share

A basic truth about human relationships is that they cannot be forced. Each relationship stands on its own. A stepparent cannot force a good relationship upon a stepchild. It must evolve on its own merits. It is a wise person who realizes and respects the level of willingness another possesses. Great relationships are built like a bridge from where they are to a better place. This is best accomplished by the principle of common consent. Find a common ground and begin to build a bridge of understanding and shared experiences. For an example of this step in assisting change, consider the following story.

The Workaholic Father

Jack was eighteen and the only member of the Church in his family. His father was cold and very businesslike. Jack desperately wanted a relationship with his father. Jack was a great athlete, but his father was always too busy with work to attend any games. Finally, Jack realized that if he was going to have a relationship with his father, it would have to be on different terms.

I suggested to Jack that he show up unannounced at his father's place of business. His dad was shocked and wondered if there was an emergency. Jack told his father that he wanted to understand what his father did for a living. The father was too busy then, but set up a time to meet with Jack. The father was excited that Jack would show an interest in the business. Jack invested many hours learning more about the business than he wanted to know. After six weeks, Jack looked up into the stands and saw his father for the first time in his life come to a game.

If our interest in changing others is only to make our lives better, we will not be successful. We need to have a sincere desire to see their lives improve and a desire to be a part of their life. Anything other than the motivation to share love is not the Lord's way of assisting in change.

Exercise Faith and Patience in God's Divine Intervention

Knowing as we do that real change comes from within, much of what we can do to assist change in others is to rely upon God to help them. As our faith in assisting change in the Lord's way increases, His influence—through a person's conscience, a witness from the Holy Ghost, or direct intervention—will become stronger in helping our loved ones change.

The Light of Christ. Latter-day Saints believe that a veil is placed over the mind when everyone is born on this earth. We have no memory of our premortal life as spirit sons and daughters of God. Because of this veil of forgetfulness, God ensured that all of us, as His children, would have an inner light to guide us back to His glorious home: the light of truth, the conscience, the Light of Christ (see Moro. 7:15–17). Despite any dysfunctional background or levels of abuse inflicted upon any of us, we can know right from wrong. So powerful is the Light of Christ that it can lead anyone to change for the better. Even the enemies of Jesus in a fallen and apostate condition were still affected by their consciences. The scribes and Pharisees had brought before Him a woman taken in adultery and demanded of Him to state her punishment:

> So when they continued asking him, he lifted up himself, and said
> unto them, He that is without sin among you, let him first cast a
> stone at her. . . . And they which heard it, *being convicted by their
> own conscience,* went out one by one, beginning at the eldest, even
> unto the last: and Jesus was left alone, and the woman standing in
> the midst. (John 8:7, 9; italics added)

Even the vilest of sinners have burning inside the Light of Christ, the first internal guidance system, to lead them back to God. It is important for every parent, spouse, and friend to know that we are not alone in our concern for a wayward loved one. God is calling to each through the Light of Christ to become a better self. When our mortal voices are out of control, when we are screaming or yelling or giving inappropriate criticism, it is hard for others to hear their inner voice of conscience. Often, it is in the quiet and reflective moments that the conscience speaks the loudest.

The Witness of the Holy Ghost. The second internal guidance system which Heavenly Father gives to each soul born on this earth is the ability to respond to a witness of the Holy Ghost. It is different from the gift of the Holy Ghost, which is given after baptism by the laying on of hands. It is the mission of the Holy Ghost to bear witness to the truth of all things. Whenever we come into contact with the truth, wherever it may be, the Holy Ghost will witness to the soul. In a classroom, in the laboratory, or when contacted by the missionaries, the witness to truth is given by the Holy Ghost (see Moro. 10:5). The Holy Ghost always bears witness of the truth. Unfortunately, it is possible for a person to be so out of touch as to not recognize the truth or the Holy Ghost. However, harsh criticism will not make a person feel the Spirit. In order to assist change, one of our jobs is to make sure that the Spirit is present, giving the other person the opportunity at least to feel that presence.

Member, nonmember, excommunicated member, Gentile, and the vilest of sinners are all alike unto God. The witness of the Holy Ghost can be available to all. It is universal. God never gives up and never gives in, in the guidance of His children. God is patient and long-suffering, not indifferent and uninvolved. Frequently our loved ones are unaware of either the light of conscience or the witness of the Holy Ghost in their lives. But God's hands are daily involved in the lives of His children. One hand of God is the conscience. The other hand of God is the Holy Ghost. Often God guides His children with His hands while He Himself goes unnoticed. When this life is over, we will be overwhelmed at God's participation in our lives and the lives of our loved ones.

Direct Divine Intervention. God, who rules the universe, is deeply centered in the life of each child on this earth. This includes the wayward and the faithful. Heavenly Father directed Jesus to "save all" except the sons of perdition who choose not to be saved (see D&C 76:44). Today is a part of God's eternity, and He does divinely intervene. We must acknowledge God's love for His children. Remember that Orson F. Whitney bore testimony to this truth in these words: "Heavenly Father loves his children more than any earthly parent loves those same children" (Conference Report, April 1929, 11). Because He sees the "big picture" with eternal perspective, God knows how, where, and when to intervene. Man's vision is blurred as he sojourns in time and peers through a darkened glass (see 1 Cor. 13:9–12). What we think is in the best interest of a loved one may not be in his or her eternal best interest. Thus, we must rely on the Holy Ghost not only to help us to know when to intervene, but also to prompt the person we want to help to change. This is a true principle which requires man to have faith in God's love and timing. Heavenly Father's plan is a plan of salvation and not a plan of damnation. God's plan is to bring back each of His children except the sons of perdition, who, by their own choice, do not want to live with God (see D&C 76:36–46). Elder Boyd K. Packer spoke of God's plan being a three-act play. Act 1 was the premortal existence. Act 2 is this mortal life. Act 3 includes the spirit world and the Millennium. Some of our loved ones over whom the most sleep is lost and the most prayers are said will not come around in this mortal life but will respond in Act 3 (see Boyd K. Packer, "The Play and the Plan," CES Fireside, 7 May 1995).

God is patient. God will find a way to save His children without violating their agency. The hands of God are manifested daily. The face of God will be unveiled to His children only when it would be a blessing for us and when we are ready for it: "For he will unveil his face unto you, and it shall be in his own time, and in his own way, and according to his own will" (D&C 88:68).

True believers in Heavenly Father are required to bow their heads and bend their knees and say what Jesus said in the Garden of Gethsemane, "Nevertheless not my will, but thine, be done" (Luke 22:42). As much as we may desire and deserve a needed blessing, the word *nevertheless* must be added to the faith-filled prayer. "Not my will, but thine, be done" acknowledges God's eternal perspective and faith in a God who loves His children. It is important to note that Heavenly Father did not remove the cup from Jesus in the garden. However, Heavenly Father saw fit to intervene in strengthening Him. There is no question of Heavenly Father's love for Jesus, or for the wayward, or for us as His agents of love.

In the imperfect lives of those who are self-destructing, the long-suffering of God is misinterpreted as disinterest or abandonment. Sins, weaknesses, and lack of worthiness add to the doubt and fear of not being loved of God. But that is simply not the case. Heavenly Father loves us so much that He allowed Jesus to suffer in the garden and suffer death at the hands of wicked and cruel men—for us. It was the supernal Atonement. Suffice it to say that we ask for the blessings of divine intervention in the name and worthiness of Jesus. We do not call upon God by virtue of our own worthiness, but in the name of Jesus, the great Mediator, whose worthiness qualifies the prayer. Because Christ is worthy, our prayers can ascend to God through Him as the Mediator (see 2 Ne. 2:27; D&C 76:69; D&C 107:19).

> Listen to him who is the advocate with the Father, who is pleading your cause before him—saying: Father, behold the sufferings and death of him who did no sin, in whom thou wast well pleased; behold the blood . . . of him whom thou gavest that thyself might be glorified; wherefore, Father, spare these my brethren that believe on my name, that they may come unto me and have everlasting life. (D&C 45:3–5)

The Lord can and will intervene on our behalf and on behalf of our loved ones, but it does require some effort on our part. Whether it is for our own life or for a loved one, the process is the same. God requires three things: humility, diligence, and the prayer of faith in Christ.

It matters not what problem we bring to the Lord. The problem could involve finances and debt, moral problems, addictive behaviors of self or a loved one, or a hardened heart. The Lord is concerned that His child be humble and diligent and exercise the prayer of faith in Christ to bring about the needed change.

Nephi was acceptable to the Lord because of these very traits. The Lord said, "The Lord spake unto me, saying: Blessed art thou, Nephi, because of thy faith, for thou has *sought* me *diligently,* with *lowliness of heart*" (1 Ne. 2:19; italics added). Moroni taught that none are acceptable before God unless they are "meek and lowly in heart" (Moro. 7:44).

As an agent of love, we must become as a child, "submissive, meek, humble, patient, full of love, willing to submit . . . to his father" (Mosiah 3:19). When we so appear before the Father, God is free to intervene in a manner consistent with the eternal best interest of all His children. The spoiled child who wants only what he wants lacks the perspective of God. The proud, willful child throws a tantrum if he does not get his way. The child's way may not be the best way (see Isa. 55:10–11). In addition, how can the Lord use a proud, lazy, willful child to serve as an instrument in His hands? The child is not willing to accept divine alternatives.

Our job, once we have humbly and faithfully sought the Lord's intervention, is to accept the way He chooses to intervene. We need to remain steadfast in our efforts, trusting that God knows what He is doing with His children.

HOW DOES THE LORD INTERVENE?

Regardless of the nature of the problem, God is more concerned that we who are offering the prayer for assistance are humble, diligent, and faithful. These requirements of God span all of time and all dispensations of the gospel. Examples of divine intervention are found everywhere in the scriptures. There are at least five ways the Lord intervenes: He can soften the heart, strengthen physically and spiritually, raise up someone to help, remove one from the problem, or remove the problem.

Softening the Heart

Notice how the Lord chose to intervene in Nephi's life.

> I, Nephi, . . . having great desires to know of the mysteries of God, wherefore, I did cry unto the Lord; and behold he did visit me, and *did soften my heart* that I did believe all the words which had been spoken by my father; wherefore, I did not rebel against him like unto my brothers. (1 Ne. 2:16; italics added)

Sometimes the first heart to be softened belongs to us as the agents of love. Then we as the agents of love can assist change in others. If we cannot effect change, then we readily accept the will of the Lord and, with faith, place the matter in His hands.

In this dispensation the Church had a problem with financial indebtedness. The Church had bills and financial obligations it could not pay. The Prophet Joseph Smith went to the Lord in mighty prayer, asking for relief. He was told that what he lacked wasn't money; what he lacked was humility, diligence, and the prayer of faith. The Lord told him:

> And again, verily I say unto you, concerning your debts—behold it is my will that you shall pay all your debts. And it is my will that you shall humble yourselves before me, and obtain this blessing by your diligence and humility and the prayer of faith. And inasmuch as you are *diligent* and *humble,* and exercise the *prayer of faith,* behold, I will *soften the hearts* of those to whom you are in debt, until I shall send means unto you for your deliverance. . . . And inasmuch as ye are *humble* and *faithful* and *call upon my name,* behold, I will give you the victory. *I give unto you a promise, that you shall be delivered this once out of your bondage.* (D&C 104:78–80, 82–83; italics added)

On this occasion the Lord softened the hearts of the creditors until the means were provided to pay the debts.

Strengthening Physically and Spiritually

There are scores of examples in the scriptures where the Lord strengthens His servants. Isaiah would plead, "Strengthen ye the weak hands, and confirm the feeble knees" (Isa. 35:3). When Alma's hand was faltering, he called upon God to strengthen him:

> Alma fought with Amlici with the sword, face to face; and they did contend mightily, one with another. And it came to pass that Alma, being a man of God, being exercised with much faith, cried, saying: O Lord, have mercy and spare my life, that I may be an instrument in thy hands to save and preserve this people. Now when Alma had said these words he contended again with Amlici; and *he was strengthened,* insomuch that he slew Amlici with the sword. (Alma 2:29–31; italics added)

A few years later, Alma prayed for spiritual strength:

> O Lord, my heart is exceedingly sorrowful; wilt thou comfort my soul in Christ. O Lord, wilt thou grant unto me that I may have strength, that I may suffer with patience these afflictions which shall come upon me, because of the iniquity of this people. O Lord, wilt thou comfort my soul, and give unto me success, and also my fellow laborers who are with me—yea, Ammon, and Aaron, and Omner, and also Amulek and Zeezrom, and also my two sons—yea, even all these wilt thou comfort, O Lord. Yea, wilt thou comfort their souls in Christ. Wilt thou grant unto them that they may have strength, that they may bear their afflictions which shall come upon them because of the iniquities of this people. O Lord, wilt thou grant unto us that we may have success in bringing them again unto thee in Christ. Behold, O Lord, their souls are precious, and many of them are our brethren; therefore, give unto us, O Lord, power and wisdom that we may bring these, our brethren, again unto thee. . . .
>
> And the Lord provided for them that they should hunger not, neither should they thirst; yea, and he also gave them strength, that they should suffer no manner of afflictions, save it were swallowed

up in the joy of Christ. Now this was according to the prayer of
Alma; and this because he prayed in faith. (Alma 31:31–38)

Jesus prayed in the Garden of Gethsemane for the cup to pass
from him. Heavenly Father chose instead to send an angel to
"strengthen" him (Luke 22:43).

Sometimes the need is physical strength; at other times the need
is spiritual strength. The God of all time and eternity stands ready to
respond to our prayers of faith. He will strengthen those of a humble
and diligent spirit.

Raising Someone Up to Help

The examples of raising people up as instruments of divine intervention are myriad. Most are not dramatic. They are manifested in
the daily lives of millions, many of whom are unaware of the direct
intervention. There are dramatic involvements that include the
appearance of angels who are raised up by the Lord to be instruments
in God's hands. Angels appeared to Cornelius at Caesarea (see Acts
10:1–8) and to Alma and the sons of Mosiah, although in the latter
case it was not due to the humility, diligence, or faith of Alma the
younger. It was the humility, diligence, and prayers of his father that
brought the angel (see Alma 27:14):

> Now the sons of Mosiah were numbered among the unbelievers;
> and also one of the sons of Alma was numbered among them, he
> being called Alma, after his father; nevertheless, he became a very
> wicked and an idolatrous man. And he was a man of many
> words, and did speak much flattery to the people; therefore he
> led many of the people to do after the manner of his iniquities.
> And he became a great hinderment to the prosperity of the
> church of God; stealing away the hearts of the people; causing
> much dissension among the people; giving a chance for the
> enemy of God to exercise his power over them. . . . And as I said
> unto you, as they were going about rebelling against God,
> behold, the angel of the Lord appeared unto them; and he
> descended as it were in a cloud; and he spake as it were with a

voice of thunder, which caused the earth to shake upon which they stood; and so great was their astonishment, that they fell to the earth, and understood not the words which he spake unto them. Nevertheless he cried again, saying: Alma, arise and stand forth, for why persecutest thou the church of God? For the Lord hath said: This is my church, and I will establish it; and nothing shall overthrow it, save it is the transgression of my people. And again, the angel said: Behold, *the Lord hath heard the prayers of his people, and also the prayers of his servant, Alma, who is thy father;* for he has prayed with much faith concerning thee that thou mightest be brought to the knowledge of the truth; therefore, for this purpose have I come to convince thee of the power and authority of God, that the prayers of his servants might be answered according to their faith. (Mosiah 27:8–14; italics added)

The question may be asked, "Do angels still appear unto men?" or, "Would God send an angel to my son, daughter, or loved one?" The answer is yes, if one is willing to qualify by his or her humility, diligence, and prayer of faith. It is also necessary that it be in the eternal best interest of the loved one. Read Moroni's inspired words:

Or have angels ceased to appear unto the children of men? Or has he withheld the power of the Holy Ghost from them? Or will he, so long as time shall last, or the earth shall stand, or there shall be one man upon the face thereof to be saved? Behold I say unto you, Nay; for it is by faith that miracles are wrought; and it is by faith that angels appear and minister unto men. (Moro. 7:36–37)

Most of the time, however, the Lord does not send angels. He sends us. He is always looking for agents of love who can serve as instruments in His hands. We must be humble, diligent, and faithful so that when the Lord calls us, we will hear. He calls to us in many voices:

- Voice of conscience ("by mine own voice")
- Voice of the witness of the Holy Ghost
- Voice of His servants (prophets, visiting teachers, and agents of love)

- Voice of ministering angels
- Voice of thunderings
- Voice of lightnings
- Voice of tempests
- Voice of earthquakes
- Voice of great hailstones
- Voice of famines
- Voice of pestilences of every kind
- Voice of "the great sound of a trump"
- Voice of judgment
- Voice of glory and honor
- Voice of riches of eternal life (see D&C 43:25)

The Lord calls us by whatever voice we as a people are prepared to hear. The issue for us as agents of love is our willingness to be the one raised up by the Lord. Great love is demonstrated by restraint. Agents of love may be the only voice the loved ones will hear. Is it not worth our effort? Is it not worth ceasing all uninvited, unauthorized, and inappropriate criticism in order to be an instrument of love?

When inspired, appropriate, and properly given criticism is involved, it can be effective. When a loved one is unapproachable and possesses a hardened heart, the burden of changing the heart rests with God. It is the Holy Ghost and the Light of Christ that are the agents of change. Would it not be a great relief to lay the burden of salvation where it belongs, on the altar of God? Is there not great wisdom in trusting God to carry out His own plan, in His own time, and in His own way? He is able to do His work and has called upon His disciples to stand in the office to which they have been called to be agents of love (see D&C 107:99).

A righteous man is not a perfect man. We are righteous when we are in the right place, at the right time, and with the right intent in our hearts (see Moro. 7:6–14). A righteous man is one who is humble and diligent and who exercises the prayers of faith in Christ.

Angels, be they glorified beings, mothers, fathers, friends, or strangers, are messengers sent by God on divine missions to help His children to return to Him.

Removing One from the Problem

There are so many examples in the scriptures of the Lord leading away the righteous (see Jacob 3:4) and turning the wicked from their pathways that it is only necessary to use the word *exodus*. In each scriptural exodus, the Lord prepares a way to escape. The first exodus began when Adam and Eve were taken from the Garden of Eden. The great Exodus of righteous and wicked led by Moses through the wilderness may be the one best known. The Book of Mormon tells of one exodus after another. From Lehi leaving Jerusalem to Nephi escaping from Laman and Lemuel to Mosiah fleeing to Zarahemla, the story is the same. But will the Lord lead away "my wayward son from his bad friends?" Yes! God will respond to our diligent, humble prayer of faith in Christ.

Removing the Problem

One of the least frequent things the Lord does is to remove the problem. Even when the Lord does remove a problem, it is only after long-suffering and many trials on the part of the faithful. For example, Pharaoh hardened his heart ten times after the Lord softened it (see D&C 105:27). Ten different plagues were inflicted before he would respond to Moses' pleas, "Let my people go." Pharaoh and his army drowned in the depths of the Red Sea (see Ex. 9–14). The problem was removed after long-suffering and patience. The same is true of Noah and the Flood: "When once the longsuffering of God waited in the days of Noah" (1 Pet. 3:20). All the inhabitants of the earth were drowned except those on the ark. Laban, keeper of the plates of brass is another example of God's patience with a wicked man. At least three separate attempts were made before Laban was removed as a problem (see 1 Ne. 3–4).

YOU ARE NEEDED

So, if change comes from within and God can intervene, what's our real role in others' process for change? Another question frequently asked at this point is, "If God loves everybody, then why am I needed?"

The answer is that not everyone can feel that love. Not everyone knows where to look for it or how to use it to change. Our job is to bring a recognition of the need to change in others by gently guiding them back to God. God needs people who can give love. He needs people who will validate the worth of a soul. He needs people who are humble, diligent, and prayerful. He needs instruments in His hands. Miracles do occur. Who knows if your spirit was not reserved to come to this earth at this time to be an agent of love for the one who is difficult to love? As Mordecai said to Esther, "And who knoweth whether thou art come to the kingdom for such a time as this?" (Esther 4:14).

Assignments for Chapter 6

1. Read Mosiah chapters 21 to 24. All five principles of divine intervention are mentioned. Find them.

2. Reflect upon your life. Who are the people the Lord has raised up to be there for you and to encourage you? List them.

3. Have you been raised up by the Lord to be an influence for good in the life of another? Maybe you have and you will only hear about it in the Resurrection, when someone will thank you for being at the right place, at the right time, and with the right intent in your heart. Write the names of those you have influenced for good.

4. Look around at the lives of friends and family. Have any hearts been softened? Has anyone been strengthened to carry on or physically restored to health? Has the Lord led anyone you know out of an abusive relationship? Can you see a problem that has been removed by the Lord?

Further Reading

Softening the Heart: 1 Ne. 2:16; 7:5; 7:19; 18:20; 2 Ne. 10:18; Mosiah 19:14; 20:26; 21:15; 23:29; Alma 19:23; 24:8; Hel. 12:2; D&C 104:80; 105:27; 109:56; 124:9.

Strengthening Physically and Spiritually: Isa. 12:2; 40:29; Luke 22:42; 1 Ne. 17:1–3; W of M 1:14; Mosiah 9:17; 10:10; 21:15; 24:14; Alma 2:18, 28, 31; 14:26; 20:4; 31:38; 43:49–50; 46:20.

Raising Up Someone to Help: Gen. 12:1–5; 45:7; Ex. 3:10; Judg. 6:17–24; 1 Ne. 3:29; Mosiah 3:4; 25:16; 27:14; 29:20; Alma 1:8; 15:1; 3 Ne. 20:26; Moro. 7:36–37; D&C 1:17.

Removing One from the Problem: Ex. 13:16; 1 Ne. 2:2; 1 Ne. 5:20; 2 Ne. 5:5; Jacob 3:4; Omni 1:12; Mosiah 2:4; 7:33; 11:26; 29:20; Alma 36:27; 38:4; 48:15; 50:22; 56:47; 57:35; Hel. 12:2; Ether 9:3; D&C 127:1.

Removing the Problem: Ex. 14:28; 1 Ne. 4:18; Jacob 7:1–3; 7:14–15; Alma 12:3, 6–7; 30:50, 60; 44:3.

CHAPTER 7

MIGHTY PRAYER

Mighty prayer is an important step in offering appropriate criticism. True prayer invites the Spirit into our lives, which can both help us to know when to criticize, and testify to those criticized of the sincerity and validity of our words. Mighty prayer also involves the Lord in our relationships, and when the Lord is an equal partner in a relationship, we cannot fail. He has counseled, "Then shall ye call upon me, and ye shall go and pray unto me, and I will hearken unto you. And ye shall seek me, and find me, when ye shall search for me with all your heart. And I will be found of you, saith the Lord" (Jer. 29:12–14).

OFFERING A MIGHTY PRAYER

Mighty prayer is different from ordinary prayer. A brief observation of the differences and similarities seems in order. Both mighty prayer and prayer assume a relationship between mankind and God. That relationship is father to child and child to parent. When we as the children of God talk to Heavenly Father, it is called prayer. When God communicates with His children, it is called revelation. As with any relationship, it requires communication and the willingness of both parties to listen. The Lord has commanded that His children call upon Him:

> And again, verily I say unto you, my friends, I leave these sayings
> with you to ponder in your hearts, with this commandment

which I give unto you, that ye shall call upon me while I am near—draw near unto me and I will draw near unto you; seek me diligently and ye shall find me; ask, and ye shall receive; knock, and it shall be opened unto you. Whatsoever ye ask the Father in my name it shall be given unto you, that is expedient for you. (D&C 88:62–64)

President Spencer W. Kimball said:

Prayer is not just words but communication. If one rises from his knees having merely said words, he should fall back on his knees and remain there until he has established communication with the Lord who is very anxious to bless, but having given man his free agency, will not force himself upon that man. (*The Teachings of Spencer W. Kimball,* 124)

It would seem that while any prayer is important, if we are seeking to truly live the Lord's higher law of love, we must seek to live a higher law of prayer. To truly make the Lord a part of our relationships, we must seek Him out in mighty prayer.

What Is Mighty Prayer?

The key word is *mighty.* There are twenty-four Hebrew words from the Old Testament that have been translated into English as "mighty." Most of them carry the notion of strength. Of the eleven Greek words in the New Testament translated as "mighty," most identify the ideas of strength, power, or fervency. In relationship to the concept of loving the Lord with all one's heart, soul, and might (see Deut. 6:5), the Hebrew word for *might* is "vehemently" or "intensely." The Greek word for *might* in the New Testament means "forcefulness, power and strength." In either case, mighty prayer is intense and strong. It is not casual, relaxed, or routine. It means we are focused and we involve our emotions. It is a prayer which is not only said, but felt. It is not rote nor detached from our feelings. Mighty prayer is honest, heartfelt, and emotionally sincere. You can see why such prayer is important to relationships; as we come to communicate with the Lord with such intent and sincerity, He will help us communicate to our loved ones this way as well.

The examples of mighty prayer listed below are from people who prayed mightily unto the Lord.

Lehi:

> Wherefore it came to pass that my father, Lehi, as he went forth prayed unto the Lord, yea, even *with all his heart,* in behalf of his people. (1 Ne. 1:5; italics added)

Nephi:

> And it came to pass that I, Nephi, being exceedingly young, nevertheless being large in stature, and also having great desires to know of the mysteries of God, wherefore, *I did cry unto the Lord;* and behold he did visit me, and did soften my heart that I did believe all the words which had been spoken by my father; wherefore, I did not rebel against him like unto my brothers. (1 Ne. 2:16; italics added)

Enos:

> And I will tell you of *the wrestle* which I had before God, before I received a remission of my sins. Behold, I went to hunt beasts in the forest; and the words which I had often heard my father speak concerning eternal life, and the joy of the saints, *sunk deep into my heart.* And *my soul hungered;* and I kneeled down before my Maker, and *I cried unto him in mighty prayer* and supplication for mine own soul; and all the day long did I cry unto him; yea, and when the night came I did still raise my voice high that it reached the heavens. (Enos 1:2–4; italics added)

Alma:

> *Nevertheless* Alma labored much in the spirit, *wrestling with God in mighty prayer,* that he would pour out his Spirit upon the

people who were in the city; that he would also grant that he might baptize them unto repentance. (Alma 8:10; italics added)

Hannah:

So Hannah rose up. . . . And she was in *bitterness of soul,* and prayed unto the Lord, and wept sore. (1 Sam. 1:9–10; italics added)

President Harold B. Lee:

I once read that scripture [Enos 1:2–4] to a woman who laughed and said, "Imagine anybody praying all night and all day." I replied, "My dear sister, I hope you never have to come to a time where you have a problem so great that you have to so humble yourself. I have; *I have prayed all day and all night and all the next day and all the next night. (Stand Ye in Holy Places,* 246; italics added)

Considering these examples, we begin to see some patterns of what it means to pray mightily. Let's take a look at the elements of a mighty prayer.

Heavenly Father's Requirements for Prayer

God's requirements are simple. Our prayers are to be sincere, and we must pray with real intent. If we pray as we ought to, the Lord will bless us. Moroni exhorts us to "ask God, the Eternal Father, in the name of Christ, if these things are not true; and if ye shall ask [pray] with a *sincere heart,* with *real intent,* having faith in Christ, he will manifest [by revelation] the truth of it unto you, by the power of the Holy Ghost" (Moro. 10:4; italics added).

It is humility, diligence, and the prayer of faith in Christ that qualify the prayer as coming from "a sincere heart, with real intent." We are also required to pray unceasingly. In the parable of the unjust judge, the Lord teaches "that men ought always to pray, and not to faint" (Luke 18:1). Our mighty prayer never leaves our hearts. Even while not actively supplicating the Lord, our thoughts and desires are sent up to Him through the intents of our hearts.

Mighty prayer is measured by the quality of its sincerity. President Spencer W. Kimball spoke about some of the characteristics of a mighty prayer:

> Could the Redeemer resist such determined imploring? How many have thus persisted? How many, with or without serious transgressions, have ever prayed all day and into the night? Have many ever wept and prayed for ten hours? For five hours? For one? For thirty minutes? For ten? Our praying is usually measured in seconds. . . . How much do you pray, my friends? How often? How earnestly? . . . Have you yet found your deep forest of solitude? How much has your soul hungered? How deeply have your needs impressed your heart? When did you kneel before your Maker in total quiet? For what did you pray—your own soul? How long did you thus plead for recognition—all day long? And when the shadows fell, did you still raise your voice in *mighty prayer,* or did you satisfy yourself with some hackneyed word and phrase? (*Faith Precedes the Miracle,* 211; italics added)

Mighty prayer is not always a long prayer, but it is emotionally sincere and reaches to the depth of the soul. Does every prayer have to last all day? Of course not! It is not about the length of our prayers. It is about faith, humility, and sincerity. There are several examples from the scriptures of short but mighty and sincere prayers. Below are three.

Hezekiah's thirty-word prayer:

> In those days was Hezekiah sick unto death. And Isaiah the prophet the son of Amoz came unto him, and said unto him, Thus saith the Lord, Set thine house in order: for thou shalt die, and not live. Then Hezekiah turned his face toward the wall, and prayed unto the Lord, and said, Remember now, O Lord, I *beseech thee,* how I have walked before thee in truth and with a perfect heart, and have done that which is good in thy sight. And Hezekiah *wept sore.* Then came the word of the Lord to Isaiah,

saying, Go, and say to Hezekiah, Thus saith the Lord, the God of David thy father, *I have heard thy prayer, I have seen thy tears:* behold, I will add unto thy days fifteen years. (Isaiah 38:1–5; italics added)

Joseph Smith's mighty prayer in Liberty Jail:

O God, where art thou? And where is the pavilion that covereth thy hiding place? How long shall thy hand be stayed, and thine eye, yea thy pure eye, behold from the eternal heavens the wrongs of thy people and of thy servants, and thine ear be penetrated with their cries? Yea, O Lord, how long shall they suffer these wrongs and unlawful oppressions, before thine heart shall be softened toward them, and thy bowels be moved with compassion toward them? . . . Remember thy suffering saints, O our God; and thy servants will rejoice in thy name forever. (D&C 121:1–6)

Jesus' Intercessory Prayer:

I pray for them: I pray not for the world, but for them which thou hast given me; for they are thine. . . . And now I am no more in the world, but these are in the world, and I come to thee. Holy Father, keep through thine own name those whom thou hast given me, that they may be one, as we are. (John 17:9–11)

It is insincere prayer, false and dishonest prayer, which is rejected by God. Sincere, honest prayer from a sinner is preferable to the prayers of the self-righteous (see Matt. 23). Those who fail to pray sincerely often do so because they miss the reasons we pray in the first place. They know they should pray but don't always know why.

Why Pray?

We pray because we "are commanded in all things to ask of God" (D&C 46:7). We pray to seek answers: "If any of you lack wisdom, let him ask of God, that giveth to all men liberally, and upbraideth not; and it shall be given him" (James 1:5). We pray because it's the only way to seek and gain the Lord's aid.

As President Kimball intimated, God will not force Himself upon His children (*The Teachings of Spencer W. Kimball*, 125). God respects the agency of man. It is up to the children of God to invite Him into their lives and the lives of their loved ones. The importance of this principle cannot be passed over lightly. Indeed, "the effectual fervent prayer of a righteous man [or woman] availeth much" (James 5:16). The prayer of invitation opens the windows of heaven and authorizes divine intervention.

Why Don't People Pray?

President Kimball asked this very question of a young man who stopped praying but wasn't sure he could answer the question as to why he had stopped praying. The prophet chided the young man:

"Why don't you pray?"

"I am not sure anymore."

"Why aren't you sure anymore? Because you have cut all the communication lines? You have lost his address? You do not have his telephone number even, and you do not have any address? The communication lines have been severed? How do you expect to know whether he is living or dead? If you went for two years without ever hearing from your parents and they were in the opposite end of the world, how would you know if they were alive or dead? How do you know if God is dead or alive if you have lost communication? Now, you get on your knees, my boy. If you want to be happy, get on your knees and crawl on your knees to the city of happiness. Only there is peace." (*The Teachings of Spencer W. Kimball*, 127)

There seem to be two main reasons why we as God's children don't pray. Weakness and unworthiness are our concerns. However, weakness and unworthiness are not disqualifiers for God. Sincerity and faith are what He requires in prayer. In other words, God is available to the vilest of sinners, regardless of our weaknesses and our unworthiness. It is fear and doubt that keep the children of God from the arms of their loving Father. The wonderful brother of Jared waited four years before he called upon the Lord. When the Lord appeared to him, the brother of Jared was chastened by the Lord: "And for the space of three hours did the Lord talk with the brother of Jared, and chastened him because he remembered not to call upon the name of the Lord" (Ether 2:14).

The brother of Jared recognized his weakness and unworthiness, repented, and began again to call upon the Lord. Notice his prayer when he calls upon God to touch the sixteen small stones to give light to their vessels:

> O Lord, thou hast said that we must be encompassed about by the floods. Now behold, O Lord, and do not be angry with thy servant because of his *weakness* before thee; for we know that thou art holy and dwellest in the heavens, and that we are *unworthy* before thee; because of the fall our natures have become evil continually; *nevertheless,* O Lord, thou hast given us a commandment that we must call upon thee. (Ether 3:2; italics added)

One of the most important words in this verse is *nevertheless.* Despite weakness and unworthiness, the brother of Jared prayed because weakness and unworthiness do not disqualify the children of God. Yet, how is it possible that God, who cannot look upon sin with the least degree of tolerance, can tolerate the sinner? God has incredible tolerance for His children. The sin and the sinner are separated by His love. While God rejects all sin, repentance is extended to the sinner. In a revelation given to Joseph Smith, the Lord declared that He could not "look upon sin with the least degree of allowance; *nevertheless,* he that repents and does the commandments of the Lord shall be forgiven" (D&C 1:31–32; italics added). The Lord always loves and wants to hear from His children. We must not doubt this, but seek His help in our relationships and other aspects of our lives. Like any parent, He will always love us, whether or not He entrusts us with all the blessings we seek.

The "I Love You" Plan and the "I Trust You" Plan of God

Heavenly Father has two approaches to His children. The first is an "I love you" plan and the second is an "I trust you" plan. There are things Heavenly Father does for us as His children because He is good. For example, everyone will be resurrected. The resurrection is a universal and unconditional blessing (see 1 Cor. 15:22). God's availability to each of His children in prayer is another. The Light of Christ and a witness of the Holy Ghost are likewise universal blessings available to all of the descendants of Adam and Eve. These are blessings which come from God because they are part of His "I love you" plan.

The "I trust you" plan of the Lord deals with the laws of obedience and blessings. It is a program that is definitely conditioned upon adherence to correct principles. A gift is different from a blessing. A blessing is earned but a gift is not. Ultimately, eternal life comes as a gift from God (see D&C 14:7). Obtaining the Lord's intervention through prayer is enhanced as His children demonstrate trustworthiness. Understanding this relationship with God helps us understand our relationships with those we must at times criticize. We are always called to love others, but not always to trust. We need the Lord in our lives, through mighty prayers, to distinguish those aspects of our relationships. We can't always trust others, but we can trust God.

Application of Mighty Prayer

The key to becoming an agent of love is to take our frustration to God in mighty prayer. We take our love to our loved ones. Until we are committed to mighty prayer, this seems idealistically unreal. The truth is that God's way is the most effective and efficient way to operate. Mighty prayer calls upon the Lord to intervene and leaves us with the responsibility to love. Of course, when spiritually moved upon by the Holy Ghost and not just by frustration, you may give appropriate criticism. It will not be all the time, rather, "betimes," in a right time and place and when our disposition is calm and measured.

SIX STEPS OF MIGHTY PRAYER

Now that we recognize the need for mighty prayer in our lives and relationships, let's explore how we proceed to pray mightily. The following is an outline of how we can really learn to pray.

1. Call upon the Name of Heavenly Father

This is very personal. Each of us as a child of God addresses our Heavenly Father in our own endearing terms. This is a relationship between a kind, loving Father and an imperfect child. Such terms as "Holy Father," "Dear Lord," "Our kind and eternal Father in Heaven" are appropriate titles with which to call upon the name of God. Our names for Him show respect and love.

2. Be Honest in Declaring Feelings at the Time of Prayer

People who do not feel their prayers are not being honest. A declaration of our honest feelings at the time of prayer brings reality. Expressing feelings to God has precedent in antiquity. I found it absolutely fascinating to research ancient meanings and expressions and compare them with modern ones.

ANCIENT EXPRESSION	MODERN EXPRESSION
"I am weary."	"I am tired."
"My soul hungered."	"My heart aches."
"Groaning in Himself."	"He was feeling overburdened."
"He cried unto the Lord."	"He raised his voice. He wept."
"I anguish, Father."	"I am impatient, Lord."
"I am brought to naught."	"I am frustrated. I am ready to tear my hair out."
"I did mourn sore."	"I'm angry. I'm mad. I'm heartbroken and disappointed."
"My spirit was troubled."	"I am upset, afraid, and worried."

"I am sorrowful."   "I am hurt, Lord. I feel hopeless.
                             I am unhappy. "
"Succor me, O Lord."   "I need help. I can't do it alone."
"Let this cup pass."   "Help me get through this."

3. Pray for People by Name and by Specific Circumstance

Platitudes and general statements create distance between God and ourselves as the prayer givers. "Bless my family and help us be good" is too vague. Also, it is difficult to recognize the Lord's answers. When people pray by name and by circumstance, it is easier to recognize the answers to our prayers.

"Father, I am frustrated with my son, Bob. He is in trouble with the law. He has dropped out of school, and I know he is experimenting with drugs. Wilt Thou intervene? Wilt Thou help my son? Wilt Thou raise someone up to reach him? He won't listen to me anymore."

"Heavenly Father, I am embarrassed and ashamed because of my pride. I lied today and I knew it was wrong. I was afraid that if I told Mary the truth, our relationship would be over. I am still afraid. Help me, Lord, to do the right thing. Soften Mary's heart. I am sorry and I promise Thee that I am determined never to buy anything again over a hundred dollars without consulting with Mary and obtaining her consent. Strengthen me, Lord."

The next time these people are faced with these situations, they will not only remember their offered prayer, but will more likely offer another prayer in their hearts in the moment and be open to the Spirit's prompting in that moment of frustration.

4. Express Sincere Love and Gratitude to Heavenly Father

Be specific. In addition to listing specifics of problems with which we need the Lord's help, we should express our gratitude and love in specific terms.

"Holy Father, in spite of my weaknesses and my many sins and my unworthiness, I am grateful for the plan of salvation, for the atoning sacrifice of Thy Son, Jesus Christ. I am thankful for the health I enjoy. I'm thankful that my son returned safely last night. Even though I am overcome with my own problems, I express my love for Thee. I love Thee, Father. I pray that thou wilt strengthen me."

Specific prayer, especially in offering gratitude, helps us to stay focused and involved with the prayer.

5. Pray in the Name and Worthiness of Jesus Christ

Jesus prayed to the Father in His own name (see John 17; 3 Ne. 19:19–32). All of the rest of mankind are to call upon the Father in the name of Jesus Christ. There are scores of scriptures which instruct the children of God to petition the Father in the name of the Mediator, Jesus Christ, but quoting from just one is sufficient, as it is instruction from the Savior Himself: "Ye shall call upon the Father in my name. . . . If it be in my name the Father will hear you" (3 Ne. 27:7–9).

When John on the Isle of Patmos saw the glorious vision of the plan of happiness, he wept because no man was found worthy to carry out the Atonement and to be man's Great Example. A strong angel told him to weep no more because Jesus Christ, the Lamb of God, was worthy (see Rev. 5:1–12). Because of His worthiness, He became the great Mediator between Heavenly Father and all His less worthy children (see 1 Tim. 2:5; Heb. 8:6; 9:15; 12:24; 2 Ne. 2:27–28; D&C 76:69; D&C 107:19).

All people are subject to the Fall of Adam. In the mortal state no man can be worthy in the sense that Christ is worthy. "Temple-recommend" worthiness means something totally different from the worthiness of Christ. Temple-worthy Saints are keeping a few fundamental commandments which qualify them to go to the temple. It is the worthiness of Christ's Atonement that qualifies the prayers of the children of God to enter into the ears of Heavenly Father. This is the principle of divine compensation. The worthiness of Jesus compensates for the unworthiness of all. Therefore, we do not pray in our own name nor by virtue of our own worthiness.

6. Say Amen with Conviction and Determination

The word *amen* means "So be it!" or "truly." Various Church leaders have given counsel on the importance of an energetic, enthusiastic, and sincere "amen!" The *Encyclopedia of Mormonism* explains its significance:

In antiquity the expression [amen] carried the weight of an oath. By saying "amen" the people solemnly pledged faithfulness and assented to curses upon themselves if found guilty (Deut. 27:14–26). And by saying "amen" the people also sealed their praises of God (1 Chr. 16:36; Ps.106:48; Rom. 11:36; 1 Pet. 4:1; Neh. 8:6).

By saying "amen," Latter-day Saints officially sustain what is said in formal and private prayer, as also in the words of sermons, official admonition, and testimony (see D&C 88:135). (Daniel B. McKinlay, *Encyclopedia of Mormonism,* 1:38)

Elder Richard R. Lyman stated:

When these prayers of which I have spoken are offered in the family circle, at church, to open a meeting or to close it, and more especially when blessings are asked upon the holy sacrament, upon the bread or upon the water, there should be silence, a real stillness, all eyes ought to be closed, all heads ought to be bowed, all hearts filled with the prayerful spirit. These appeals are not to be made by one individual, they should be the hope, the faith, the united appeal of all who are present. And if in every heart there burns an earnest hope for Providence to hear, and for the united appeal to be answered, then every pair of lips should express the fervent feeling of each and every heart by saying, Amen when the prayer is finished. (Conference Report, April 1933, 51)

President Spencer W. Kimball said:

I was glad to hear you say, "Amen." Sometimes we forget to do that and it is a very pleasing word to those who speak or pray or preach, and we hope that that will always be very important in your life and in your sacred services. That sounds better every time. Every time that a sermon is concluded or a prayer is offered, every man, woman, and child should say "Amen," loud enough so that the person next to him or her can hear it. (*The Teachings of Spencer W. Kimball,* 520)

In a similar talk given at a priesthood session of general conference, President Kimball, I recall, chided the brethren for their weak
and somewhat infirm "amen." When he concluded his sermon he said
stoutly, "AMEN," and turned around to sit down. The Tabernacle
resounded with a loud chorus of "AMEN!" President Kimball turned
around and with a raspy whisper said, "That is more like it!"

Most of us make prayer difficult. It is not unusual to hear a
myriad of reasons why we don't pray. Many simply feel it doesn't
matter. Some are embarrassed and feel awkward. Others lack faith in
God's intervention because of their sins and weaknesses. It's as if
prayer works for apostles and prophets, but not for the average
member. This is the issue. But there are no average people for God.
Heavenly Father is the God of the living and the dead. Truly, He is no
respecter of persons. He hears and answers the prayers of all of His
children whether on earth or in the world of spirits, whether they are
members of the Church, "less active" members, or non-members. I
have a personal testimony of mighty prayer that I'd like to share.

"Someone Prayed Me Here"

The thought of bearing one's testimony at a church of a different
denomination without being invited is scary. Yet that is exactly what
happened to me. At the time I was serving as the stake mission president. In a very vivid dream, I saw myself walking into a certain
church. After a few moments, I stood upon my feet and bore witness
of Jesus Christ, the Prophet Joseph Smith, and the truthfulness of the
Book of Mormon. Then the dream ended.

When I arose in the morning, the details of the dream were
engraved upon my mind. The church was a white building made of
wood with a large oak tree in front. There was a graveled parking lot and
a large sign announcing the meeting times. Try as I might, I could not
rid myself of this dream. I prayed unto the Lord in mighty prayer to seek
His guidance. I asked the Lord to take the dream away and give me
peace of mind. If, however, this was of God, I prayed that He would
open the way before me. I felt a strong confirmation that I should go to
this particular church on the upcoming Sunday. It was in a town off of
the main highway. I consulted with my stake president, and he encouraged me to go forth. I doubted my sanity, even though I felt the Spirit.

It was not until I turned the corner and saw the church that I knew for sure this was a mission from God. The sign, the tree, the building, and the graveled parking lot were exactly as I had seen them in my dream. I wondered how the Lord would open the door for me to bear my testimony. I thought of Nephi going for the plates of brass, not knowing beforehand the things which he should do. I entered the church on a hot August Sunday and sat down on one of the pews.

After a few songs and several prayers, there was a period of silence. I felt the Holy Ghost move upon me as I had felt before in a Mormon fast and testimony meeting. It was "time." I stood up and went to the pulpit, not knowing what I should say. The moment I opened my mouth to speak, the Lord gave me the words. I witnessed of Jesus; I bore testimony of Joseph Smith and of the Book of Mormon. Still I did not know why I was there. Then it came to me. It was clear. Someone had "prayed" me to the church. I bore testimony that I had been "prayed" to this meeting, and I was there in answer to one of their prayers. At the time, I did not know that the church I was attending that hot August day was built by my grandfather. He died when I was six, and I barely remembered him. He had been a faithful member of that church. Although he was dead and in the spirit world, his mighty prayer to God had inspired me, his grandson, to bear my testimony. It was he who had "prayed" me there.

A good thing happened as a result of that experience. Many of those people, including the minister, investigated the Church. I look forward to the day when I will meet my grandfather and acknowledge the power of his mighty prayer.

CONTINUING IN MIGHTY PRAYER

At some point, like the prodigal son, each of us must come to himself (see Luke 15:17). The intent of mighty prayer is to accept the Lord as the changer of the human heart. When we are frustrated with a loved one, it is hard to focus on loving instead of criticizing him or her. In mighty prayer we can take our frustration to God; then we can take our love to our loved ones. The Father will intervene. Humility, diligence, and the prayer of faith qualify us. The Atonement of Jesus

Christ, His love, and His worthiness divinely compensate for our lack of worthiness. Our mighty prayers are notarized by the Holy Ghost. They are sent directly to the Father, and He does that which is in the eternal best interest of each of His children.

Assignments for Chapter 7

1. We are commanded to pray. Read Doctrine and Covenants 46:7. Write down what that scripture means to you.

2. Read Ether 2:14. How does this scripture relate to you?

3. Look at 2 Nephi 32:8–9. What would you tell a loved one who felt unworthy to pray?

4. Prayerfully select someone for whom you are greatly concerned because of poor choices he or she is making. Take your love to the one for whom you are concerned. Go to the Lord and pour out your heart on behalf of that person.

5. Frankly, which of the three will be hardest for you: humility, diligence, or the prayer of faith? Why? What course could you pursue to strengthen yourself in this area?

6. In getting to the point where they can "feel" their prayers, many people have found it helpful to make an honest statement to the Lord declaring their current state of mind. For example: "Heavenly Father, I'm tired tonight and don't feel much like praying, and also I don't feel worthy to approach thee; however . . ." How would you preface your prayer to God, now?

7. Read Ether 3:2. What does the word *nevertheless* mean in this scripture?

8. Read Luke 18:1–14. How does this relate to you?

CHAPTER 8

ACTING OUT OF LOVE UNFEIGNED

No power or influence can or ought to be maintained by virtue of the priesthood, only by persuasion, by *long-suffering*, by *gentleness* and *meekness*, and by *love unfeigned.* (D&C 121:41; italics added)

Unfeigned love is genuine and sincere. It is not phony or faked. The admonition of Jesus was to love one another. Sometimes we don't understand what love is. Here is another way for us to understand love. It is affection, acceptance, and appreciation. Acting out of love ought to include hugs of affection from us. We need to speak words of sincere praise and approval. We ought to show forth little acts of kindness that visually reinforce the message of love. How hard we work at our employment or as a homemaker does not compensate for our neglect of affection, acceptance, and appreciation. Courtesy, a smile, and concrete expressions of love communicated daily are the things of which love is made. Each relationship stands on its own merits. The quality of the relationship will rise or fall on the mutual love, respect, and caring concern that each of us invests into the relationship. However, as disciples of Christ, we are called upon to love those who may not love us in return. Acting out of love unfeigned requires a clear head and the ability to separate loving someone from trusting someone.

If everyone we loved were also trustworthy, that would be wonderful. The naked truth is that many of our loved ones are not trustworthy. This creates a dilemma. How do we love someone we cannot trust? It's easy. Actually, every parent confronts this apparent paradox of loving and not trusting, usually about the time children reach the teen years. The answer is profoundly simple. There must be an "I trust you" plan as well as an "I love you" plan.

As imperfect as we all may be, acting out of love unfeigned requires that our words be consistent with our actions. A righteous intent and an unrighteous means will never convince anyone that he or she is loved. It will only label the professor of the double standard as a hypocrite. When our words and behaviors are negative, the words "I love you" fall on deaf ears.

Defining a set of specific behaviors as loving and following through consistently will allow others to trust us and give us credibility as one who truly loves, even if we cannot trust them. This is not just about how we give and receive criticism in the Lord's own way. It is about being an instrument for love in the lives of those who matter the most to us. It is about how we eliminate unnecessary and inappropriate criticism from our conversations. But it is more than that. It is about empowering our love to influence those we love to become their highest and best selves.

Sam's Story

Sam was a responsible seventeen-year-old in every respect but one: he drove too fast. In a single month he received three speeding tickets. There was an important prom dance coming up. Sam asked his father if he could borrow his father's expensive car. The father responded, "No."

Sam was disappointed and naively asked, "Why?"

Dad's reply was straightforward, "I love you, son, but I don't trust you once you get behind the steering wheel of a car."

Sam pleaded, "How can I ever prove to you that I can be responsible if you never trust me?"

The father replied, "When you have paid me back the money I loaned you to pay the speeding tickets, and if you receive no more traffic violations for three months, I'll be willing to extend trust once again and loan you the car."

Sam said, "But, Dad, the dance is this Friday night. In three months it will be too late. I promise I'll drive responsibly."

Sam's mother would have let him take the car. In her heart she thought it would be the loving thing to do. She looked at her husband with pleading eyes.

The father stood firm. "I'm sorry, son, the answer is no."

Sam stomped off angrily and slammed the door to his room. The mother was also upset with the father. She felt that mercy was needed. The dad explained that doing the responsible thing is almost always the truly loving thing to do.

We have already established that trust and love are two separate issues. The mother would have caved in to the disappointment she saw in her son. She would have given trust in the name of love. Trust, however, is unlike love, respect, and forgiveness, which can be gifted. But to forgive doesn't mean that one is trusted. A child molester can be forgiven, but never trusted again with children. An alcoholic can be forgiven, but not hired as a bartender. Trust must be earned by responsible behavior. Sam would agree with the statement, "If you love me, trust me." So would his mother. The problem is that the mother winds up being an enabler. Sam wanted freedom without responsibility for the past. The father's decision was a correct one, a loving one, and a very unpopular one.

Trust means that a person is where he says he is going to be, doing what he says he will be doing. You cannot give someone trust. Trust is earned by credibility and by a history of being trustworthy. Trust is about them, and love is about you.

To reiterate, a person can see that with each relationship we need to have two plans. One is an "I love you" plan, and the other is an "I trust you" plan. The two plans should be kept separate. When love and trust become mixed up, people begin to act in bizarre ways. They set themselves up to be taken advantage of and then are hurt and wounded. In the name of love, they trust the untrustworthy. Genuine love does not mean unconditional trust.

We have a responsibility to protect ourselves from the untrustworthy. To allow another to take advantage of us in the name of love is to be foolish. It is to be an enabler in the worst way. It reinforces manipulation as a reward for the untrustworthy. The wounded party decides to withhold love as a punishment for not being trusted. When the "I love you" plan is separated from the "I trust you" plan, clear-headed decisions can be made. Indeed, love and trust need not be related at all. The "I love you" plan has a simple governing value.

The "I Love You" Creed

Because I love you, I will assist you in becoming your
highest and best self. But I will not help you one inch
to hell, nor will I enable your self-destructive choices!

There, in a nutshell, is the affirmative statement which declares
your position of loving. In regard to the "I trust you" plan, the
governing value is a simple declaration.

The "I Trust You" Creed

I will trust you as you demonstrate responsible behavior.
I will trust you because you are where you said you
would be, doing what you said you would be doing!

Offending parties frequently demand trust as a sign of being
loved. Only the foolish will be convinced by this faulty reasoning.
Those who are unable to separate love and trust often wind up
enabling unhealthy behaviors to continue in the name of misplaced
love. Love or a positive approach does not mean we have to be stupid,
taken advantage of, or made to feel a fool. Love is something we give
because we are good people, not because our loved one deserves it.
However, the loving thing is almost always the responsible thing. The
loving thing is to help a person become his or her highest and best
self. It is not love to enable someone in poor judgment decisions. "I
will not help you one inch to hell" is a loving stance. Irresponsible
people want to play upon the love others have for them in order to
escape the responsibility of being trustworthy.

Creating an "I Love You" Plan

Maybe the most profound way to effect change in others is to be
positive with them, to strengthen them and their self-worth in such a
way that they come to believe in themselves. The power of a positive
approach has yet to be measured. This much is known: it is difficult

to resist forever the positive affirmations of another. There is so much to say about the power of love, of acceptance, affection, and appreciation. There are some cautions. As we have abundantly pointed out, love and trust are two different things. You can love someone and not trust him or her. Also, you can trust someone and not love him or her. You can both love and trust, or you can both not love and not trust. Trust is the function of freedom and responsibility. A boss or parent might say, "I will give you as much freedom as you demonstrate responsibility to handle." Look at Chariti's story:

Chariti and Her Father

Chariti was a fourteen-year-old girl with a passion for animals. Horses and dogs seemed to be her obsession. Since they lived in a suburban area on a quarter-acre lot, getting a horse was out. But she could get a dog. Chariti spent weeks going to the library and reading about every breed of dog. Finally Chariti decided she wanted a schipperke. She had pictures on her walls of this little, black dog without a tail. It looked very much like a black fox and was about that size. Every Saturday Chariti and her father would drive around looking at pet stores and checking out the newspaper ads.

Then Chariti broke one of the family rules. It was not a difficult rule to remember. The rule was that if the children's plans changed while they were with their friends, they must contact either parent in person or over the phone. If the parents could not be reached, the answer was no. The penalty for disobeying was two weeks of being grounded from all activities except school and church. Chariti knew the rules. One Friday night she and a girlfriend were going to the movies. At the last minute her girlfriend canceled, and Chariti called another girlfriend and spent the night at her house without informing her parents. When the mother and father came home at midnight, they did a bed check. They found the other seven children sound asleep in their beds. Chariti was gone.

The mother called up the first girlfriend's parents and was told the girls never got together. The plans had been canceled. Chariti's mother began to imagine the worst. Maybe she was dead. Maybe she had been hit by a car and was in the hospital. All of Chariti's friends were called except the one at whom she was mad. This happened to be where she was. The police were called, the hospitals were called, and the mother drove around in the car to see if she could find her. It was 4:00 A.M. when the mother and father commended her spirit to God and went to bed.

Chariti had spent the night with Jeannie, less than one-half block from her home. About nine o'clock on Saturday morning, Chariti came bounding through the front door, all smiles and good cheer. After the gravity of her insensitivity was explained to her, she was grounded for two weeks. Chariti cried. Through her tears she said to her father, "Does this mean we are not going to look for a dog today?"

The father replied, "We are still going to look for a dog today because I love you. You are still grounded for breaking the rules, but this is a different thing."

This was the father's "I love you" plan. It was independent from the "I trust you" plan. It was part of the father's unconditional love. Each week the father would hold a sharing time with each child. It was a time to talk or play games. In Chariti's case the time had been allocated to go looking for a dog. It was not a time to be withdrawn as a punishment or taken away at any whim or infraction. This was an unconditional act of love.

Separating love from trust is easy for most parents of teenagers. We can love them and still not trust them. There are loving behaviors we exhibit toward our teenagers at the very time we don't trust them. Parents separate love from trust repeatedly. Because love and trust are different, it is possible to have a set of behaviors called an "I love you" plan separate from a set of behaviors called an "I trust you" plan. This can happen for all of our relationships.

Before proceeding with the creation of either a trusting or loving plan, be aware of the dangers of withholding love as a punishment. The major danger involves the relationship between love and acceptance. Withholding love or acceptance will drive our loved ones into the waiting arms of those who will give them acceptance but often will not contribute to their becoming their best selves. Defining love and certain things we are willing to do in the name of love as unconditional does not mean we have to tolerate inappropriate behavior. In other words unconditional love does not mean unconditional acceptance of poor choices.

In the story, the father was acting out of love. Love should not be used as a punishment. When we withhold love as a punishment, we become emotionally unsafe. The one being criticized withdraws. As critics we become less and less effective. The distance increases with each new critical statement.

THE CRITIC ◄───► THE CRITICIZED
Criticism equals distance.

THE CRITIC ◄─────► THE CRITICIZED
More criticism equals even greater distance.

THE CRITIC ◄────────► THE CRITICIZED
*More criticism equals separation, divorce, abandonment,
or constant conflict.*

Now the critic must scream or yell to be heard because the emotional distance is so great. The more out of control the critic becomes, the more emotionally unsafe he or she is to the one being criticized. What the critic doesn't realize is that the one being criticized is not focusing on the message but the messenger. The only message being received is that he or she is not acceptable, not worthwhile, or not valuable. The critic's frustration is only intensified. However, if someone doesn't understand Spanish, whether it is whispered or shouted doesn't matter. Until the one being criticized is confirmed, validated, and secure in the love of the critic, the message will never be the focus; it will be on the negativity of the messenger. Eventually, the one being criticized will leave the relationship. If he or she hasn't left it physically, he or she will definitely leave it emotionally. Most critics are blind to the fact that others have stopped caring about what they think or feel. Depending on the nature of the one being criticized, responses vary from rebellion to apparent compliance. The compliant individual listens to the critic and agrees to abide by the critic's counsel. Yet once out of sight of the critic, the apparently compliant person does whatever he or she wants. Both types of people will lie to get the freedom they crave— freedom to be with those who accept them. People want to be where they feel accepted and appreciated. They avoid being with critics. Unfortunately, more problems arise if the person who is being criticized is driven into the arms of friends who do not have his or her best interest at heart. Rational people "hang out" with people who are losers, bums, druggies, and self-destructive because they seek acceptance and a sense of belonging. They feel more emotionally safe with loser friends than they do with critical family members. In the following story, Donna is an example of a person who is apparently compliant.

Don and Donna

Don is a very hard-working father. He shows his family how much he loves them by providing well for them. He is also a man of few words and high expectations. Most of his comments are critical in nature. He tends to notice what hasn't been done instead of what has been accomplished. Don doesn't yell or scream. He just gives a lot of corrective advice. Donna is his sixteen-year-old daughter. Frequently, when Donna hears her father come in the front door, she will exit out the back door without a word to avoid being criticized. Don is unaware of his daughter's avoidance behaviors.

Donna has a boyfriend whom her father doesn't like. Her boyfriend's life's ambition is to be a drummer in a band, and Don measures people by their productivity and ambition. Donna has recognized the futility of arguing with her father. She listens to her father and says that her boyfriend and she are just casual friends. She assures her father that she is going on to college and has no intentions of ever marrying him. She lies about going to a girlfriend's house in order to flee her home and sneak off to be with her true love. Donna is an apparently compliant child. Her world is built on acquiescence, avoidance, and lies.

The essence of the gospel of Jesus Christ is to love. It is to help others become their best selves. This is not psychobabble or some socially acceptable thing to do. It is not about being politically correct. It is a gospel principle. "Reproving betimes with sharpness, when moved upon by the Holy Ghost; *and then showing forth afterwards an increase of love toward him whom thou hast reproved, lest he esteem thee to be his enemy*" (D&C 121:43; italics added).

Donna feels that her father doesn't accept her and has no confidence in her. Don hasn't paid a price to understand his daughter's world. He doesn't "reprove betimes"; he reproves all the time. It is obvious that Don is moved upon by frustration and the lack of performance in others and not by the Holy Ghost. There is no increase of love after a criticism. There is nothing but more criticism and silence.

Cynthia and Her Mother

Cynthia and her mother have been arguing since Cynthia was potty trained. It doesn't matter what the topic is. These two women yell and scream after being in the same room for fifteen seconds. Usually Mom will make a comment about Cynthia's immodest clothes, her freaky hairstyle, her pierced belly button, the tattoo on her ankle, or the poor quality of her choice of friends. Cynthia is so upset at her mother's nonacceptance and she craves her freedom to fail so desperately that she rejects even reasonable requests from her mother. Cynthia is involved in a power struggle over who will make the decisions for her life. She is determined to win even if the course she is pursuing is self-destructive. The mother feels that her job description is to make Cynthia a responsible person and that she is a failure as a mother if she does not point out Cynthia's poor choices.

When I suggested to the mother that she focus on loving her daughter and stop trying to mold her, the mother was upset. The answer to my question, "Is the approach you are now using working?" was an obvious no. "Are you willing to try a different approach? Are you willing to take your love to your daughter and your frustrations about your daughter to the Lord? By this I mean that you cease all criticism of your daughter. Tell the Lord about your frustrations with the tattoos and pierced belly button. For thirty days, focus on being positive and loving in spite of her continued poor choices. Each time you become aware of a poor choice on her part, go to the corner of your mind or a private spot and pray to God to help her."

No one will be surprised to learn that Cynthia and her mother now have the best relationship they have ever had. Cynthia is beginning to ask herself if she likes the direction of her life. To this point, she had simply done the opposite of what her mother wanted.

It is important that we show love *before* reproof is given. A solid "I love you" plan complete with weekly shared-time experiences may be necessary. We need to treat a loved one with respect. It enhances the possibility of not being perceived as an enemy. The kindness of a "thank you" and "please" engenders respect. If our loved one is treated consistently with respect, the credibility of our criticism increases. When we as critics are unwilling to develop an "I love you" plan and an "I respect you" disposition, we will almost certainly come to be viewed as enemies, as was the father of a young man who spoke with then Elder Gordon B. Hinckley. Elder Hinckley related,

> I happened to know his father, and I know that his father did not hate him. He loved him and mourned and grieved for him, but that father had an uncontrolled temper. Whenever he disciplined his children, he lost control and destroyed both them and himself.

> As I looked across the desk at that trembling, broken young man, estranged from a father he considered his enemy, I thought of some great words of revealed truth given through the Prophet Joseph Smith. They set forth in essence the governing spirit of the priesthood, and I believe they apply to the government of our homes. Let me read them to you. "No power or influence can or ought to be maintained . . . only by persuasion, by long suffering, by gentleness, and meekness and by love unfeigned by kindness and pure knowledge which shall greatly enlarge the soul without hypocrisy and without guile."

> I believe those marvelous and simple words set forth the spirit in which we should stand as fathers. Do they mean that we should not exercise discipline, that we should not reprove? Listen to these further words:

> "Reproving betimes with sharpness (When? While angry or in a fit of temper? No—) when moved upon by the Holy Ghost; and then showing forth afterwards an increase of love toward him whom thou hast reproved, lest he esteem thee to be his enemy;

that he may know that thy faithfulness is stronger than the cords of death" (D&C 121:41–44).

This, my brethren of the priesthood who stand at the head of families, is the key to government in the home directed by the Holy Spirit. I commend those words to every man within the sound of my voice and do not hesitate to promise that if you will govern your families in the spirit of those words, which have come from the Lord, you will have cause to rejoice, as will those for whom you are responsible. (Conference Report, October 1967, 91–92)

The term *enemy* is such a strong word. Enemy! Is it possible that what the prophet Micah said is true across all time? "Trust ye not in a friend, put ye not confidence in a guide: keep the doors of thy mouth from her that lieth in thy bosom. For the son dishonoureth the father, the daughter riseth up against her mother, the daughter in law against her mother in law; a man's enemies are the men of his own house" (Micah 7:5–6). Jesus quoted this scripture in Luke 12:53 and taught a higher law. This higher law will create a division. The division is between those who treat people with love and respect and those who do not.

Relationships Require Common Consent

Acting out of love unfeigned does not require common consent. One party acting unilaterally can gift love to another. However, for a relationship to grow requires common consent. When two free agents choose to interact, a relationship is born. Once a relationship has been established, there is no such thing as not communicating. Silence and not being available for a relationship send a loud message of indifference, apathy, or abandonment. Common consent is the basis of all healthy relationships. Mutual agreement is a key principle. In Isaiah we read, "Come now, and let us reason together" (1:18).

Frequently one party—or both—must do a lot of compromising in order to share the world as friends, spouses, or parent and child. Our best relationships are built by sharing. We share time together. Often we share our hopes and dreams. The nature of a relationship depends on age, interests, and mutual respect. Sometimes the best way for two people to cultivate a relationship is by taking turns choosing the shared activity. However, priorities prevail, and some relationships have to settle for the best efforts of each person. For example, Ellen and Susie had been roommates in college. They both worked and had very busy but separate lives. Each would have liked to spend more time together, but their schedules never seemed to match. The years went by, and each lamented the loss of contact. They finally decided on a luncheon date once a month and a phone call every other week. This was all the time they had for each other. Because it was mutually agreed upon by common consent, it was a good relationship.

Another factor we must consider in our relationships is age-appropriate activities. Frequently, adults try to bring children into an adult world instead of entering the world of the child. Granddaddy learned this lesson the hard way.

Granddaddy and His Grandson

Granddaddy wanted to take his grandson to a football game. The grandmother asked the grandfather if he was sure he wanted to take a four-year-old to a football game. "He will get bored, he won't understand, and he will be going to the bathroom all the time," she said.

The grandmother could not have been more right. It was a terrible experience for both of them. Granddaddy had purchased root beer and popcorn for the little guy. He spilled all the popcorn on the people below them. However, he did drink the pop. Granddaddy had to leave the game at exciting times to take his grandson to the bathroom.

Upon their return, the grandmother didn't need to ask how it went. She could see it upon their countenances. Granddaddy was frustrated because he tried to bring a four-year-old into an adult-world activity. The grandmother suggested that the grandson would have been happy just to go to the park and play on the swings. The next time they went into the world of a four-year-old. It was wonderful. Grandmother winked at her husband and said, "If you want to build a relationship with a four-year-old, you have to think like a four-year-old." Granddaddy said that the way his memory was slipping, he would catch up with their grandson in no time at all. They laughed.

There is an old saying that goes, "If you don't have time to do it right, when will you have time to do it over again?" There is time now to love. There is time to develop, if necessary, a one-sided, unilateral "I love you" plan with each significant person in our life. Maybe it's a postcard, a phone call, an enthusiastic hug, a smile. Acting out of love doesn't always have to cost us money. It does require from us thought, effort, and some time.

Some Relationships Require Strategic Retreat

A relationship cannot grow beyond the willingness of each to participate. This means that one party or the other will have to sacrifice and compromise in order for the relationship to progress. God was willing to have the children of Israel behold His face. He was ready for a better relationship. However, the children of Israel were not ready. Moses came down from the mountain with the higher law written on tables of stone. The children of Israel were neither willing nor prepared for this higher relationship: "Now this Moses plainly taught to the children of Israel in the wilderness, and sought diligently to sanctify his people that they might behold the face of God; but they hardened their hearts and could not endure his presence" (D&C 84:23–24).

Rather than abandon the children of Israel altogether, the Lord agreed to a lesser relationship called the law of Moses. This is called "strategic retreat." It is not abandonment. It is common consent. It is working at the level of mutual agreement. It is sharing at the level of our loved one's willingness to share. A relationship cannot be forced.

Alfred the Smoker

Alfred promised his fiancée that he would take her to the temple and be sealed. He did so, but shortly thereafter he picked up his habit of smoking again. His wife felt betrayed and cheated and nagged Alfred on every occasion. Alfred has many good traits and qualities. He is a good provider, a responsible and supportive father, and a faithful husband to his disgruntled wife. It is Alfred who is out first with his snowblower to clear the widows' walks and driveways. Alfred is a great neighbor, a good friend, and a responsible citizen. He is a major in the Air Force National Guard.

After four children and twenty years of marriage, I suggested to the wife that she offer her husband two gifts: peace and appreciation for what he is, rather than criticism for what he is not. Her first choice would be that he give up smoking. He is simply unwilling to do so and is willing to let her rant and rave in her frustration and to endure whatever misery she attempts to inflict upon him. All of her tears and pleadings have not moved him.

Next, I suggested that they negotiate about his smoking. Would he agree not to smoke in the house or around the children?

"Yes," said Alfred, "I will agree to that."

His wife agreed that she would never mention his smoking again. She had retreated to her next best option. He would not smoke in the house or around the children. They had come to common consent and to a level of willingness they could each support. They agreed to support this decision with a good attitude. They agreed to disagree without becoming disagreeable.

Common consent respects the preparation of each person in the relationship to function at his or her level of willingness. To criticize another requires common consent. Compulsion and improper criticism will not achieve common consent. It is only when we are acting out of love that real progress can be made.

Assignments for Chapter 8

1. Develop an "I love you" plan independent of an "I trust you" plan. As a parent or spouse or friend define how you would have an "I love you" plan and a different "I trust you" plan.

2. Gift respect to all people because you are a good person. Would others say that you respect them or their opinions? What would be an example of you respecting someone else's opinion in your family?

3. Work by common consent. Read D&C 26:2 and Amos 3:3. What do these scriptures mean to you?

4. Learn to "strategically retreat." Pick an issue that is not illegal or immoral but represents a difference of opinion or a difference in willingness. What are you willing to do to compromise to reach a less-than-ideal outcome?

CHAPTER 9

AN INCREASE OF LOVE

After people have been reproved or criticized, they often question their worth, feeling unappreciated, unaccepted, and hurt. The worth of their soul, although great in the sight of God, doesn't feel very valuable in the sight of their critics. Everyone has felt misunderstood, improperly judged, and unappreciated. A common reaction to criticism is to flee from the critics. Often those criticized are angry with their critics, and since most critics are mortal and flawed themselves, they question their right to correct them even when they are wrong. Depending on the level of confidence they have in the critic, they assume a very defensive posture. That is why we are to show an increase of love after we criticize, "lest [the criticized] esteem [us] to be his enemy" (D&C 121:43). Even when the criticism is properly delivered and spiritually inspired, those we criticize will question our motives and wonder if we are indeed their enemy.

It becomes apparent then that this criticism must be prompted by the Spirit. If not, it will be misinterpreted and will not lead to a more loving relationship. One man said, "If I had to wait until the Holy Ghost moved upon me before I could criticize, I would live in eternal silence." Perhaps, if he is not supposed to criticize, this is the best and most loving way to live. Elder Dallin H. Oaks counseled, "When truth is constrained by other virtues, the outcome is not falsehood but silence for a season. As the scriptures say, there is 'a time to keep silence, and a time to speak' (Eccl. 3:7)" (*Ensign*, February 1987, 68–78).

LOVING BY THE SPIRIT

The art of criticism may be the art of listening to the Holy Ghost. The doctrine of learning to live by the prompting of the Spirit is called sanctification. It is not impossible, nor is it an unreachable star. Sanctification is achieved by exercising our agency and making choices which would not offend the Spirit. Sanctification is not something the Spirit does; rather, sanctification is up to us as individuals. Helaman teaches that "sanctification cometh because of their yielding their hearts unto God" (Hel. 3:35). Therefore, the scriptures admonish would-be believers to "sanctify yourselves" (D&C 88:68; see also Isa. 1:16). For baptized and confirmed members of the Church who have been authorized to "receive the Holy Ghost," sanctifying ourselves is making decisions that allow the Holy Ghost to stay with us.

Decisions that drive the Spirit away are antithetical to sanctification. They cannot be loving actions if they drive away the Spirit. The Lord has stated in all four of the standard works that His "spirit shall not always strive with man" (see Gen. 6:3; Ether 2:15; D&C 1:33; Moses 8:17).

Some doctrines are taught but once. Imagine how important it must be for the Lord to have this specific phrase recorded in each of the standard works. The meaning of *to strive* is to "stay with or abide" or to "exert much effort or energy" (*American Heritage Dictionary*). The Lord has conditions which must be met in order for the Holy Ghost to abide with the individual. The phrase "I lost the Spirit" reflects the notion that someone did something contrary to keeping the Spirit with him or her.

Some have argued that one either has the Spirit or not, that it is a black-or-white issue. Others talk about the Holy Ghost being with a person in degrees. The sons of Mosiah prayed that the Lord would grant "unto them a portion of his Spirit to go with them, and abide with them" (Alma 17:9). It may be that having the Holy Ghost or having it withdraw is a matter of degrees, depending on the choices we make. It may also depend upon the magnitude of the choice that is made by the individual. Murder or adultery may cause a total withdrawal of the Spirit. Other choices, such as an unkind word from us, may offend the Spirit, causing it to withdraw a ways but not completely. Remember the experience that Joseph Smith had with translating the Book of Mormon. He and Emma had cross words one with another, and when Joseph returned to the task of translation, he could not do it until he apologized to Emma and made things right. After he and Emma were in accord, the Spirit returned and he was able to resume the process of translation. Joseph made a choice to say or do something that offended not only Emma but also the Holy Ghost.

Apparently the companionship of the Holy Ghost is indeed a conditional gift. It is bestowed with the understanding that it can be withdrawn from us when the Spirit is offended by the poor choices we make to speak, act, or even think in inappropriate ways. Learning to keep the Spirit in our lives and to enjoy the various gifts of the Spirit is often a lifelong process. It all begins with the desire to always have His Spirit to be with us.

FIGHTING GOD:
LOSS OF THE SPIRIT OF LOVE

In one sense, the Lord is using classical conditioning and reward to teach us as His children. We may have His Spirit only as long as we are humble, teachable, and ready to make choices that do not offend His Spirit. When we think in unkind ways, when we act in the ways which are not in our or another's best interest, and when we speak the critical word without the authority of the Holy Ghost in any degree of unrighteousness, "behold, the heavens withdraw themselves; the Spirit of the Lord is grieved; and when it is withdrawn, Amen to the priesthood or the authority of that man. Behold, ere he is aware, he is left unto himself . . . to fight against God" (D&C 121:37–38).

Fight against God? How do we fight against God? The answer is that we fight against God by going against God's way. If God is love, then fighting against Him means to live without loving, without having His Spirit with us. Our Heavenly Father's stated goal and objective is to bring about the growth and development of each of His spirit children: "For behold, this is my work and my glory—to bring to pass the immortality and eternal life of man" (Moses 1:39).

It is not sufficient for us to do God's work. How God's work is done is as important to Him as what is done in His name. The end does not justify the means. Forcing someone to go to church is not of God. Compelling someone to pay tithing is not of God. Coercing someone to do his home teaching is not of God. We may say that we are doing these things because we love the one we are trying to compel. But such force is not how God works and will result in the loss of the Spirit. The gospel of Jesus Christ is based upon invitation, enticement, and gentle persuasion. It is based on showing love, not fighting it.

In one of the most informative and insightful revelations about the premortal existence and the events that transpired there, Moses was taught how God's relationship with His children works. The idea of coercion was not of God, but of Satan:

> That Satan, whom thou hast commanded in the name of mine Only Begotten, is the same which was from the beginning, and he came before me, saying—Behold, here am I, send me, I will be thy son, and I will redeem all mankind, that one soul shall not be lost, and surely I will do it; wherefore give me thine honor. But, behold, my Beloved Son, which was . . . from the beginning, said unto me—Father, thy will be done, and the glory be thine forever. Wherefore, because that Satan rebelled against me, and sought to destroy the agency of man, which I, the Lord God, had given him, and also, that I should give unto him mine own power; by the power of mine Only Begotten, I caused that he should be cast down; and he became Satan, yea, even the devil, the father of all lies, to deceive and to blind men, and to lead them captive at his will, even as many as would not hearken unto my voice. (Moses 4:1–4)

Agency is a premortal gift which God has bestowed upon each of His children. When any of us presumes to take away the agency of man, woman, or child without the specific authority of the Holy

Ghost, we are fighting against God and God's ways. God will not sustain us, nor will He permit His Spirit to abide with us. King Benjamin's words remind us as the disciples of Jesus to watch ourselves:

> If ye do not watch yourselves, and your thoughts, and your words, and your deeds, and observe the commandments of God, and continue in the faith of what ye have heard concerning the coming of our Lord, even unto the end of your lives, ye must perish. And now, O man, remember, and perish not. (Mosiah 4:30)

In the journey to return to Heavenly Father's home, the road is clearly marked. It is clear that both what we do and how we do it are essential, or we will stray from the path.

LOVE: THE LORD'S STANDARD

What is the Lord's standard? The answer is comforting. It is to love much (see Luke 7:47) and to do what we can (see Mark 14:8). We need to learn to follow the promptings of the Holy Ghost and to grow line upon line and precept upon precept. It is proclaimed in the beautiful hymn "If You Could Hie to Kolob" that "improvement and progression have one eternal round" (*Hymns,* no. 284).

Even when what we have to say is true and in the eternal best interest of others, we are not justified in sharing it unless we can do so in a loving manner which allows the Spirit to abide with us. Just in case we are unsure of the concomitant characteristics, the scriptures enumerate them. They are persuasion, long-suffering, gentleness, meekness, love unfeigned, kindness, and pure knowledge. The frosting on the cake of criticism is that afterwards we show forth an increase of love toward the one reproved. Together these comprise the "approaching skills" necessary to criticize in the Lord's own way.

We must understand the worth of souls in God's eyes. We are precious to Him—so precious, in fact, that He does not want His children attacked by uninspired criticism. Many Church leaders have counseled us in this matter.

President Hugh B. Brown said, "Let us be very careful about this matter of reproving . . . [and] let us be careful how we trample on the feelings of our brothers and sisters. Let us lift them and bless them and benefit them as we go forward and never be guilty of humiliating them or causing them to think that we do not appreciate their work" (*The Abundant Life*, 146).

Hugh B. Brown related the following poem in general conference:

> Oh, the unkind things we say to those we love.
> We have kind words for the stranger
> And smiles for the sometime guest,
> While oft to our own
> The bitter tone,
> Though we love our own the best!
> (Conference Report, October 1965, 16)

Elder Neal A. Maxwell has stated:

> Practical and spiritual meekness also provides a helpful context for giving and receiving correcting candor, when such candor is needed. Graciousness makes easier the following of the injunction of the Lord: "Reproving betimes with sharpness, when moved upon by the Holy Ghost; and then showing forth afterwards an increase of love toward him whom thou hast reproved" (D&C 121:43). Graciousness facilitates providing the increase in love. President Brigham Young counseled the Saints, "Never chasten beyond the balm you have within you to bind up." Gracious individuals will heed Brigham's counsel. Paul spoke similarly: "Brethren, if a man be overtaken in a fault, ye which are spiritual, restore such an one in the spirit of meekness" (Gal. 6:1). (*Meek and Lowly*, 94)

President David O. McKay counseled:

> "Reproving betimes with sharpness, . . . and then showing forth afterwards an increase of love toward him whom thou hast reproved, lest he esteem thee to be his enemy." Why, it is a wonderful admonition and lesson in regard to the government,

not only in quorums of the priesthood, . . . but also in our home
life and in all phases of association in society! Consider, again,
the suggestion in regard to the worth of souls. (*Gospel Ideals,* 150)

Who would attack the worth of a soul? How does anyone deni-
grate another's value? The opposite of enabling love is disabling love.
When one is giving uninvited, unauthorized, and inappropriate criticism, he is disabling himself as a purveyor of love. He is also denigrating the recipient of his criticism. Any form of abuse disables love.
Even the truth, when inappropriately given, is harmful meat that
"they cannot bear" (D&C 19:22). To physically, emotionally, or spiritually abuse a child of God is to risk destroying his or her self-worth.
It is to send a message that he or she is not worthwhile. With unkind
and critical words one attacks the very core, the spiritual essence of a
person. A constant bombardment of criticism will convince even the
noblest that they are worthless. Consider the following quotations
from Church leaders that specifically address criticism.

President Gordon B. Hinckley has stated:

> There is not a man or woman in this vast assembly who cannot
> be depressed on the one hand, or lifted on the other, by the
> remarks of his or her associates.

> Criticism is the forerunner of divorce. . . . [Speaking of a young
> married couple:] They had thrown away with careless and sour
> words the hopes and dreams of eternity. With criticism and
> shouting, they had violated the sacred promises that might have
> taken them on to exaltation. (Fireside, BYU Marriott Center, 6
> March 1994)

President J. Reuben Clark Jr. advised:

> Brethren, be careful, be prayerful, be wise, when you undertake to
> make your reproof, when you undertake to direct. . . . Be careful
> of their feelings. Speak kindly and in such a way that there never
> will be any question as to your love for them and your desire
> merely to be helpful. (Conference Report, October 1958, 83)

President Brigham Young counseled:

> Parents should never drive their children, but lead them along, giving them knowledge as their minds are prepared to receive it. Chastening may be necessary betimes, but parents should govern their children by faith rather than by the rod, leading them kindly by good example into all truth and holiness. (*Discourses of Brigham Young,* 208)

Elder Dallas N. Archibald of the Seventy said:

> It is impossible to emphasize the good in others if negative words or phrases are readily available on the tips of our tongues or expressed through our gestures. . . . When correction is necessary, it must take place "betimes"—meaning early on—under the direction of the Holy Ghost and not in anger.

> The instructions on how to correct are clear and simple: early on, with the peace of the Holy Ghost, with enough of the healing power within us to make sure that self-esteem is never wounded, ensuring always that the individual feels important and capable. . . . Enlarge the soul. (*Church News,* 10 October 1992, 11)

And Robert L. Simpson stated:

> Let us place first things first and mention love as the prime ingredient. I rather think that Heavenly Father would like the idea of love heading our list, for his Only Begotten, the Savior of the world, had unlimited capacity for love. This single trait of love was most typical of his brief mortal ministry. (Conference Report, April 1964, 68)

This vast array of counsel from the Brethren reemphasizes the Lord's ancient command to love. It also shows what a concern it is that we are still not properly living this higher law of love. In theory we all believe and support this loving way of life, but what about our practice? Consider the impact of showing love and concern in the following story:

Working for Bill

It had come to Bill's attention that Sue had been coming to work twenty minutes late every day during the week. Some of the other employees complained about the apparent double standard. Why should she be allowed to come to work late and the others held to a higher standard? When Sue came to work twenty minutes late on Friday morning, Bill called her into his office and confronted her with her tardiness. Sue reported that she had a very sick child, and the day-care center would not take the responsibility to care for him. She had to drive thirty miles one way to take the child to the home of her mother who had agreed to care for the infant. Sue informed Bill that even though she came twenty minutes late, she stayed an extra half hour to compensate for her tardiness and to ensure that she gave an honest day's work.

Bill paused and expressed concern for the child. Then he proceeded to upbraid Sue for not coming to him on the first day and giving him the information. Sue cried and told Bill that as a single mother she really needed this job. Bill agreed that Sue could alter her schedule as long as she continued to stay the compensating half hour. Sue was relieved that she was not fired, but her feelings were hurt; she felt unappreciated and wondered about looking for another job. Sue had worked hard for the company and had gone out of her way to empty the wastebaskets of several employees and frequently cleaned up the employee break room, which was a disaster. Sue was the one who made sure there was paper in the copy machine and a dozen other things. Now Sue didn't feel like doing any of those things. In the court of her mind, she was innocent of any wrongdoing. She probably should have explained her situation to Bill, but she had felt she wasn't hurting the company. By 4:00 P.M. Sue was ready to quit her job and find a place that appreciated her extra efforts.

At 4:30 P.M. Bill called Sue back into his office and said, "Sue, concerning what I said to you earlier this morning, I hope if the situation ever happens again you will come to me first so we can work it out. I want you to know how much I appreciate all you do for the company. I know you give way more than your job description requires. I've seen you emptying wastebaskets, cleaning the break room, and keeping paper in the copy machines. We don't have an extra-mile award in our company, but if we did, Sue, I would give it to you. Thank you for all you do for us here. I hope your child will get better soon. That's all I wanted to say."

Two weeks later Sue was offered a different job for slightly more pay. "No, thanks," she said. "I like working for Bill."

In this story Bill showed forth an increase of caring concern after giving appropriate criticism.

The scriptures place a heavy responsibility upon the givers of reproof. Not only are they required to package their criticisms in gentleness, but they are expected to be Spirit-directed. Additionally, the givers of reproof are to show forth an increase of love toward the one criticized. In this way of dealing with people, the true disciples of Christ are identified. This is what is meant by loving as Jesus loved. This is the higher law.

Assignments for Chapter 9

1. Write down your thoughts about the phrase "It takes a revelation to share a revelation." How does this relate to the giving of criticism?

2. Read Doctrine and Covenants 88:68; 133:4; 67:10; 93:1. If sanctification is the doctrine of living with the companionship of the Holy Ghost by making wise choices, what choices do you need to make so that you can sanctify yourself?

3. Define an increase of love in concrete behavioral terms. What does that mean?

4. The next time you criticize someone, how will you let them know that your genuine concern for them is stronger than the cords of death?

CHAPTER 10

GIVING APPROPRIATE CRITICISM

Now that we have worked on the other four steps of giving criticism in the Lord's way—properly assisting change, seeking divine help in mighty prayer, acting out of love, and showing an increase in love—it is important to combine these efforts in giving appropriate criticism. Here is a checklist to help ensure your criticism is appropriate. We'll explore these points in more detail throughout the rest of the chapter.

QUICK CHECKLIST
FOR GIVING APPROPRIATE CRITICISM

Step 1: Before You Speak
- Before you speak, ask yourself two questions:
    1. Is the criticism a part of my stewardship?
    2. Is the criticism necessary and helfpful?
- If the answer to either question is no, *back off!*
- If the answer to *both* questions is yes, proceed.

Step 2: Ask for and receive permission to criticize.
- Be alone with the one being criticized at a mutually agreeable time and place.
- Be in emotional control and logically explain concerns.
- Stay focused on the issue. Do not attack self-worth!
- Separate the issue from ego.

Step 3: Affirm his or her worth to you!

STEP 1: BEFORE YOU SPEAK

Before you open your mouth with "you should, you need, you ought," consider the consequences of your words. An out-of-control critic destroys his or her own credibility and effectiveness. Some refer to this as the "Ready-Fire-Aim" approach. We are always ready to criticize with no regard for the feelings of the one being criticized. "They didn't think about me, so why should I think about their feelings?" We fire our mouth off without thinking of the time, place, circumstance, or ability of the one being criticized to receive it. The consequences are usually disastrous and create unnecessary fallout. In the process of justifying our criticism, we now try to aim our comments to some productive purpose. We persist in putting the blame on others. The more we talk, the more we try to attribute our hostile response to being tired, upset, or worried about something. We live in denial of our toxic reactions. We refuse to admit that our approach was insensitive, nonproductive, and poorly handled; or if we do admit it, we justify it.

People giving appropriate criticism should always respect the time, the space, and the ability of the recipient to manage it. Before you speak, it would be wise to mentally walk through the experience and anticipate the reaction and the desired outcome.

Before you proceed with any criticism, there are two questions that need to be answered in the affirmative.

Question 1: **Is the criticism a part of your stewardship?**

If the answer to the above question is no, and if it is not illegal or immoral, then allow others their own poor relationships and their right to fail. If your concerns are serious enough to warrant outside intervention, then report the information to one who has the appropriate authority and *back off!*

For example, in a family of eight children, the youngest child frequently grows up thinking he has nine parents. They include Mom, Dad, and seven brothers and sisters. In addition to two real parents, the child has brothers and sisters who feel authorized to tell the youngest what he or she should, needs, and ought to do. The siblings give themselves permission to criticize because they are older. Sometimes we assume the right to criticize because we are bigger, faster, smarter, or stronger than the younger sibling. There are those of us who feel we have a right to criticize anything that any family member may do which might negatively reflect upon us, and therefore we are constantly correcting others and interjecting what should, needs, and ought to be done. The older siblings should not criticize the youngest; they don't have the stewardship. When people assume a stewardship they do not have or if they have the stewardship but act inappropriately, it is called "unrighteous dominion."

Each of us is entitled to our own space and the right to manage our life within that space. This includes the right to succeed and the right to fail. There is much to be learned from both success and failure. As already discussed in this book, there are three major ways of learning: through observation, instruction, and bumping into boundaries. Sometimes, paying the consequences for inappropriate behavior is the most effective lesson.

In regard to human relationships, it is important that we allow people their own poor (or good) social interactions. Consider the following scenario:

Mom as Traffic Cop

A father and son had a poor relationship because neither of them was willing to make the effort to improve it. They needed to accept responsibility for what they had. It was ineffective for a third party, like the mother, to try to improve their relationship by being a go-between. This type of mediator is eventually blamed by one or both for contributing to the poor relationship. She winds up being a judge or umpire. The real damage done by the third party is taking away the responsibility which the father and the son have to make the relationship work. Also, it creates an illusion that the relationship is somehow better than it truly is.

On occasion, a counselor will ask this question to the well-meaning and well-intentioned meddler: "Where would this relationship be if you were killed in a traffic accident tomorrow?" The answer is that the relationship would be where it was before the meddler got involved. Assume that the father stopped communicating with his son when the boy was a teenager. All messages were carried between them by the mother, who served as a mediator, negotiator, and arbitrator. They were more than willing to let her carry the messages. Although she was frustrated, it gave her a sense of being needed.

Assume that the mother died when the boy was eighteen. The father and his son had to go back to the point where the relationship was abandoned. From that point they had to communicate to make it better. They were willing to do so. If one or both of them had been unwilling to communicate, it would have revealed the true nature of their dysfunctional relationship. They needed to face reality. A third party cannot have a relationship for two other people who need to have their own "lousy" relationship.

The mother in this example was acting outside her stewardship. She was simply trying to compensate for the poor relationship of the father and the son. The mother should have felt free to communicate with her husband and to communicate with her son as two separate relationships. In a situation like this, the best alternative for the mother would have been to become a "traffic cop." This means that she should have directed the negative verbal traffic to its proper destination. When approached by her husband with a complaint about the son, a more appropriate response would have been, "You are so right, dear. May I suggest that you go to him and tell him what you have just told me?"

Instead, many well-meaning guardians of the peace scurry off to warn the other party that Dad is really upset. The son justifies his behavior to the mother, who shuttles back to explain the son's message. The mother would be better off if she offered understanding to both her husband and son without letting herself be drawn into the middle. She should not accept responsibility to communicate for her husband or her son. In like manner, when the son brought his concerns to her, she should have been a verbal "traffic cop" and directed him to his father. This could have been done by her sympathizing with her son. "It must be very hard for you, son, not to feel like you can communicate with your father. However, I think you have a point. It's important that he hear from you. Perhaps you may want to write him a note." This way the mother would have been free to love her husband and to love her son independent from feeling the responsibility to make the relationship better.

Verbal and emotional abuse are exceptions to the rule. Sometimes the question is asked, "What about verbal or emotional abuse? Would I not be justified in intervening in a dysfunctional relationship if my husband was verbally or emotionally abusing my son or daughter?"

In the case of a child, the parent does have a stewardship to protect his or her offspring. This does not, however, give the parent license to act unrighteously or inappropriately. Each situation is unique. All of the circumstances need to be considered carefully and prayerfully. There will be times when intervention under serious verbal and emotional battering is an appropriate response.

If someone is so emotionally unhealthy as to be constantly assaulting his or her spouse or children with verbal and emotional abuse, the questions should be asked, "What is being done to protect the child? What is being done to obtain help for the abusing spouse?" Most want to run off and get a divorce. The nonabusive mate needs to approach the Lord in mighty prayer and petition for divine intervention. The gospel has clear guidelines for approaching an offending party. It is the responsibility of the one offended to attempt reconciliation. This is to be accomplished in the spirit of helpfulness (see D&C 42:88–89). Assume that this attempt is rejected. According to Doctrine and Covenants 98:34–45, an "offering of peace" is to be made three separate times. Between each attempt, the nonabusing person should mightily pray unto God for divine intervention. He or she should consult with a bishop and priesthood leaders. After the fourth offense, these testimonies are to be brought before the Lord. They will not be blotted out until the abuser repents (see D&C 98:44). This does *not* mean that in the case of physical abuse someone is to tolerate being beaten three times before he or she protects himself or herself. What is being discussed here is verbal and emotional abuse.

The nonabusive person has to be willing to put his or her relationship with the abuser on the line and say, "You cannot verbally or emotionally abuse these children anymore. If you do not go and get professional counseling help, I am leaving you for a week (or some other specified time period)," and then do it. A decision of this magnitude should be made only after mighty prayer and consultation with priesthood leaders. Why? Because a third-party priesthood leader can be more objective. Nevertheless, we have the first right of revelation for our lives, and we cannot transfer that responsibility to others. This is a proper response to someone who is out of control with verbal or emotional abuse.

People will say they can't leave because they have nowhere to go, they can't afford it, they fear for their safety, and so on. Seldom are these valid reasons. There are women's shelters in every major city, and anyone with determination will find religious and charitable groups willing to help. The Lord does not lead people away from a problem until His ways have been followed.

The purpose of this entire explanation is to give permission to leave when necessary. In general, this will not be the rule. It is more appropriate to approach the Lord in mighty prayer and call upon the powers of divine intervention and to consult with priesthood leaders. Professional counseling may be in order. The more people are in tune with the Spirit, the greater will be their confidence in the outcome. Take a look at how Wendy handled an abusive situation.

Harry and Wendy

Harry is a verbally and emotionally abusing father and husband. He is always criticizing his wife and children. He is constantly calling them names like "stupid" and swearing at them. Wendy, his wife, has managed to deal with Harry but fears the children will suffer irreparable damage. Every time Harry begins to criticize the children, Wendy jumps in to defend them. Then Wendy and Harry wind up in a fight. Wendy accuses him of being verbally and emotionally abusive. Harry accuses Wendy of interfering with his relationships. He also feels that she is parenting him by telling him what he should, needs, and ought to do. He sees Wendy as being disloyal to him in front of the children. Furthermore, he is tired of her choosing the children over him.

Harry is right that Wendy has been mothering him. Unwittingly, Wendy, by mishandling her response, gives Harry issues to argue, and thereby he can escape focusing on his abusive behavior. Because she parents him in front of the children, she is viewed by Harry as being the problem. This is typical of most arguments. Each party is arguing a point of view he or she can defend. Wendy wants to talk about Harry's abusive actions, while Harry wants to talk about Wendy's inappropriate interference. But there is another way that Wendy could handle these situations that would take away all of Harry's complaints about her. First, Wendy can go to the Lord in mighty prayer, seeking His guidance and asking for the companionship of the Holy Ghost. She can also discuss the matter with their bishop. Then she can ask Harry for permission to criticize him. Maybe a letter or note could be written by Wendy asking for permission to meet with Harry to discuss a painful issue which threatens their relationship. The middle of an emotionally charged encounter is not a good time to ask someone if now would be a good time to discuss inappropriate conduct.

When Harry and Wendy do meet alone, at a mutually agreed upon time and place, Wendy is nervous and maybe a little afraid, but she says to Harry, "I've asked to meet with you privately because I did not want to criticize you in front of the children. It's my way of respecting you. Also, I did not want you to think that I was choosing the children over you. Our relationship is worth working on, and I love you. I know that the children are frustrating you, and I want to help. I have a problem with the way you talk to the children. I'm concerned about their self-worth. Also, I know I'm not perfect myself, and I am willing to work on being better. I'm really looking for solutions, Harry. You love the children, and you work hard to provide for us. I will try to help them be appreciative of what you do for all of us. I worry when I see either fear or despair in the children's eyes when you swear at them or call them names.

"This is the issue I have, Harry, and I honestly believe it's hurting your ability to have a good relationship with the kids. You are entitled to have a poor relationship if that is what you want, but not an abusive one. I love you and I love them, and I want to help if I can. What can I do to help? I have made several phone calls, and I know where and when different anger management groups meet. I'll go with you, if you would like. Think about it and we can talk later."

People in Wendy's situations might say that their husbands would never let them complete the first sentence without interrupting them. In such cases, write out the whole concern and the consequences in a letter. Obviously, Harry is going to be defensive. However, Wendy has not compounded the problem with insertion, disloyalty, and face-loss for Harry. If Harry is a good man, he will think about it and try to improve. Wendy needs to go to the Lord in mighty prayer. She needs to bring the same calm spirit to at least three such encounters. If he is a "bad" man, then Wendy needs to confront him with an ultimatum to get professional help for anger management or leave for a specified period of time. And she must be prepared to leave. What Wendy is attempting falls under the category of seeking for common consent. By following the Lord's approach Wendy takes the focus off herself and places the responsibility for the behavior directly in Harry's lap.

Earlier, it was pointed out that we can only share to the level of willingness of the other person. In the illustration, Wendy did what she could. She went to the Lord in mighty prayer and consulted with the bishop. Next, she asked for and received permission from Harry before she criticized him. She made sure she and Harry were alone at a mutually agreeable time and place. She was in emotional control of herself and logically explained her concerns over Harry's abusive language and her fear of its impact on the children's self-worth. Also, Wendy gave Harry a viable alternative. She prepared a way for him to be successful. Wendy is only one-half of this relationship. She can control only her actions and reactions. She can model proper behavior for Harry in interacting with the children. She can love Harry for the good he does in generally protecting and providing for the family. She may not feel she can trust Harry and his abusive relationship with the children, but Wendy can have an "I love Harry" plan and do an unconditional deed of love every day for him independent of Harry's language with the children. She will do this deed of unconditional love, not because Harry deserves it, but because Wendy is a good person. She wants to be a loving individual. By strengthening the overall relationship with Harry, Wendy creates a supportive environment conducive to change.

Some might ask, "Isn't it a form of intimidation to threaten Harry with leaving if he does not change his abusive language?" Yes, and it depends on how serious Wendy is about the issue. This should not be a ploy. Wendy cannot threaten to leave over everything, or she is simply trying to blackmail Harry emotionally. Saying that she will leave if Harry continues to verbally and emotionally abuse the children is a simple statement of fact, not an idle threat. Wendy may want to leave for a month or a week to underscore her words if Harry's behavior is not modified. This is setting boundaries to protect herself and the children.

For Wendy, this is a preferable and more appropriate overall response than to insert herself into every conversation that Harry has with the kids and wind up always arguing with Harry. Even if Wendy divorces Harry, he is still going to have some kind of relationship with the kids. This may include every other weekend, six weeks in the summer, and holidays. In the end, Harry has to be responsible for his own poor relationships. Wisdom would dictate that Wendy criticize sparingly so that when she does speak to Harry, her input will be considered, evaluated, and weighed. Otherwise, Wendy will be perceived as a nagging, never-satisfied person, and the content of her messages will never be given sincere consideration. She dealt with Harry as a wife. She also dealt with Harry as the mother of their children. What she decided not to do was constantly interfere directly with Harry's relationships. By acting the way she did, Wendy acted properly in her stewardship position.

Question 2: Is the criticism necessary and helpful?

Your criticism may be true, but is it necessary? Is it edifying and in another's best interest to hear it? Just because something is true does not mean that anyone needs to know it. An aging mother does not need to hear about all of the sins of her children while they were teenagers. We must remember that "that which doth not edify is not of God, and is darkness" (D&C 50:23).

Wisdom would dictate that the sharing of truth be appropriate to the ability of the receiver to appreciate it. There are many truths which should never be spoken. Just because they are true does not justify their publication. Elder Dallin H. Oaks gave a powerful discourse on the evils of criticism, in which he said:

> The fact that something is true is not always a justification for communicating it. . . . The critical consideration is how we use the truth. . . . A Christian who has concern for others exercises care in how he uses the truth. Such care does not denigrate the truth; it ennobles it.

> Truth surely exists as an absolute, but our use of truth should be disciplined by other values. For example, it is wrong to make statements of fact out of an evil motive, even if the statements are true. It is wrong to threaten to reveal embarrassing facts unless money is paid, even if the facts are true. We call that crime blackmail. . . . Modern revelations direct us to avoid backbiting, evil speaking, and finding fault one with another (see D&C 20:53–54, D&C 42:27, D&C 88:124, and D&C 136:23). (*Ensign,* February 1987, 68–72)

The real issue here is the matter of a higher law than "Is it true?" The higher law asks, "Is it edifying?" The story that follows illustrates the difference between the two.

True and Edifying?

A neighbor girl went away to have a child out of wedlock. She then decided to place the baby up for adoption. The baby was adopted by a loving, caring couple. She later returned home, desiring with all of her heart to start her life over.

The girl is now doing well and the truth is known only by a small circle of family members and medical personnel. However, quite by accident, her neighbor who was visiting another town, encountered the couple who had adopted the child. Putting two and two together, the neighbor suspects the truth. A little investigation confirms it.

Later the neighbor is involved in a conversation with someone who asks what she thinks about the girl.

If she were to tell all she knows it would not be a lie. It is, after all, "only the truth." She would only be relating what she knows. But it is not edifying, and in this case it is gossip. To spread the tale of what she knows could affect the young girl's future. If our standard of judgment is, "Is it true?" then we could prattle away and tell all. If, however, our standard is a higher one, a standard that asks, "Is it edifying?" then our lips will be closed. It is not necessary. It is not needed or called for; it is a truth which never needs to be spoken.

In conjunction with the question, "Is it edifying?" is the issue of whether it is in another's best interest to hear it. If the knowledge and criticism we have to share are truly in another's best interest to hear, then we need to have the courage to share it. If, however, no good thing can come of it, then we need to exercise restraint and control the impulse to share it with anyone. A very important part of self-mastery is the ability to keep harmful knowledge to yourself. People are more respected for constraint than indulgence. We will possess greater self-respect and self-mastery when we speak only the truths which edify.

An Old Lie

Barbara and Doris have been the best of friends since junior high school. Now, both are married and preparing to attend the same ten-year class reunion at the old high school. Barbara has found out that Doris didn't make the cheerleading squad in high school because of a false rumor. Another girl lied about Doris to the teacher who was the class advisor. Both Barbara and Doris will see the teacher at the reunion. Also, the girl who spread the false rumor is the class vice president and will be there also.

It certainly is true that Doris suffered as a consequence of a false rumor. But answer the following questions. Is it edifying for Barbara to tell Doris? What earthly good could it do for Doris to know that now? Would it change the past? Will Doris feel better about herself just knowing that she might have made the team had someone not spoken ill of her to the teacher? Will it improve Doris's self-worth? How will it impact the relationship between Doris and her former teacher who acted on false information? Currently, Doris doesn't feel badly about the teacher or about the gossiping classmate whose lie kept her from the cheerleading squad. What do you think would happen if Barbara told Doris? Would the ten-year reunion be edifying for Doris? Would it be in Doris's best interest to hear this information about the past, and would it be wise for Barbara to disclose all she knows? The answer is no! If it would not edify, *don't say it*. Let it go!

However, if you *are* in a stewardship position in which you know some truth, and imparting that knowledge would help someone become a better person, then you should proceed with step 2 in offering appropriate criticism.

STEP 2: ASK FOR AND RECEIVE PERMISSION TO CRITICIZE

Asking for permission to criticize does not mean that permission will always be given. It is as important to receive permission as it is to ask for it. If we criticize without asking and receiving permission, we are not treating the other person as an equal or with respect. If we criticize without permission, we are assuming a parental role over the other person. We do not have a right, even if we do have authority, to treat another with disrespect. If we do not receive the permission to criticize verbally, we may ask for permission to communicate our criticisms in writing. The one being criticized could then read them and respond within a certain amount of time, perhaps twelve hours. This option gives the frustrated critic a place to take his criticism. Writing down criticism removes much of the intimidation factor and allows the one being criticized to focus on the content of the criticism. Otherwise, the packaging of the criticism and the delivery system supersede the message. People interpret meaning by looking at a person's facial expression and interpreting his or her body language. Tone of voice can also distract from the content of the message. Writing down the criticism provides focus for the critic and greater emotional safety for the one being criticized. Often they will be open and give permission in this way. In getting permission to criticize, there are other steps we need to take to set the stage for a critical scene. Part of our arrangements should include privacy for the one criticized, emotional control on our part, and protection of the ego.

Be Alone with the One Being Criticized at a Mutually Agreeable Time and Place

Once permission to criticize has been verbally received, decide when and where you can be alone. The meeting should be at a mutually agreed upon time and place. Criticizing anyone in front of others is a bad idea. A person criticized in front of others suffers humiliation. They feel belittled and are more concerned about other people who may be present than they are about the content of the criticism. This is especially true of children being criticized in front of their friends. If we as critics are truly concerned about effectiveness, we will be alone with the one being criticized at a mutually agreed time and place. For example, "Johnny, I would like to talk to you right after dinner, before your friends come to play," or, "Mary, I can see this is a bad time; could we talk before you go to bed, about nine o'clock?"

A parent, employer, or one who is in a position of authority may ask, "What if he or she refuses to give me permission to criticize?"

An appropriate response would be, "That is not an option. I was asking out of respect for you. Your options are to choose within the next twenty-four hours a time and a place that will be convenient for both of us."

It shows respect and restraint when we are willing to be alone at a mutually safe place. The opposite is also true. It shows disrespect and lack of restraint when we insist on the here and now. For those of us who want to enjoy a close relationship, being emotionally safe is enormously important. In addition, through respect and restraint, the critic who is willing "not to criticize" in front of others is displaying loyalty to the relationship. It is hypocrisy to expect loyalty from others when loyalty is not given.

There are consequences attached to humiliating someone in front of others. Emotional closeness will suffer. Respect will be replaced by resentment. Most of us as critics are either unaware of or unconcerned about these consequences. In this case, it is as though we felt justified for giving the ridicule or criticism in public. Ridicule is a justifiable consequence in our mind. Therefore, we feel we have done nothing to deserve alienation. We expect that being "right" gives us permission. Too many critics assume that there will be no consequences for their self-justified behavior. Their criticisms were just compensation for the behavior of the one who was being criticized.

Behavior which says, "I am free to criticize anytime, anyplace, and in front of anyone I choose," is naive. It could be amusing, except for its tragic consequences. Ironically, even when our criticism is right, we are wrong in not being alone to share the criticism. To criticize in front of others and hope that social pressure will be on our side as the critic is foolish. *The sympathy goes to the one being criticized.*

Imagine, in a classroom setting, a misbehaving boy who is truly guilty of rude and insensitive conduct. The teacher calls him by name and chastens him in front of the other students. In spite of the fact that the student is wrong and the teacher is right, the students will sympathize with the one being embarrassed in front of others. In this case, the teacher is right in principle but wrong in delivery.

Be in Emotional Control and Logically Explain Your Concerns

No yelling, crying, swearing, threats, or physical or emotional intimidation should accompany our criticism. Facial expression and body language represent more than half of how communication is interpreted. It is vitally important to be in control of these bodily signals. When neck muscles are taut and the blood vessels at the temple are bulging, the focus is going to be on the messenger and not the message.

Sue and Her Father

Sue's father caught her breaking curfew, not doing her chores, and lying to him. He began yelling at her, grabbed her arm, and pulled her downstairs. Sue tripped and broke her arm in the fall. Child protective services was called, and the father was mandated to take an anger management class by the court. He was required to report for regular counseling. As the counselor talked with Sue and her father, it was obvious that there was a great deal of hostility between them. Sue confessed that she had been wrong. She had fully expected to lose phone privileges and to be grounded for the weekend, which were the punishments prescribed by the father. With childlike wisdom she said, "But I didn't deserve to be treated that way. Certainly I would not have broken my arm if you had not pulled me down the stairs."

The father was in bewilderment that somehow he had become the focus. He felt that Sue's misconduct justified his behavior. The counselor had to explain to them what it means to be emotionally healthy. It is important that each accept responsibility for his or her behavior. They role-played the situation over again to determine what should have happened. Sue accepted reluctantly the responsibility for each poor judgment decision she had made.

Then it was the father's turn. He had a very difficult time accepting responsibility for his angry and aggressive behavior. It took several tries before he could admit that her behavior did not justify his reaction. The counselor talked with him about the "abuser mentality," discussed in the following scenario.

The Abuser Mentality

A man hit his wife because she had not done something he had asked her to do. The abusive man felt justified. He tried to explain that he would not have done it had she only accomplished his expectations. It was her fault she got hit; she "made" him do it. This, of course, negates individual accountability. Each of us is responsible for our own behavior, regardless of the actions of others. Each of us has a right and opportunity to act and to react. We cannot always choose the circumstances, but we can always choose our response. When we try to say that someone else made us do it, we are not accepting responsibility for our own behavior. We violate the first principle of emotionally healthy people, to accept responsibility for our own behavior. Abuse is never justified.

It is important to talk about how the husband could have handled the situation differently. He should be in emotional control before he speaks to her. This might mean a time-out, a mind walk, or any number of anger-control mechanisms—deep-breathing exercises, counting backwards, going for a trip in the mind, or actually walking around the block.

When we logically explain our concerns, it removes the element of emotionalism with its attendant distractions. Credibility is on the line when we say we are being logical, but our behavior says otherwise. Criticism is difficult to receive under the best of circumstances. Adding emotionalism to the criticism only confuses the matter. Our focus should be on the issue or behavior in question. It is best for us not to become angry, to swear, or to cry. Some of us feel that this display of emotionalism adds emphasis to our point of view, or we justify it by saying we can't help ourselves. But we only succeed in making ourselves the focus. Those of us who use physical or emotional intimidation as a part of our presentation once again dilute the message and divert the focus to the messenger.

It is a dysfunctional and self-defeating behavior to criticize anyone in the heat of emotionalism. If it is too sensitive an issue and tears cannot be restrained, it would be better to write it down. Involving a third party may be necessary. A counselor or priesthood leader can deliver the content in such a way that the emphasis remains on the issue or behavior in question. Men feel manipulated when women cry. They resent it. They feel diverted from the true issue. Many women have this same response when men yell at them. Both yelling and crying shift the focus to the person and away from the issue. This is so frustrating that many men and women just give up. Breaking this nonproductive behavioral pattern of joining criticism and negative emotionalism is a difficult habit to modify. Nevertheless, logically explaining our concerns in a letter can be practiced. It develops into a skill and contributes to the process of better communication.

Separate Ego from Issue

As we have discussed already in this book, part of the art of giving criticism relates to this important ability to separate *ego* from *issue.* Let's look at this idea a little more closely. Ask yourself, "Is the criticism an attack on self-worth?" Focus on the issue or behavior. Be specific in separating self-worth from the issue or behavior.

Ego means the whole person, the self, the "I." It represents our personal identity. Ego is expressed as "in my opinion" or "I feel this way." Self-worth, or ego-worth, is the value we place on our personal identity. It manifests itself by asking three questions:

- What is my worth?
- Are my input, effort, and time appreciated?
- Am I loved, and am I lovable?

Self-worth is how we feel about ourselves. Each relationship helps us to evaluate our self-concept. The sum total of all the messages received from others assists us in forming self-perception. Job satisfaction, marital happiness, and self-acceptance are all impacted by self-perception.

Our family is the greatest contributor to self-worth and self-perception. A child who is raised with a constant bombardment of "You are worthless," "You are no good to anybody," "You are dumb, stupid, and lazy" is going to have a problem with ego and with low self-worth. In a family where these messages are constantly sent, the child will seek for acceptance outside of the home. Even in a home where "positive ego strokes" are given, people will still look outside the home for validation from friends and acquaintances. The combination of friends, school, marriage or dating, work, church involvement, and feedback from society either reinforce the perception of self received from the home or negate it. One of the most important contributions a parent, a family member, or a friend can make is to acknowledge a person's worth to God. The next important contribution we can make is to reinforce that knowledge by treating the child, spouse, or friend with respect and love.

The Atonement of Jesus Christ in Gethsemane established the worth of a soul. Imagine facing the Savior on Judgment Day and explaining to Him our right to attack the worth of a soul. All souls are valuable unto God. There can be only one standard that is universally acceptable, and that is to respect the worth of each as intrinsically valuable. Once again, the only defensible goal any of us can sustain is to help each child of God to become his or her highest and best self. Anything we do less is an insult to the Atonement of Christ.

In order to be a disciple of Christ, we cannot belittle the worth of another. *Ever!* It cannot be tolerated. We never have the right to attack the inherent value or self-worth of another—not in jest, not in the heat of anger, not out of frustration, not out of our own weakness, *never! never! never!* This means no name-calling, no swearing at someone, no epithets. It means no spiritual, physical, or emotional abuse. This is a nonnegotiable. When someone is called "dumb" or "stupid," it is an attack on his or her worth. To attack self-worth is presuming a right that we as critics do not have.

It is a testimony to the futility of criticism when people lash out at others and attack their worth as human beings in an attempt to deal with an issue or behavior. When we are in an emotional, irrational state of frustration, we are seldom possessed with enough presence of mind to separate the real issues from the self-worth of the one being criticized.

Appropriate criticism is that which separates self-worth from the unacceptable behaviors of the one being criticized. The difficulty of this task is enormous because so many of us have been programmed from our youth to equate our own worth with the criticism from others. But it can be done. The art of giving and receiving criticism is the art of separating self-worth from the behavior or issue to be criticized.

The following is a personal story and relates to my wife, Bonnie, who possesses a natural gift for separating her love from the obnoxious behaviors of others.

Dirty Socks

For a young married couple, there was considerable latitude given by both parties for each other's shortcomings. However, I possessed a habit that truly made life difficult for Bonnie. We were both college students and took turns with cooking, housekeeping, and the washing. However, I was in the habit of taking my dirty stockings, rolling them together to form a ball, and then throwing them from wherever I was to the closet in the bedroom. Frequently, this would require a bank shot off a wall. Just as frequently, the stockings would miss the closet and roll under the bed, down the hall, or wherever. Bonnie's newlywed patience wore thin as days of this became weeks. Apparently, the final straw was a missed shot that wound up on top of the refrigerator. The stockings rested unnoticed on top of the refrigerator until the next day. Some of my wife's friends were sitting around the kitchen table when my wife opened the refrigerator door, releasing the stockings and sending them on a downward flight, giving the appearance that they had emerged from the refrigerator itself. This might be a difficult thing to explain to friends: why do you keep your husband's dirty stockings in the refrigerator?

I do not know what Bonnie said. I do know that that night, when I returned home from an evening class, that there was something unusual about her countenance. I sat on the couch, removed my shoes and stockings, and began to roll my stockings up into a ball. Bonnie was standing in the pathway of the projectile. While I still had the germ-riddled stockings in my hand, ready to fire, Bonnie asked permission to share a concern of hers. She said something like this; "Honey, there is something silly I would like to talk to you about. It really is a small thing, but it is something that would mean a lot to me."

"What is it?" I asked, totally unaware of the stockings in my hand.

"I bought a clothes hamper today, and it would really, really mean a lot to me if you would throw your dirty socks into the hamper."

Bonnie had managed to separate my self-worth from my bad habit. There were a number of unproductive ways she could have approached this same situation. She could have attacked me and criticized me and said, "You have a disgusting habit of throwing your stockings all over the house. It's a sick behavior. Your mother never taught you anything. I'm not your slave, you know; I'm not here to pick up after you. How dumb are you, anyway? Don't you know it's only common courtesy to pick up after yourself?" She could have, but she didn't. She spoke to me with respect. She was very much in control of her emotions. She had asked for and received permission to express herself. She logically explained her concern. We were alone at a mutually agreeable time and place. I felt no intimidation. She owned her expectation. The issue was indeed one that was a part of her business as well as mine. It was, after all, a shared stewardship. The criticism was not only true, but it was in my best interest to hear it. Eliminating the behavior in question was edifying to us both. There was no attack on my self-worth; she had focused on the issue with great clarity. I almost felt like a hero for putting my stockings in the clothes hamper.

Learning how to separate ego from issue on the little things helps us prepare the way to deal with more serious matters. The mother in the next story did everything right.

Two Wrongs

Billy was ten, the older sibling. The younger child, Micky, went into Billy's room and, without permission, took his remote control car and hid it. Billy confronted Micky, age five, and Micky lied about taking it. Angry and upset, Billy hit Micky, then he asked his mother to make Micky give him back the expensive toy. Micky was crying, "Billy hit me! Billy hit me!"

The mother comforted Micky and then said to Billy, "Why did you hit him?"

Billy responded, "Because he stole my remote control car. Make him give it back, Mom! Right now! Or I will go into his room and break his toys!"

Mother sent Micky downstairs with these words. "I'll be down in a few minutes and we can talk about it."

Before Mother spoke, she thought about the desired outcome. Next she said to Billy, "I'm sorry that Micky took your car without permission. That was wrong, and I will get it back for you. Billy, I need to talk to you about hitting Micky. Would now be a good time or would you like to wait ten minutes?"

Billy responded, "I just want my car back."

"So would you prefer we talk about your hitting now or in ten minutes?" repeated Mom.

"In ten minutes," grumbled Billy.

"Fine, I'll set the timer on the stove for ten minutes. When it buzzes I expect you to be ready to talk to me," declared Mom.

The buzzer went off, and Billy and Mom sat on the edge of Billy's bed. "Billy, what Micky did was wrong," said Mom, "but what you did in hitting him was also wrong. Two wrongs don't make a right."

"He deserved it, Mom; he is just a little thief. He's always taking my things," blurted out Billy.

"Right now, Billy, we are talking about your behavior. I love you, son, and I know you will grow up to be a fine man. For now, I want you to know that it is never right to abuse someone. You must accept responsibility for what you did, in spite of what Micky did. After I talk to Micky, I want you to apologize to him for hitting him. Also, I want you to take a time-out for fifteen minutes for hitting your little brother. I meant what I said about loving you. I know a good boy like you will want to overcome a bad habit like hitting when you are angry. You go and set the timer on the stove for another fifteen minutes. Then sit at the kitchen table while I talk to Micky. When the buzzer rings, you turn it off and come and find me."

Billy was reluctant, but he did it. Mom went to Micky and said, "Micky, may I talk to you now or in two minutes?"

Micky looked puzzled and said, "Now, I guess."

Mom responded, "Thank you for letting me talk to you. Micky, right now there are only three people in the house—you, me, and Billy.

I didn't take Billy's car. That means you had to have taken it. Don't lie to me, because it will only make matters worse for you. I want you to go and get Billy's car right now and bring it to me." She was firm and looked him directly in the eyes. Micky returned with the car.

Mom continued, "It is wrong to take things that don't belong to you. Do you know that, Micky?" Micky nodded his head. "Would you like to get one of your own?" Micky again nodded. "I will talk to you later about some work I need done, and maybe you can earn some money and you can buy one. Micky, I love you. You will always be special to me because you are my little caboose. Someday, when you grow up, you will be a missionary and you will teach people about Jesus. So you need to act like a little missionary right now. Missionaries don't take things that don't belong to them. You are a wonderful boy. A good boy like you doesn't want to do a bad thing like take someone else's toy without permission." Micky shook his head from side to side. "Here is the right thing to do. First, I want you to give the car back to Billy. Next, I want you to say you are sorry to Billy for taking his car. Afterwards, I want you to take a fifteen-minute time-out and think of something nice you could do for your big brother. Billy should not have hit you. That was wrong. Two wrongs don't make a right. He is going to apologize for hitting you. Right now he is taking a time-out for fifteen minutes."

The buzzer sounded, and Billy appeared at the door. "Come in, Billy. Micky has something he wants to return to you."

Micky handed the remote control car to Billy and said, "I'm sorry, Billy."

Mom prompted, "I'm sorry I took your car without your permission." Micky repeated it. Mom continued, "Billy, I want you to say 'Micky will you forgive me for hitting you?'" Billy said it. "Now, Micky, I want you to say, 'I forgive you, Billy.'" Micky did so. "All right, Billy, I want you to say, 'Micky, I forgive you for taking my car without permission.'" Billy repeated it.

"Okay," said Mom, "Now Micky is going to take a fifteen-minute time-out and think about what has happened here. Afterward, I thought I would go for some ice cream. Would my two future missionaries like to go and get some ice cream with a mother who loves them both very much?"

Remember our discussion earlier on the "greatest revelation?" This is the Lord's counsel on correcting and criticizing in our relationships (see D&C 121:34–46). Notice how in the previous story all the elements of "reproving betimes with sharpness" were present:

- It was within the mother's stewardship, and the criticism was necessary.
- She asked for and received permission to criticize them.
- She was alone with each one at an agreeable time and place.
- She was gentle and direct.
- She stayed in emotional control. There was no yelling, crying, or abuse. She logically explained her concerns.
- She focused on the improper behavior, and she separated the issue from the worth or self-worth of each. She was fair and evenhanded.
- She confirmed their worth to her. She showed forth an increase of love.

This last step is one of the most important steps in our criticism. We must continue to love, even if the person never positively responds to our criticism. Remember, as disciples of Jesus Christ, we are first called to love. We must never miss this crucial step in our relationships.

STEP 3: AFFIRM HIS OR HER WORTH

Affirming worth is another way of saying that after we have reproved or criticized, we need to show "an increase of love toward him whom thou hast reproved, lest he esteem thee to be his enemy" (D&C 121:43). The greatest thing we can do to convince the one reproved of his or her worth is not to repeat improperly given criticism. We need to *show* respect by restraint. The greatest revelation that God has ever given to man says "showing forth"—not telling of—"an increase of love" (D&C 121:43).

How do we follow up a message of criticism with a message of love? It is made difficult by the fact that the one criticized may feel rejected, withdrawn, and alienated by the giver of criticism. Human nature being what it is, inappropriately given criticism will add to the difficulty of showing forth an increase of love. We as the critic will often find that before we can show forth love, we have to apologize for the inappropriate way the criticism was given. We are apologizing not for the content, but for the delivery. If, in giving criticism, we allowed ourselves to be angry or to lose emotional control by yelling or by attacking the worth of the one being criticized, we have a self-imposed higher mountain to climb. First, we must undo the damage done by improper criticism. Then we must show love.

What if we as critics appropriately criticize and show forth sincere love, and then we are totally rejected on a consistent basis? Assume that the one being criticized is not only hostile but interprets loving behaviors as a mockery. Under these circumstances, the appropriate giver of criticism must realize that he or she is dealing with a toxic person. This means that we will not be able to say enough, be enough, or do enough to ever satisfy the toxic person (we will discuss this idea more fully in a later chapter). However, when we give criticism in the Lord's own way we have the satisfaction of pleasing God. It is consistency and patience that will ultimately triumph. It may take years. The power in the principles of the gospel of Jesus Christ will overcome the most hardened heart. No one, except sons of perdition, can resist forever the power of infinite love.

Is there an art and a skill to the giving of criticism? Yes, very definitely. It is time for us to practice. Remember, like bowling, golfing, or anything we do for the first time, it will feel awkward. And, just like playing the piano or violin for the first time, it sounds awkward. In spite of feeling clumsy, a little embarrassed, and ill at ease, we do it! It is time for us to put it all together. It is time for our profound adventure into self-mastery. When beginning to practice the art of giving criticism, it is a good idea for us to say, "I'm very concerned about saying something that will hurt your feelings; I would like to be able to talk to you about an issue or behavior without you feeling that I'm attacking your self-worth," or "I love you," or "I care about you," or "I'm sincerely concerned, and I just want to help you be an even better person than you already are. This is why I'm not yelling or crying. I am genuinely concerned."

You may want to copy the guidelines for giving criticism onto a card and carry it in a pocket or a purse. Here they are, one more time:

- Think before you speak. Is the criticism within your stewardship, and would it be in the best interest of the other person to hear it? If not, don't say it. If it is, then proceed.
- Ask for and receive permission before criticizing.
- Be alone with the person at a mutually agreeable time and place.
- Be in emotional control and logically explain the concern. No yelling, crying, swearing, or physical or emotional intimidation is allowed.
- Do not attack the self-worth of any human being. Focus on the issue or behavior. Be as specific as you can in separating self-worth from the issue or behavior.
- Affirm his or her worth to you.

It is also a very good idea to invite a friend or loved one to practice the process together. It can be a very bonding experience to develop this art and skill with a spouse. Sometimes it is impossible because our friend or spouse is unwilling or unprepared to do so. Coworkers are a potential resource. This is a talent to be developed whether anyone else chooses to do so or not. Think of it as a spiritual mission. Remember, we are never alone. Self-mastery is a journey that ultimately must be taken with the help of Jesus (see John 16:32–33).

LOVE BEGETS CHANGE

Realizing that all this is a long process and requires patience and diligence, many people begin to feel discouraged. They begin to ask questions that amplify their frustrations: How much unnecessary suffering is enough? How many tearful nights are enough? How much hurt, heartache, and sorrow are enough?

When will he or she ever learn? At what point do we cry out, "It is enough"? The heavens weep over all these injustices, but agency belongs to man. When will we, as the children of God, come to treasure the worth of a soul? When will we stop giving improper criticism? When will the natural man yield to the Holy Ghost? When will words of love be matched with loving behaviors? The answer to all of these can be summed up in another question: When will we as critics reprove in the Lord's own way?

When we can learn to love as the Lord does, our suffering can begin to ease. When will it all end? When we start—start living and loving as He does. Real love will beget change—if not in others in our lives, then, at the very least, in ourselves.

What is real love? To some, love is a romantic ideal. To others, love is a feeling. Music, poetry, and the movies have removed love from reality. Conceptually, love is a nebulous, elusive, and difficult concept to understand. Behaviorally, love is easier to understand. Love is acceptance, affection, and appreciation. Love is treating people with respect. Love is kindness, gentleness, meekness, and, at times, long-suffering (see Gal. 5:22–23). True love is manifested by acting in the eternal best interest of a loved one. It is also loving in a manner that is consistent with the principles of righteousness. The phrase "that he may know that thy faithfulness is stronger than the cords of death" (D&C 121:44) bespeaks an eternal perspective. Love is not lust in the selfish present. It is confirmed with a view of eternity. Love that is "stronger than the cords of death" is a commitment to the souls of our loved ones. It is a willingness to lay down our life if necessary to help them on their journey to their highest and best selves. We need to learn to love as Jesus loves. He taught, "This is my commandment, that ye love one another, as I have loved you. Greater love hath no man than this, that a man lay down his life for his friends" (John 15:12–13).

People deserve to be loved because they are children of God. Love should not be the reward for behaving well. People should be loved even if their deeds cannot be. We are still loved by God, even if our deeds are not looked upon with the least degree of allowance. What kinds of behaviors are consistent with that love? The answer is behaviors that reflect the acceptance of the person's worth to the critic.

Respect, smiles, and sincere praise are concrete evidence of appreciation. For those of us who are comfortable with them, hugs and kisses are great signs of affection. Love is a reward for being, not a reward for behaving. Encircling loved ones in robes of acceptance, affection, and appreciation will keep them warm during the winter of reproof.

Assignments for Chapter 10

1. Using the Quick Checklist for Giving Appropriate Criticism, try all three steps in the giving of criticism.

2. Focus on a key relationship in your life. Ask the person if he or she would be willing to help you in an assignment. Explain to the person that you are learning the art of giving criticism. Tell him or her what you have learned. Invite him or her to practice with you the important step of asking for permission before you criticize. Do not be surprised at the reluctance of some who may act very wary or even defensive at your request. Some may even trivialize your efforts and mock you. However, persist and ask if they will try for one day not to criticize anyone without first asking that person for permission. Get with them later and discuss the experience.

CHAPTER 11

RECEIVING CRITICISM

The main focus of the book thus far has been primarily on giving proper criticism. However, each of the principles discussed throughout is crucial in receiving criticism as well as giving it, so it is important that we carefully consider this aspect of criticism in relationships. The following is a quick guide to gracefully and effectively receiving criticism. Keep this list in mind as we explore each of these steps in more detail.

QUICK CHECKLIST
FOR RECEIVING CRITICISM

Step 1: STOP and remove your ego from the issue; LOOK at the person; and LISTEN.

Step 2: Write it down so you can evaluate it.

Step 3: Repeat it back without emotion.

Step 4: Excuse yourself from any immediate response and set a time and place to respond.

Step 5: Evaluate the criticism and your resources for dealing with it.

Step 6: Respond at the appointed time and place.

STEP 1: STOP, LOOK, AND LISTEN!

Stop!

One of the most important things to remember in receiving criticism is slowing down. Too often, our defenses come up before we even have time to consider whether there is any truth to the criticism or our critic's perspective. As we do when we criticize, we immediately react to others' criticism and force the relationship into a downward spiral of negative reaction. Let's take a look at a counseling session with Betty to see why it is important to slow down and consider how to respond to criticism.

Stopping for a Mind Walk

Betty felt as though her husband was hypercritical. He was a good man in so many ways, but he was emotionally unsafe for her. She wanted to know what she could do to fix him, because his pride would not allow him to come in to see a counselor. Ed, her husband, was a critiholic and was negative about most things and people. I asked Betty if it was also true that she was hypersensitive to being criticized. She confessed that she was and admitted that this compounded the difficulties in the marriage. I asked Betty if she would describe for me a typical evening with Ed.

"First, even before he sets foot in the house, he will be upset about bikes in the driveway or the yard and comes into the house mumbling. I've gotten to the point where I feel sick to my stomach when I know he is coming home. He seldom has anything pleasant to say at all. Immediately he will begin to check to see if I did all the things he feels are important. It's like the Gestapo going over a checklist. He thinks we are talking, but I feel like it's an inquisition. If I fail to do one thing, I get a lecture. When I try to explain my schedule or my reasons, he gets angry and I cry. It's the same pattern day after day. If we make it through the checklist, we have some kind of dinner. I hate to cook anymore. He criticizes everything I make, and now he criticizes me because I don't cook as often. After dinner, he goes into his computer room until it's time for bed. If he ever comes out to watch a ball game on TV, he yells and criticizes the entire time. Our intimacy is almost nonexistent. I don't want to be seen by him. I never feel like I perform to his expectations. I find myself making excuses to stay up until he has gone to bed so that I won't have to be with him. He knows something is wrong. He is always telling me I don't appreciate what he has provided for me and the family. He is a good provider and a hard worker. In his own way, I know that he loves me and the children, but I'm getting to the point that if something doesn't change, I'm going to leave. I just can't take it anymore. That's why I am here."

"Betty, there are two things you can do immediately to improve your situation. First, protect yourself, and second, learn how to live with a 'toxic personality.' Do you accept responsibility for protecting yourself against uninvited or unwarranted criticism?"

"What do you mean?" she asked.

"You are choosing to be hurt. You are giving him a perfect target at which to shoot. What you have told me is that you have a whole series of expectations of how a loving person would treat you if he truly loved you. For example, if someone truly loved you, he would never criticize you or your efforts. You said it yourself; Ed does love you. It is also true that Ed is hypercritical. These are coexisting truths, and they are not mutually exclusive. If you were to say that Ed doesn't love you because he criticizes you all the time, I would say that your conclusion is false. 'Ed loves you' and 'Ed criticizes you' are both true statements. Betty, I want you to focus on Ed loving you, and for now, ignore any thought to the contrary. As much as anything, you object to how Ed packages his criticisms and their quantity.

"Let me teach you about criticism, about the art and skill of giving and receiving criticism. Giving criticism deals with the ego or self-worth of others, while receiving criticism relates to your own ego. Developing the art and skill of receiving criticism is more difficult than applying the principles involved in giving criticism. Giving criticism properly has been defined as the art of 'telling someone they are going to hell in such a way they look forward to the journey.' This is the art of focusing on a negative issue or behavior in a way that preserves the sense of self-worth of the one being criticized. This acquired talent of 'giving' criticism while respecting the value of the individual happens because of being 'other-centered.' The art and skill of receiving criticism requires that we extend to ourselves that same respect for our self-worth. Appropriate self-respect means that we do not empower others to devalue us.

"I know that you are a deeply committed religious person. I want to appeal to the ultimate worth of your soul. Do you have any idea how precious you are to Heavenly Father? Your worth has been established by the Atonement of Jesus Christ. He paid a price beyond death for your soul. We may never know the height and breadth of His atoning sacrifice until we resurrect. A price has been set on the worth of your soul, Betty. It is above all the combined wealth of a million worlds. No mortal man can even begin to match the price that Jesus paid for the worth of your soul. Do you believe that?"

Betty responded, "Intellectually I do, but frankly, I am not sure I feel it."

"Because we share a common faith, let me tell of a personal experience. I didn't feel it either, until I went to the Lord in fasting and mighty prayer. I asked Heavenly Father in the name of Jesus to fill my soul with His love. A few days after that, I awoke one morning and I was absolutely confident that Jesus Christ would have come to this earth if I had been the only son of God who needed the Atonement. Before that experience, I knew that the worth of my soul was great, but after that I really felt it. Our worth is not a topic for debate or discussion. Those who want to do so are outside their stewardship. It is not their right to pass judgment upon our worth. No one can hit you over the head with an emotional club that you don't first put into his or her hand. Being able to protect yourself from the negative effects of criticisms is a part of the art and skill needed.

"There is a desire you must possess. It is the desire to become your highest and best self. Without that desire, you will never be able to truly learn the art of receiving criticism. What if the criticism is valid? If you are not committed to become your highest and best self, you will not even evaluate the criticism on its merits. Instead, you will be distracted by the way it was said. Your desire to defend your self-worth, your personal sense of value, your ego will prevail.

"If you are going to be successful in receiving criticism from others, it will require that you live a higher law. The single greatest challenge to receiving criticism is the ego. The higher law that you will be asked to live demands that you place your ego in a safe place—remove it as an issue. Protect yourself. Otherwise, every conversation with anyone about anything becomes an issue for ego validation; he or she must agree with you, you must be right, or you have no value. This means that you become so emotionally involved in defending your ideas and behavior, which are really your ego, that you cannot receive valid criticism. You wind up defending your sense of worth, your ego, and you are not open to hear what the real issues are. Taking your ego out of the picture is a necessary step.

"Let me tell you what I do. I have a very special box. When anyone criticizes me, I immediately take my ego, my sense of worth, and mentally put it into the box. It takes me a half second. Then, in my mind, I walk to the temple and place the box on the altar for Jesus to take care of until I return. It works for me. However, each person has to find a way that works for him or her."

I told Betty that a "mind walk" is a mental journey people can take the moment someone begins to offer uninvited criticism. I said, "Imagine in your mind an alarm going off, just like those noisy, irritating car alarms that go off when someone touches the car. Or think of your ego being in a bank vault, and when the alarm sounds, all the doors automatically close. Huge, impenetrable, solid steel doors two feet thick close off every window, door, or exit. Your ego is protected. It is safe. Now you can venture outside the bank, because your ego is safe within the vault." I asked Betty if she would like to know how other people handle criticism by taking a mind walk. She did.

I described one man who said his mind walk included a visual image of the critical person asking for the combination to a safe, and he would say, "I'm sorry, it's not available to you." He saw himself putting a package containing his ego into the safe, closing the door, and spinning the dial. Then I mentioned a very inventive woman who said she had a secret personal identification number, like one uses at all automatic bank-teller machines, that represented her ego, and she didn't let anyone who was toxic know it. If someone became ego-toxic, she changed her secret number.

Taking a mind walk doesn't work for everyone. Some people simply choose to ignore unauthorized criticism. That works too. There are unproductive and relationship-defeating behaviors like becoming confrontational, abusive, and more toxic than the giver of criticism. Becoming totally passive, like a doormat, to be verbally abused, is equally unacceptable. The fight-or-flight alternatives don't work.

I told Betty that I had suggested to several people that they reward themselves twenty-five cents each time they were criticized and stopped to take this mind walk before responding. One woman said that a quarter wasn't enough, but a dollar would be! Each time she was criticized, a dollar sign flashed in her eyes. Her ego was safe in the cash register. One man bought himself a new fly rod with his mind-walk earnings. At twenty-five cents a criticism, one young married wife bought a new pair of shoes in only a month.

I continued with Betty, "Let's assume that you develop an effective mind walk that works for you. Your ego is safe. This means that you have removed self-worth as an issue, thereby avoiding any emotional meltdown. You are Spock on Star Trek. Dr. McCoy comes ranting and screaming at you because you are not responding to his emotionalism. Although he calls you names like a pointed-eared, green-faced, half-human freak, it doesn't bother you. But you look at him and say, 'Very interesting, but quite illogical.' Disregard the 'how' and examine the 'what' of the message. This takes practice and is a highly developed mental skill, to separate your ego from the criticisms of others. It can and must be done.

"Your objective with Ed is to focus on the content of his criticism. If the content of his criticism is an attack on your worth, you must protect yourself by leaving or ignoring it. You are Spock. Now, bring on the criticism, for 'sticks and stones can break your bones,' but words shall never harm you. You are going to pan for gold. You are going to separate the mud from the gold nuggets. The packaging of the criticism is the mud, and the golden nugget is a truth covered in mud. Accepting that truth may help you reach your objective of becoming your highest and best self. Yes, it is a poor job of packaging. However, by separating your ego and placing it in a safe place, you are prepared to evaluate the criticism logically and pan for gold. If there is no substance to the comments, they can be disregarded as having come from frustration or a contentious spirit. If there is merit in the criticism, regardless of packaging, it can be evaluated for future benefit."

Betty was beginning to learn to slow down and separate her worth from the criticism given, whether it was well-founded or not. This half-second delay in response could save so much time spent in grief. It puts the moment in perspective and allows us to focus instead on the message.

Look!

Continuing with our case study of Betty, let's consider the importance of shifting the focus to the true message of the criticism.

Look Him in the Eyes

"Remember, Betty, the art of receiving criticism is much more difficult than giving reproof. It will take a concerted effort to separate your self-worth and ego from the criticism. It will take practice and time, and more practice and more time. However, the process works.

"With practice, you can separate your ego and put it in a safe place, then you are ready to focus on the message. Remember, you do not have to tolerate abuse. Walk away; go to another room; just say, 'Excuse me, please. I'll be back when you are ready to focus on the issue.' If Ed gets physically abusive, call the police. He is out of bounds. If you tolerate it, he will give himself permission to continue.

"Let's assume that Ed is frustrated and criticizing you. You are going to defang the tiger. Here is what you do. You look him directly in the eyes. If you look down, it means you are letting his criticism impact your self-worth. Even if his eyes are bugging out of his head and his neck muscles are strained, look him sincerely in the eyes. Your objective is to focus on the issue or behavior about which he is being critical. You are in control of yourself. If you cave in to your emotions, you will be rewarding him. You have the power. There is a protective shield around you. This level of self-mastery and dissociation may even cause you to smile inside. His once-effective techniques have no effect on you. It's almost an out-of-body experience, Betty; it is as if you are a third party watching. You are an actress on stage. Sincerely look into his eyes, searching for the message."

Such control of self allows one to choose the action to be taken, rather than reacting without any thought of the results. It provides the opportunity to actually hear the critic's message and possibly understand the intentions.

Listen!

Listening seems like an obvious part of this process, yet too often when we are criticized we want to justify ourselves and avoid hearing more. There is a definite art to really hearing and grasping the message. Let's continue with Betty's story.

An Old Record Player

"Truly listening and not reacting is difficult. There is a strong urge to want to explain, justify, or defend. Betty, this is where you 'zip your lip.' Don't apologize. Don't make excuses. Don't speak. Just gaze into his eyes and listen.

"You are too young to remember the old-style record players. Maybe you've seen one in an attic or a museum. They played records of different sizes. The records of the same speed were placed in a stack on a metal center post. An automatic arm would extend from the side once the record was in place. A needle protruding from the arm fit perfectly into the record grooves. It was quite primitive compared to the CDs of today. However, the old record players had an unusual characteristic. No matter where the record was playing—the beginning, the middle, or the end—if you bumped the record player, the automatic arm would stop and go all the way back to the beginning and start over again. That is just like someone who is criticizing. If they are interrupted, they go back all the way to the beginning and start over. Sometimes they increase the volume of their voice because they believe you are not listening. So I want you to listen for the issue or behavior which is the object of Ed's concern so that he won't have to start all over again and so that you won't have to hear it over and over."

There are plenty of books written on active listening and communication. Suffice it to say here that we must be sincere and intent, truly wanting to learn. As we listen this way, without defenses, we can have the Spirit with us and can actually become stronger through the criticism experience, whether it is warranted or not.

STEP 2: WRITE THE CRITICISMS DOWN SO THAT THEY CAN BE EVALUATED

It we are to truly listen, it makes sense that we should really try to remember the message. Any student knows that the best way to remember something is to take notes on it. But there is more to this writing process than that, as I explained to Betty:

Out of Your Mind, On the Paper

"Next, I'm going to ask you to write down his criticisms. This may sound like a contradiction. I've already asked you to look into his eyes and to listen to what he is saying."

"Won't writing it down distract me from looking and listening?"

"The answer is no, if you will only look down to write and look up into his eyes. It works, and I'll explain why.

"Years of experience have verified the importance of writing down criticisms. The difference between those who succeed in receiving criticism and learning from it and those who fail is their willingness to follow this counsel. There are two important reasons why you should write down Ed's criticisms. The first is psychological. Writing down the criticisms will allow the criticism to enter your ears, flow through your brain, down your arm and hand and to the paper. Otherwise, the criticisms will stay in your brain. Maybe the greatest benefit is spiritual. By writing down the criticism as an issue or behavior, you are protecting your self-worth and value as a daughter of God. You are focusing on the issues or behaviors in question. This is a legitimate process.

"The second important reason for writing down the criticism is to evaluate it at a later time. There are a myriad of secondary benefits.

- It alerts the critic to how often he is criticizing.
- It shows that you are willing to listen.
- It demonstrates a sincere attempt to improve.
- It increases your credibility.
- It helps you focus."

"What if Ed objects to my writing down the criticisms?"

"Most critics are suspicious of people writing down their criticisms. Ed may wonder if you are preparing for divorce. He might fear that you are building a case against him. Critics hate being reminded of how frequently they criticize. Most will object. They will also mock your efforts. This is especially true of the insecure. Be prepared for Ed to object to your writing down his criticisms. He doesn't want a record kept. Nevertheless, write down the criticisms.

"When he asks you, 'What are you writing down, Betty?' say to Ed, 'I'm writing down your criticism of my behaviors and issues so that I can honestly evaluate them.'"

"Ed may say, 'Why do you have to write it down in order to remember it?'"

"I want you to say, in your own words, something like this, 'Ed, if it is important enough for you to say it, it is important enough for me to write it down. I'm sorry if it makes you uncomfortable, but this is my way of dealing with it.'

"Obviously, this will require courage on your part not to back down. If he fails to agree, offer him the alternative of writing you a letter expressing his criticisms so you can evaluate them. If Ed persists in being verbally critical, write it down.

"Now I am going to ask you to keep a writing pad and pencil within reach at all times. This may require writing pads in every room in your house, especially the bathroom, bedroom, and glove box in the car. There will be at least two times when it will be difficult to do so. One is when you are in the shower or bath, and the other is when you are driving. Even under these two conditions, I would like you to write down the criticisms on paper afterwards. Remember, from a psychological view, you are taking the criticisms from your mind and transporting them out of your body onto the paper."

Even as I spoke, Betty was taking notes as rapidly as she could. "What you are now doing with me is what I want you to do with Ed. The difference is that you feel safe here and not with Ed. But what you are doing now is perfect. You are looking, listening, and writing. Are you clear so far as to what to do? What are the first two steps in the art and skill of receiving criticism from Ed?"

"Protect my ego. Stop, look, listen, then write down the criticisms."

"That's right. No one has the right to physically, emotionally, verbally, or spiritually abuse you. If you feel any of these are happening, excuse yourself. Simply announce that you are leaving the room. You are not leaving the relationship. Tell Ed you will be back when he is in emotional control (or when you are in control) and can logically focus on the concerns.

"Just because Ed is upset or frustrated does not mean that you are being abused. However, you be the judge as to whether you are prepared to receive it.

"We will assume that you are and that Ed is on a critical binge, but he is not yet abusive.

"Let's review the steps so far. When verbally criticized, do not defend yourself, do not make excuses, and do not justify your behavior. Just STOP, LOOK, LISTEN, and WRITE. A defensive response or an excuse or a justification is perceived as 'not hearing' and usually results in the critical person repeating his verbal criticisms. Ed believes that you are not focusing on the content of what he is saying to you. It's as if your ears fell off and he has to speak louder in order for you to properly get the message. Frequently, your excuses only upset him and add fuel to his fiery words."

By taking the steps outlined thus far, we take control of the situation and can then choose to receive the criticism in the proper way—the Lord's way. We can learn to lovingly accept criticism, whether valid or not, rather than retaliating with an emotional rampage.

STEP 3: REPEAT BACK
THE CRITICISM WITHOUT EMOTION

In receiving criticism, it is difficult not to feel hurt. Sometimes it is the intent of our critic to hurt us. But a strong emotional response on our part will only make the situation worse. Staying calm and collected is a better defense than any witty jab at the other person or any string of shouted threats and complaints. Let's see how Betty dealt with this situation.

Making a List

"There is another benefit to listening and writing it down. When you choose not to be combative, you help create an atmosphere which can allow you to focus on the issue or behavior in question. If you choose to be combative, the content will be lost in a war of words and a new issue will emerge—the self-worth of one or both of you. Soon a crisis of individual worth is created and the focus of the original criticism is lost. It will not be long until a hurt feeling, the argument itself, or some threatened divorce becomes the diverted battleground. Unchallenged allegations given in the heat of frustration soon lose their fervor. Once they are challenged, however, adrenaline begets adrenaline, the heartbeat speeds up, the bodily energy increases, and fatigue gives way to a newfound power to combat.

"Betty, some people feel that unless one is emotional, one is not serious. This is a characteristic learned in the family. It's not healthy. About half of all men feel manipulated when women cry. They feel that it is a diversion from facing facts. Almost always, when someone is crying or yelling, it is a plea for understanding and acceptance. However, it is a diversion to the ego and takes the focus away from the issue. Consciously or unconsciously, crying when criticized is a reaction to feeling rejected. Sometimes, unless a person is emotional, he or she doesn't give himself or herself permission to express feelings. There are appropriate times for tears. While you are receiving criticism is not one of them.

"Continue to write down the expectations or the frustrations of Ed. Be a court reporter. Eventually, he will finish. After he is through criticizing you, feed it back to him without emotion. Do it just as if you were reading a recipe from a cookbook. For example, 'So what you are saying, Ed, is that I spend too much time talking on the phone with my friends. If I spent less time on the phone, I would have more time to devote to cleaning the house and cooking.' This does not mean in any way that you agree with him or with his evaluation or criticism. It means that you heard him. This acknowledges his concerns and gives him an opportunity to clarify or expand. It will have an end. Ed may launch into a repeat of the items. Just put a check mark by the criticism he has already mentioned."

Although Betty knew the things which were a source of frustration for Ed, she never let him fully express himself. Before he could complete a thought, they would be fully engaged in a verbal battle. Name-calling, swearing, yelling, and another night spent on the couch by one or the other ensued. The pattern was well established. The next day, no one talked. Eventually small talk would cautiously give way to a guarded peace. Neither was emotionally safe for the other. At the slightest hint of any criticism, Betty would go into a tirade and harangue Ed on his lack of appreciation, his insensitive nature, and his own weaknesses. I asked Betty to hear him out, even if it involved repetition.

"Keep track of his criticisms. Which ones are recurring? After a while, you will be able to number them."

A few weeks later she had a list. Ed was critical of five things:

- Betty was overweight.
- She allowed the kids to eat in the car.
- She was a poor housekeeper.
- She wasn't a good mother.
- She was a poor money manager.

Betty wanted unconditional acceptance. She wanted Ed to overlook the fact that the doctors had told her she was borderline diabetic. Weight loss would help her. I asked Betty if she remembered why she originally came to me. She said, "I was concerned about how to stop my husband from criticizing me. I really wanted you to fix him through me."

"I know you are reaching your wit's end. I sense that you feel overwhelmed. What I am sharing with you is the answer to your question. You may not see it clearly. But by taking control of your ability to protect your ego and committing to become your highest and best self, you are on the way to changing the interaction between you and Ed."

This calm demeanor does more than keep the volume of the conversation down. It allows the critic a chance to express himself or herself and feel heard. It also gives the one criticized a measure of safety in controlling his or her own reactions.

STEP 4: EXCUSE YOURSELF FROM ANY IMMEDIATE RESPONSE AND SET A TIME AND PLACE TO RESPOND

Just because you've managed to control your emotional reactions thus far does not mean that you are not boiling with fury inside. It is commendable to be in control this far, and in order to stay in control, it is important not to retaliate as soon as the other person is finished. Give yourself time to cool off and sincerely consider the message you have just received. As I told Betty:

Make an Appointment

"Avoid the very, very, very big temptation to respond verbally or emotionally when he criticizes you. This is not the time to cry, to become angry, or to stomp out of the room and slam a door. After this great exercise of patience, it would be a pity to lose all that effort. An immediate response shows no effort to honestly evaluate the content of the criticism. Ed may just want you to promise you will improve. However, when you do not keep your promise, he will use that to tear you down.

"This is what I want you to say to Ed. 'I've heard you, Ed. It wasn't easy, but I have heard you. I'm not prepared to respond now. I need some time to think about these things. I want to evaluate my ability, willingness, and energy to make the changes you've suggested. I'm not capable of anything now but an emotional reaction. Give me three days to evaluate. I propose that we meet on Wednesday at 7:00 P.M. at the park. I will be prepared to talk to you then.'

"Do not allow him to draw you into a conflict. Excuse yourself and be civil and kind. This reaction will disarm him. He may not know how to respond except with a negative statement like, 'Right! I'm sure you'll think about it and nothing will change.'"

It doesn't always seem natural just to step away from such an experience without a defense or explanation, but it is a necessary part of receiving criticism in the right way. It gives your critic a chance to calm down and think about what he or she has said, and it gives you a chance to really consider the experience and the message. Doing this will spare you spouting out something you may later regret, and may even help you learn something.

STEP 5: EVALUATE THE CRITICISM

Often criticism given in a negative way is hard to accept. We don't want to consider that our critic may be right, especially when he or she delivers the message in such a demeaning way. However, we have no control over the packaging of someone else's message. We can only control how we receive that message. Back to Betty:

Panning for Gold

"It's time to be honest with yourself. It's time to pan for gold. Maybe you have never given yourself permission to be honest. Is there any truth whatsoever to these criticisms? Until you honestly evaluate the situation, you will be an emotionally unhealthy person.

"I want to review with you quickly what an emotionally healthy person is.

"An emotionally healthy person accepts responsibility for her own happiness, unhappiness, and behavior. She realizes that life is a gift and that it is her responsibility to improve her life. She escapes denial by facing reality. She does not have to live with God or the devil, or with anyone else. She does have to live with herself, "eternally" with self. Self-improvement is her job. This is why she is committed to become her highest and best self.

"An emotionally healthy person is able to forgive herself and others.

"An emotionally healthy person will make a plan to take herself from the reality of where she is to a higher and better self.

"Betty, are you in agreement with these three basic characteristics of an emotionally healthy person?"

"Yes," she said.

"Your willingness to accept personal accountability for your behavior and happiness, forgive yourself and Ed, and make a plan means that you can now look at the criticism. For now, we are not talking about Ed. It is not Ed's meanness, insensitivity, and improper criticism. Ed is not the focus. It is you, Betty. If you would like, I'll walk you through how to evaluate the criticism."

"Yes, I would like that. It's kind of scary. I'm not sure I'll like what I find."

"Do you remember where you put your ego?"

Betty and I met for six hours over the next two days. She was trying very hard to protect her self-worth around Ed. At the same time, she worked on loving behaviors. Her mind walk consisted of a fairy-tale image of a woman surrounded with a bright light, like an aura, that protected her from all harm. Her ego was safely guarded in the midst of the light. Like some powerful electronic field or bug zapper, the criticisms would come toward her ego and be destroyed by the protective field. Betty was learning to take her frustrations to God and her love to Ed. We began to discuss Ed's five criticisms.

Betty was overweight. She was borderline diabetic. Independent of Ed, she needed to lose thirty pounds for health reasons. I asked Betty to evaluate her ability, her willingness, her time, and her energy in relationship to losing thirty pounds. It was obvious that she did not lack knowledge. She had the ability, the time, and the energy. What she lacked was willingness.

"Betty, independent of Ed's criticism, would it be in your mortal best interest to lose weight?"

"Yes," she said.

"Remember that emotionally healthy people accept responsibility for their behavior, happiness, and weight. They forgive themselves, and they make a plan to become better. For our purposes, a goal depends upon you, and a wish is something that depends upon others."

I asked Betty to put together a realistic program wherein she could lose thirty pounds over the course of a year. "Make it a plan that does not depend upon Ed. It is your goal to eat more wisely and to lose about half a pound per week over the entire year. Are you willing to build a program or join a support group on weight management and commit to stay with it for a year? This is not a commitment to me. This is a commitment to yourself to become your best self."

In like manner, each of Ed's criticisms was evaluated. As Betty looked at "allowing the kids to eat in the car" she thought that what Ed really wanted was a clean car. She determined to ask Ed for a clarification. Regarding housekeeping, she decided that she and Ed needed to agree on a common standard of what it meant to keep the house clean. She decided to ask Ed for a clear definition of "what he considered a good mother to be." She also made a commitment to establish a realistic budget and to stay with it. All of these decisions, she believed, would indeed help her to become a higher and better self, wife, mother, and sister in the Church.

Rather than reject the message altogether because of how it was delivered, this woman was able to take a very negative situation and make it positive. She gleaned the good information and discarded the bad packaging. This is what we must do in order to receive criticism effectively. We can't choose how others will criticize us; we can only choose our response.

STEP 6: RESPOND AT THE APPOINTED TIME AND PLACE

After taking all these steps, now it is time to respond. Remember the importance of staying in control of your response. If you fail to do so and instead go off on an emotional rampage, all your work will have been for nothing. Take a look at how Betty handled her situation and what resulted:

The Result

"Betty, when you meet tomorrow night with Ed at 7:00 P.M. in the park, stay in emotional control. This is a time of great defensiveness for the both of you. If he loses control, excuse yourself. If you feel you are going to go off the emotional deep end, excuse yourself. Set up another appointment. *Do not let this turn into an argument.* There is a tendency to let that happen.

"Do not overcommit. Remember, actions speak louder than words. These last two days have been a good experience because you've changed your approach. Ed hasn't changed. He is reacting to you.

"Your responses will probably fall into one of these categories:

- I will change.
- I disagree, and this is why . . .
- I need more specific information before I can make an intelligent evaluation.
- I am unwilling.
- I am unable.

"Go prepared. Write down in black and white what you are willing to do. Also have a specific list of questions that will clarify his definition of a clean house, a good mother, a reasonable budget."

Betty told me on her next visit that Ed could see some positive efforts on Betty's part as a result of counseling. Ed finally agreed to come and see me as a counselor. When I visited with Ed and Betty, I explained that there are always three issues in any relationship. First, there was Ed with Ed. Second, there was Betty with Betty. Third, there was Ed and Betty. Each of them have issues separate from the person they married. Ed agreed. I asked Ed if he felt he was critical.

"No," he said, "I am just honest."

"Do others perceive you as critical, other than your wife?"

He admitted that they did.

"If you were killed in a traffic accident tomorrow, would all of Betty's challenges go away? Would she automatically lose weight? Would her skills as a mother and homemaker suddenly improve? If she were killed, would your ability to control your tongue go away as an issue?"

"I suppose not," admitted Ed.

"No. Your issues and her issues are independent of each other. Ed, you have issues as a father that don't concern Betty."

It was obvious that uninvited criticism had taken this relationship to an all-time low. Ground rules were established, to which each agreed. Betty was to work on her issues; Ed would work on his issues; and the two of them together, with my guided help, would work on the relationship. Maybe the tool that was most helpful for both of them was the requirement that they each give the other person a way to approach them with criticism. Ed wanted it verbally and to the point, while Betty wanted the criticism written down. Both agreed to follow the steps in the art of giving and receiving criticism.

Giving respect took practice, as did asking for and receiving permission to criticize. After a few weeks, they were prepared to work on the art of receiving criticism. Betty was firmly entrenched in hypersensitivity. It took a great effort and considerable hard work, tears, and diligence before she was able to separate her self-worth from an issue or behavior. She learned to read the criticism from her husband without comment. They also agreed that if Ed had a blind spot and Betty felt like she was being criticized, even if Ed didn't mean it as a criticism, she would write it down. Ed was a zealous hypercritic. Yet the miracle that took place was that Ed became aware of his hypercriticism. How? Every time Betty picked up a pad and pencil and began to write, he was reminded of who was criticizing and how often. This awareness alone had the effect of decreasing the sheer volume of his negative comments. The second miracle was that he was able to complete his thoughts and fully express himself. The third miracle was his confession of how silly he felt, listening to himself being out of control with body language and tone of voice, while his wife sat there writing it down. He became less intimidating and calmly related his concerns. Betty began to feel a sense of power in not letting his criticisms hurt her ego. She would feed back his criticism like a secretary reading the dictation of a letter to a boss. He would usually add a word or two, and this part was over.

I suggested to Ed that what he was doing in criticizing Betty had not succeeded in changing her. I wanted him to let go of all five expectations. He wasn't sure he could. His moment of truth was about to happen. He was ready for the biggest "aha" of his life.

"Is there any doubt—even the slightest—that your wife is unaware of your concerns about weight, the kids eating in the car, overspending the budget, her poor housekeeping skills, or her not being the kind of mother you would like her to be? Listen carefully to your own words."

"No. I know she knows. She just doesn't care."

"You are absolutely right, Ed. Betty does not lack knowledge of your concern. What she lacks is motivation to do anything about it.

Betty is motivated by her dreams and her desire for acceptance, not by yours. She does not share your values. She is not convinced that your values should apply to her.

"Think about it," I said. "Of what value is your criticizing her? If she doesn't lack knowledge, why are you giving her knowledge? You ought to work on motivation and encourage her. Your criticisms of her are counterproductive. They only frustrate the both of you and destroy any desire she might have to want to change. She resents you."

"You mean I need to work on building her up and not on tearing her down?"

Aha! Shazam! I wasn't about to let him off the hook!

"Why?" I said.

"Because what I'm doing isn't working, and my trying to punish her and intimidate her by yelling only causes her to withdraw from me."

"Exactly. What Betty lacks is a commitment to your values. She doesn't lack knowledge of what your values are. Currently, you are not her friend. You are not committed to helping her become her highest and best self. Ed, do you even know what her values are, her hopes, her dreams? Remember, all people are motivated by their own goals, not by yours. Your agenda is to change her, to make her into your image of what you think she ought to be. The truth is that she is not acceptable to you, and both of you know it. You, my friend, are at a crossroads. You can decide to focus on loving Betty as she is, or you can do nothing about it. Let things go on as they are until one of you has truly had enough and leaves the relationship.

"If anything I have said makes any sense to you at all, then stop criticizing her today and apologize to her for trying to make her into your image. Tell her that you are not going to criticize her weight anymore. It is her body. It is her health. She has the responsibility to care for it. Negotiate with Betty on the budget. Be flexible, but also realistic. Let her see the true picture of your finances and give her the option of selling the house and moving to a less expensive one, where you will be able to spend more on other things, or enlist her support in making the sacrifices necessary to stay where you are.

"It's reasonable to expect hungry children to want to eat in the car. It's also reasonable to expect them to clean up after themselves. Give Betty some options. Prepare a way for her to be successful. For example, 'Betty, it would mean a lot to me if you would teach the kids to clean up after themselves. However, if they don't, would you please just do it yourself or hire a neighbor boy or girl to do it?' As far as the housecleaning is concerned, agree on a standard of cleaning that may be less than what you would wish and a little more than Betty would want. If you are still not happy, then you need to either hire outside help to come in on a periodic basis and clean to your standard or do it yourself. After all, it is not her standard; it is yours. You must own it. If you want to spend time cleaning the house because you feel better about it, then do it with a good attitude and don't attempt to put a guilt trip on her.

"Betty is entitled to define for herself what kind of a mother she would like to be. She is also entitled to her own poor relationships. She must also accept the consequences of her choices as they relate to the children and to you. She does not trust you. You are emotionally unsafe to her. It will take time and responsible behavior on your part. She can come to trust and love you again. My many, many years of experience have seen many couples grow in and grow out and grow back in love again, sometimes several times in the same marriage."

I asked Ed if he would be willing to try. With quiet determination, he nodded his head. Next, I asked him to commit to treat Betty with respect by never criticizing her again without her permission. Also, I asked Ed to focus on the art of giving criticism. Again, he nodded his head. This is a man who has been a "critiholic" all of his life, agreeing to reasonable behavior.

Betty, who was hypersensitive, was to specialize in the art of receiving criticism. What previously had been a weakness was now becoming a strength. In order to finish her training in the art of receiving criticism, she was to evaluate the criticism. She was to look for truth in the criticism and decide if changing would help her become her highest and best self. This was not according to her husband's standard, but according to her own. The next step in the art and skill of receiving criticism was to evaluate her resources. Did she have the time, the energy, or the will to accomplish the change? What choices could she make within the limits of her circumstances to make it happen?

Betty worked on her issue of hypersensitivity to criticism. Ed worked on his issue of being hypercritical. An amazing thing happened; their relationship began to improve. As respect was gifted to each other, their mutually defensive attitudes were replaced with more loving dispositions. Each came to the awareness that true progress in a relationship is made only by common consent and by moving at a pace mutually agreeable to both. Everything isn't perfect in their relationship today, but they are emotionally bonded and walking a common path. Things are better than they have ever been, and neither of them is willing to go back to the dysfunctional way it was before.

Most relationships fail because the parties involved do not know how to resolve conflicts in healthy ways. Loving and being loved are often sacrificed on the altar of criticism. It doesn't have to end that way. We are capable of change. I have seen it. I have experienced it. The gospel of Jesus Christ requires and facilitates it.

Assignments for Chapter 11

1. Using the Quick Checklist for Receiving Criticism, follow the six steps by breaking the process down into its component parts. Practice step 1: Stop, Look, and Listen. Whenever you are criticized, put your ego in a safe place.

- How will you separate your ego from the message and from the emotions of the messenger?
- Create a mind walk. This is a defensive mechanism that will allow you to focus on the content of the message and not on the way in which it was packaged.

2. Listen to the criticism, whatever it may be. Listening does not mean that you agree or disagree with the criticism. The skill at this point is to understand the critic and the message.

3. Practice writing down the criticisms you hear. How many of them are about the same things?

4. Repeat back to the critics their criticisms without emotion. Your objective is to let them know that you understand their concerns.

5. Excuse yourself and tell them a specific time when you will get back with them.

6. With paper in hand whereon you have recorded their criticism, find a solitary place where you can honestly evaluate the criticism. Will making the change asked of you make you a better person? Do you have the will, the energy, and the resources to make this change?

7. Report back to the critic your response.

8. In a journal or in a letter, write down the hardest parts of this assignment and try to ask yourself why it is so hard for you to receive reproof.

CHAPTER 12

TOXIC PERSONALITIES

This chapter is in large part adapted from another book of mine entitled *How to Hug a Porcupine*. I am including it in this book because a person with a toxic personality is extremely critical. Dealing with someone toxic requires even more faith and love, in addition to specific, extra coping skills. By amazing coincidence, while writing this chapter on a Sunday afternoon, I was interrupted by an emergency phone call in which I was asked if I could meet with a couple who said they desperately needed to meet with me as a relationship and communication counselor. I consented, and in a matter of minutes they were in my den at my home. They told me their story.

Not Enough

Theirs was a ten-year marriage with four children. The parents of the wife had arrived from out of state at the wife's request with a U-Haul truck. They were to take their daughter and four grandchildren back to another state. The husband was frantic and willing to do anything to save this marriage. The mother and father of the wife were loading the truck while I was counseling with the couple. I met with them individually and then as a couple. "Tell me," I said to the wife, "what is so frustrating to you about your marriage that you are willing to pack up and leave?"

What follows is as near as I can come to her exact statements, which were interspersed with tears and soul-rending sobs. "He is so critical of everything I do, or wear, or cook. He yells at me for the stupidest things. I can't even hold a map right. He is so controlling. He has to comment on everything I'm doing or not doing. He is always mad at me for something. He is so intense. He snaps at me, and I can never have an opinion of my own. He is always angry at me. I can't take it anymore. I called my parents and told them to come and get me. I've tried to talk to him, but he discounts everything I say. He has to be right. He is so dominating. Every time I attempt to express myself, he shuts me off with rude remarks. Well, I'm not going to take it anymore. It's not just me; he does the same things with the kids. I can't be criticized anymore. I feel no love for him—only resentment. Well, I guess I do feel some love for him, or I wouldn't be so hurt . . . but not enough to stay in this marriage."

After they left, I picked up my manuscript to continue my writing. What more could be said as a testimonial of the negative effects of a toxic personality? It is important that we consider the aspects of a toxic personality so that we can both avoid becoming one and learn how to deal with one in a loving, safe way.

DEFINING THE TOXIC PERSONALITY

A toxic personality is a person we *cannot please.* He or she appears incapable of giving us total acceptance. A toxic personality is one for whom the other party will never be good enough. Frequently, the toxic person dangles acceptance like a carrot on a string. The person who wants to be accepted and appreciated can never quite reach the carrot. Toxic people only give partial acceptance for pleasing them. They fear that if they accept a person fully, that person will stop trying to please them. They fear losing that power. They withhold love as a punishment. They are consistently inconsistent. They promise a reward which is often denied. The earned privileges are never secure. Toxic personalities come in many varieties. Some are gruff. Some are pleasant. Some appear indifferent. They can be very affable, but one still walks away emotionally empty. Most toxic people have a very difficult time accepting blame. They always have to be right.

Often toxic personalities will change their "rules" for acceptance. They have long lists of expectations, but just as one appears to meet all of the requirements, they change the items on the list. With a toxic person, the agenda is constantly changing in order to keep us off balance. The focus for the toxic is always on others. When the toxic person becomes the focus, he or she will quickly move to a crisis in order to divert attention from himself or herself. If a crisis does not exist, the toxic person will create one. They feed on pitting people against each other. The toxic person seems always to be offended.

It is not uncommon for the toxic person to pick out a "favored one," who seems exempt from all the harshness of criticism. This keeps the hope alive in the hearts of others that someday they may be a "favored one." Someday they may be "enough." In addition to one's not being "enough"—not rich enough, thin enough, good-looking enough, a good enough provider or housekeeper or parent or human being—the toxic person feels the need, or the divine call from God, to point out other people's flaws, shortcomings, weaknesses, errors, mistakes, and lack of perfection. The devastating thing about toxic people is their ability, consciously or unconsciously, to offer hope of acceptance and love.

Toxic people are aware of their power. They tend to be controlling, judgmental, highly critical, and manipulative. Toxic people create crisis. Often, under the guise of perfectionism, they justify their rejection of others. On one hand, the toxic person holds out acceptance as a bribe, while on the other hand he or she uses rejection as a method of control. This sends a message to others: "Beware, or you could be the next person put on the blacklist of rejection." Toxic people have a difficult time forgiving others. Why? Because withholding forgiveness is one more means of control.

Often, even when giving a compliment, there is some holding back of full acceptance, or some "trailing barb." A "trailing barb" is a statement added to a compliment which implies that a "better job could have been done." For example:

"That's so nice that your boy Gary got a B+ in math. Did you know that his cousin Darrell got an A?"

"Dinner was great tonight. If we could have had a dessert, it would have been perfect!"

"The lawn looks really nice; thanks for mowing it. We need to do a little better job on the trim, however."

The toxic person does not seem to be able to give a complete compliment and let it stand alone. Even when someone else pays him or a loved one a compliment, he finds a critical thing to say in the name of balance, or fairness, or "being honest." One cannot please a toxic person. One cannot make him happy. One cannot keep him from being unhappy.

Toxic People Are Emotionally Unhealthy

This statement of ill emotional health may be blunt in surmising the situation, but it is painfully honest as we consider how toxic people infect relationships. For a relationship to be emotionally healthy, it takes two emotionally healthy individuals. Emotionally healthy people have the following characteristics:

- As emotionally healthy people, we accept responsibility for our own happiness and unhappiness, and we own our expectations and behaviors. We are able to say, "I was wrong. It was my fault."
- As emotionally healthy people, we can forgive self and others. We do not hold grudges, nor withhold loving behaviors.
- As emotionally healthy people, we make a plan to move ahead in becoming our highest and best self, in spite of difficult circumstances. We will not act out the role of a victim. We will not get easily offended.

Toxic people are constantly blaming others for their unhappiness. The world they live in is an "if only" and "it could have been" world. Most toxic people are experts in transferring blame. If they are wrong, it is because someone else gave them false information, or they will define their behavior in such a way as to justify it. They weren't really wrong; it only appeared that way.

Toxic people want freedom to criticize anyone, anywhere, anytime, because of their unique circumstances. They may assume a role of superior position, wisdom, knowledge, or insight. Another favorite role of toxic people is that of victim or martyr. However, whichever role they choose, they are easily offended and hypersensitive to being criticized themselves. The very ideals they cite in criticizing others cannot be applied to themselves. There is a big-time double standard. They have high expectations of others, but resist those same expectations being applied to them.

Frequently, a gruff exterior hides toxic people's vulnerability. They are incredibly insecure. They mask their insecurities by claiming to be a perfectionist, a control freak, or a giver of constructive criticism. The victim or martyr uses his status to control others. He does this by defeating all solutions to his problems. A common phrase is, "I've tried that and it didn't work."

Most toxic people cannot make a personal progress plan for their own individual lives. In order for them to be happy, everyone in their circle of influence must live according to their expectations.

Examples of Toxicity

Toxicity comes in degrees. Everyone may recognize a toxic characteristic in his or herself. However, when several of these characteristics exist, we may come to the sudden awareness that we are a toxic person. Here are some of the common toxic personalities:

Amy the Perfectionist

Amy is the mother of five children, two from a previous marriage and three with Phil, her current husband. Amy is a perfectionist. She takes a great deal of pride in being a person of high expectations. Her first two children were girls. They never came to accept Phil. The relationship between Phil and the girls was strained at best. Amy blamed Phil and resented him for not connecting with her daughters. However, every time Phil attempted to assert himself as a father, Amy would rush to the defense of her daughters. Phil quit trying. This was one more reason Amy was frustrated with Phil. He wasn't involved enough in their lives, and when he did involve himself, he overreacted, according to Amy.

The first daughter ran away from home at sixteen and never returned. The second daughter married at seventeen. The premature exodus of these two daughters was blamed on Phil. When the third child, a boy, also left home at sixteen, Amy was perplexed. She wanted to blame Phil but could not quite settle on a reason. When the fourth daughter ran away at sixteen, they wound up in a counselor's office.

Amy came to the realization that although Phil had his problems, she did too. It was a revelation to her that she was the major reason for her children leaving. Her perfectionism had translated into constant criticism. Phil, with all of his shortcomings, had not driven off her oldest two daughters. She had. Her smug attitude about her perfectionism was shattered. Amy worked hard to keep her house looking good. In her mind, it was her job to criticize others into helping. The more she criticized, the less they did. When they became lazy, rebellious, and unwilling, her criticisms were backed by punishments. The privileges they enjoyed, such as having their friends over for a night, driving the car, going out on weekends, and so on, were restricted. All of their freedoms were being curtailed. Being grounded was the norm.

Some of Amy's children were verbally abusive to her. They were "in her face." Two of her children were passively aggressive. They dragged around, were always late, and left most jobs incomplete. Even when the children did what they thought was a good job, Amy's perfectionism would find something that could have been done better. They were never quite good enough. The result of Amy's constant carping was hopeless alienation. She was emotionally unsafe. Her true feelings of love were never able to break through her aura of negativism. Her habit of criticizing had become a self-defeating behavior. In her mind, she was right. They were wrong. It was her *duty* to point out the flaws. She had the truth on her side. Amy was toxic.

There is an axiom in psychology which says that the more insecure one is on the inside, the greater the need to control the outside. In order for the control freak to feel good about his or her world, he or she must stay in control of it. This means controlling others. Being a control freak is a form of criticism. The message it sends is, "I must control you because you are not smart enough to control yourself. You are incompetent. You must do as I say because you are not capable on your own."

The Kingdom of Lester the Controller

Lester was a CPA and operated his own business. He had a rigid schedule, and few employees would work for him for any extended period of time. He experienced a high turnover. Everything was black or white for Lester. There were few grey areas. Things were right or wrong. Anything that was different from what Lester thought was wrong! Life was absolute. Everything needed to be done a certain way. Lester's way was the right way. It wasn't just a "different" way, but the "right" way. "King" Lester could control his world. He had power at home and at work. It was his way or the highway. This rigidity carried over into his home life as well, and some of his family chose the highway rather than his way.

Lester was of one religious faith; his wife belonged to another church. They had four daughters. There was no television in their home, and only classical music was allowed. There was a very strict dress code enforced. Each of the daughters had a huge list of chores to perform each day. One half hour of free time was granted if the day's homework from school had been completed. School let out at 2:20 P.M., and the girls were expected to be home by 2:45. The daily vacuuming, yard work, cleaning, and laundry would take an hour and fifteen minutes. At 4:00 P.M., all five women would begin to prepare for the evening meal. Dinner was always formal. There were always cloth napkins and fresh flowers. A display of poor manners or laughter at the dinner table would result in one or more of the girls being sent to their rooms without dinner. A mandatory apology was required first. After dinner, the girls were sure to be quiet while they cleaned up after the meal. Excessive noise was forbidden. Shoes were not worn in the house, but neither was one allowed to go barefoot. Slippers were the preferred standard, and stockings were tolerated.

The girls spent the remainder of the evening, either in their rooms, or practicing the musical instrument chosen by the parents. They were adamant that each daughter learn the piano and one stringed instrument. Guitars were not an option. After music practice, it was time for homework. The parents met regularly with the teachers and knew precisely how each girl was doing. At 8:30 P.M. the girls prepared for bed. They were expected to be in their rooms by 9:00 P.M. All lights were out at 9:15 P.M. The father made a personal bed check on each daughter. Each girl had her own room; however, it was made clear that the room was on loan to her. The beds had to be made immediately after arising.

This routine was followed religiously from Monday to Friday. A music lesson after school or a preapproved school activity were the only exception. Friends were not permitted in the house except on Saturday afternoons between 12:00 and 4:00 P.M. The girls were not permitted to sleep over at someone else's house and, of course, they were not allowed to have friends sleep at their place. The truth is that the girls were afraid to have their friends over. They were embarrassed by the strictness of their lifestyle. Even minimum exposure to others at school made them aware of their limited freedom.

When the girls began to became teenagers, trouble started. The oldest was outwardly conforming. However, behind her parents' back she was living a double life. She smoked. She sneaked out of her window at night and was immoral. She had earphones and listened to acid rock when her parents thought she was listening to classical music. She had cleverly exchanged the inside of her personal classical cassettes by opening up the plastic and supergluing it back. On the outside it read Mozart; on the inside was the obscene music of Black Sabbath. This reflected her own life, on the outside she was the perfect daughter, but on the inside she was a "wild thing." It all came to a point of crisis when the father heard a noise in the house about midnight. He opened the daughter's bedroom door. There he found his daughter and a young man. He went into a rage and ran for his .45-caliber gun. The youth fled from the house. The house was in an exclusive wooded area with a long, serpentine driveway. The police report stated that as the youth fled, the father pursued, firing his gun as he ran. Large pieces of bark flew as bullets ripped through them. I was the court-appointed counselor. The oldest daughter ran away from her parents and lived in a foster home until she was eighteen. The second daughter had an abortion at fifteen and was sent away by the father to live with one of his sisters.

People like Lester have a hard time learning that the art of parenting is not the art of hanging on, but the art of letting go. When a baby is born, it is helpless. Abandoned, it will die. A parent or caring adult must assume full responsibility for the life of the infant. True parenting involves gradually transferring the responsibility for life to the shoulders of the child. Lester could never let go. His need to control everything extended to the lives of those around him. His control style of parenting did not allow for personal growth. Obedience, conformity, and outward performance replaced individual value judgments. The girls had no personal values. They were not allowed to have their own opinions. Therefore, they rebelled. Even in rebellion, they did not form their own set of values. They were only reacting to their father's control of their world.

Tragically, Lester died in his midforties. The mother immediately changed her hairstyle. Lester had liked it only one way. She redecorated the house and started to discover who she was. She loosened up considerably and found out that she had a sense of humor. Her marriage to Lester had been an exercise in fear. She had constantly been afraid of his disappointment or disapproval. She had enabled him as a control freak out of her own fear. Yet she was equally responsible for supporting this unhealthy environment which tried to enforce obedience. This was the principle that Lester and his wife did not understand: criticism is external; change is internal.

Remember the example of the sponge. One can force it to conform by external pressure, but it has only temporarily altered its shape. As soon as the hands which hold it let go, it will return to its natural state. Threat, intimidation, and criticism are external forces. They may alter a person's behavior in the presence of the critic. However, in the absence of the critic that person will find his or her own way. What most critics fail to recognize is the real issue. The criticized seldom lack knowledge of their weaknesses and flaws. What they lack is a commitment to the critic's value. No one can change a person who is unwilling to change. Not even fear of death by cancer will stop the smoker who is unwilling to change. People don't change people. People change themselves or are changed by the Holy Ghost.

What toxics often don't understand, and what we need to understand in order to avoid becoming toxic, is that all we can really do in our relationships is try to show others a better way; we need to educate. This doesn't mean to force, though. The word *education* comes from the word *educe,* meaning "to draw forth." True education is that which is drawn from within the person. Change can be encouraged. It can be brought forth by enticing, by inspiring, by rewarding, and by loving. Again, most people do not lack knowledge of their need to change; what they lack is the inspiration to change.

Continued criticism leads to rebellion and stubbornness. It breeds contempt for the critic. Defiance, justification, and excuses will abound, but behavior will not change. It engages the giver and receiver of criticism in an adversarial relationship with no winner and two losers. All of the external criticism, job loss, or family humiliation will not substitute for a decision which can only be made on the inside. We learn this from Belinda's story:

Belinda the Critiholic

Belinda was a very hard worker. She gave 110 percent all the time. She had high expectations of herself and others. She had no time for anything unproductive. Her whole value system revolved around her work ethic. Few could match her, stride for stride. She was generous and dependable. She received great praise at work from her employers. She had been advanced several times on merit alone. Her replacements were not able to accomplish as much work as she accomplished. Extra workers were hired. Belinda took her work home and came in nights, worked weekends, or did whatever else the job required. She was a workaholic. From her perspective, she was a hard worker, dependable, and reliable. To her family, husband, and friends, she was out of balance.

But because Belinda gave much of herself and expected others to do the same, all of her relationships were strained. Few wanted her help if it obligated them to return it in kind. She was not sought out, and yet she worked hard to please.

The problem with Belinda was her tongue. She had no tolerance for the lazy. The slow were only endured. Belinda honestly felt that she was entitled to be critical of others. Her hard-working efforts gave her the right to be judgmental of others less committed. She felt that she did not need their permission to be critical. As a mother, a wife, and a sister in her own family, she found herself alienated and isolated. Not one wanted to be around her. She was devastated and deeply hurt. Not only was she frustrated by their lack of commitment to her work ethic, but their rejection of her seemed unwarranted. She felt unappreciated. After all she had done and continued to do, why would she be treated with such aversion?

The issue in Belinda's story is not about being a workaholic. It is about being a "critiholic." Granted, she had issues with overdoing it at work, but her main problem was bringing that same drive to all her relationships. She pushed everyone to work as hard as she did, and ended up pushing others away. Her other problem—or, rather, another extension of her controlling problem—was that her demands were often unwarranted and always unsolicited. People started avoiding her because they didn't want the criticism, yet she forced it on them anyway. By not seeking the permission of others before she criticized them, she violated the fundamental tenet of relationships, which says, "Common consent is the basis of all healthy relationships." Mutual agreement is a key principle.

Parents, employers, and those in authority can get away with criticizing those they command for a while. However, if common consent is not achieved at some point, their relationships will fall apart. Usually, the one criticized will exit first. Children will leave home, desperate to get away from the critical parent. Employees will change jobs or quit. The spouses will flee. The commanded will avoid the commander.

The perfectionist, the control freak, and the critiholic who give themselves permission to criticize without receiving the permission of the one criticized are a law unto themselves. Eventually, they will be left alone. They will be frustrated. They will live a life of regret and complaint, a life of what should have been. They will feel unappreciated and puzzled at their loved ones' reaction to their "helpful" criticism. Do they change? Maybe. Mostly they continue to give themselves permission to be "constructively critical." Those who refuse to see the toxicity of their nature will instead offer themselves the self-righteous comfort of the Toxic's Creed:

Toxic's Creed

Give me your emotionally poor, your hypercriticized hungry for acceptance, your fearful, low-self-esteemed huddled masses yearning to breathe free and be loved. I will constructively criticize them into being emotionally rich, self-actualized, filled to the eyelids with self-confidence. They will brim with love for themselves and others. No longer will they be huddled masses yearning to breathe free. This I will do. I will point out their areas of needed improvement. I will focus on their weaknesses. I will shine the light of truth on the unacceptable. I will concentrate on the flaw and remove their blemishes. All I need are willing subjects who can see the wisdom of my counsel.

DEALING WITH THE TOXIC PERSONALITY

Understanding toxicity is helpful, but will only take us so far in these relationships. What we must do now is learn to deal with the toxic person. Sharon's story is a good illustration of where to begin.

Redefining Enough

Sharon wanted to be loved. She wanted her husband, Aaron, to be happy. One of her dearly held values was a peaceful home where everyone was kind and people got along with each other. To Sharon, this meant that one sacrificed what one wanted for the greater good. No matter how hard Sharon tried, however, she was unable to accomplish her dream.

Aaron was constantly criticizing Sharon. She couldn't try hard enough. Not matter what she did, it didn't quite measure up to Aaron's expectations. Sharon was convinced that if she tried harder, then her efforts would be enough for Aaron. Sharon was a codependent who felt responsible to make Aaron happy. She could not do it, but she kept trying. She just wanted affection, acceptance, and appreciation for trying and for accomplishing what she did. She wanted no more or less. Sharon, however, kept coming for her approval to a "toxic source"—her unhappy and "never-pleased" husband, Aaron.

When I talked to Sharon, we started immediately on a program where she accepted responsibility only for her own happiness and unhappiness. I explained to Sharon, "You are not responsible for Aaron's happiness, or unhappiness. That is his choice. You are hereby released from trying to make him happy. If he is unhappy, that is his choice.

"For the purpose of our discussion, I want you to think about a goal as something over which you have control. It depends solely upon you. A wish, Sharon, is an expectation that depends upon others for its fulfillment. According to this definition, is making Aaron happy a goal or a wish?"

"It's a wish," she said.

"Is making yourself happy a goal or a wish?"

"It's a goal, because it depends upon me," she responded.

"Is getting acceptance, affection, appreciation, and love from Aaron a goal or a wish?"

"It's a wish," she said dejectedly.

"Sharon, it is your own expectations that are setting you up for failure. They are based on a false premise that if you are good enough, you will receive acceptance. All your frustration comes from these unmet expectations. You are going to a dry well for water, and no matter how many trips you take to the well, your expectation for water is never going to be met. Aaron is a dry well. You have 100 percent control over being a loving person. That's a worthy goal. You have no control over being loved by others. That's a wish.

"If you choose to stay in this relationship with Aaron, you will have to change the rules of engagement. You will need to establish a new set of goals which truly depend upon your doing what you can. It is up to you, Sharon, to take control of your happiness and commit to one objective—to become your highest and best self. You have your own natural resources, your own gifts, talents, and abilities to accomplish this task. Your expectations must be reasonable and within your sphere of control. Do not depend upon Aaron for your acceptance.

"Sharon, let's go over some ground rules which will allow you to stay married to Aaron and to survive a toxic personality:

"Become emotionally healthy yourself. This means that you accept responsibility for being a happy person, or an unhappy person, and for your behavior. You own it. You do not need to make Aaron happy. You cannot, even if he agreed. He alone is responsible for his happiness and unhappiness. It's his choice. It's your choice to take control of your life and to forgive yourself for your past. You must also make your own plan to become a higher and better self, independent of Aaron or of anyone else. Regardless of the past, you have positive choices in the present. Do not trade happiness for pity or sympathy. It's a poor trade. Many do it everyday. It is a cop-out. Give yourself permission to be emotionally healthy.

"Define your own standard of excellence. In other words, define what is enough for you. Do not let other people set the parameters of what a good mother is, what a good wife is, what a good person is. Let go of the expectation of measuring up to their definition, their wants, their needs, their expectations. The way to release yourself is to stop trying to please them in order to be loved by them. Codependents find it hard to let go of wanting to please others and frequently wind up becoming enablers.

"Let others accept responsibility for their own happiness. As long as you act in such a way that gives them the impression that you have the power to make them happy or unhappy, why should they accept responsibility for their life? When things go wrong, they will blame you. It's your fault. 'You should have . . .' or 'shouldn't have . . .' 'You need to . . .' or 'didn't need to . . .' 'You ought to have . . .' or 'ought not to have . . .' They will transfer to you the responsibility for their unhappiness if you let them. It's so easy for others to blame you for their lack of happiness. That is what toxic people do.

"Live to your own definition of enough. You can at least please yourself. If your expectation is pleasing others, you have no control over doing so, because the toxic personality will keep redefining the standard in such a way that you can never measure up. The thing to keep in mind about toxic people is that you are darned if you do or darned if you don't. They are going to be frustrated with you, regardless of your behavior. You cannot be governed by their frustration. Most toxic people use their frustration with others as one of their tools of manipulation, of control, of intimidation. Toxic people have endless lists of expectations. Just as you get close to doing everything on the list, Aaron will change the list. He can never let you 'be enough.'

"Sharon, when you see the insanity of this treadmill, you will come to realize that toxic people are 'crazy makers.' They drive you crazy trying to please them. The crazier your life becomes, the more in control they become, and because you are going crazy, the focus can be on your aberrant behavior. You are the one out of your mind, and they are the ones who are justified. Most toxic people were raised that way in their families. They were never enough as individuals, as children, as siblings, so the accusation of not measuring up or not being enough, the trailing barbs, constant criticism, and the blame-fixing are all normal for them."

If Sharon chooses to stay in this relationship with toxic Aaron, she will have ample opportunity to practice the art of receiving his criticisms. In addition, she will need to set up her own goals for improvement, wherein the judge and jury of her performance is herself. She already knows what the verdict will be for anything she does as judged by Aaron. It won't be enough for him! But it will be enough for Sharon. At last, Sharon can succeed. The rules of the game cannot be changed arbitrarily. The boundaries cannot be shifted. There will be a chance for success if Sharon takes control of her own mental health and sets her own standards of excellence.

The solution for Sharon is to commit to becoming her highest and best self and to embark upon a solo course to becoming emotionally healthy. Sharon committed to apply the rules she learned for surviving a toxic personality. Armed with new determination and a fresh writing pad, she was ready to deal with Aaron's complaints.

One of Aaron's main complaints was about Sharon's housekeeping. Aaron's standard of housekeeping as stated to me was, "I'm reasonable. I just want a clean house." The unstated, unrealistic expectation by Aaron was, "Anything less than perfection will be criticized."

Sharon's standard of housekeeping was, "I'm reasonable. The house is clean, but not clutter-free. I like to keep some of my projects out where I can see them. It reminds me of what I need and want to do with them."

Sharon reviewed Aaron's criticism, set her ego aside, and determined that it was not reasonable to have several projects out in the open all the time. After thinking about it and talking it over with one of her friends, she came up with a plan to obtain some orange boxes, label them, and place her different projects in them. She decided she would keep only one project out at a time. The other undertakings would have to be stored and rotated. This now became Sharon's personal standard of excellence.

Aaron's actual words when he found out about Sharon's plans to put her projects in orange boxes and store them were, "That's great. I'm really proud of you, but why don't you put all the projects in boxes and only take out the one you want while you are working on it, and then put it away again?" Notice the trailing barb.

If Sharon's expectation was to please Aaron, she would be disappointed by his response. In Aaron's mind, Sharon's solution was a step in the right direction, but it "wasn't quite good enough."

I told her, "It will take time and practice to free yourself from feeling disappointed with Aaron's responses."

Sharon asked me, "How am I supposed to respond to a trailing barb?"

"Why don't you smile when he gives you a trailing barb and say in your heart, 'That's Aaron.' Your verbal reaction to Aaron could choose to focus on the positive part of his statement. You could say, 'I'm glad you were proud of me. Frankly, I'm proud of myself, and I feel good about it.'

"Don't respond to the negative trailing barb. Ignore it. When you choose to comment on it, you are reinforcing its worth. If he won't let it go and continues to fuss and fume over the one project you have out at a time, acknowledge his frustration and continued criticism by saying, 'I'm sorry you're still frustrated over my one project being out, but it's just the price you pay for being married to a wonderful person like me!' Your resolve must be firm and consistent. If you waffle or give in, you will only encourage his criticism."

Another area of expectation for Aaron was about Sharon's level of education. Aaron had remarked, "I think Sharon needs to get a bachelor's degree. It will make her more marketable if something happens to me. Also, women who are college educated are more interesting to talk to."

Sharon's response was, "I don't want to take the time to go back to college right now. I want to be a wife and a mother. I'd rather increase your insurance or look at some other options."

Sharon reviewed Aaron's criticisms and set her ego aside to evaluate his concern. "Education is important and it would make me a better self if I were to expand my mind. I have time to do something, but I don't have the time or the will to be a full-time student." Sharon pondered her options. She visited with some friends and family. She bounced some ideas off them to see if she was being reasonable. Finally, she explored her proposal with Aaron, the toxic, whom she knew in advance would not find her solution "good enough." This time it was not his acceptance she sought; she just wanted to inform him of the options she could support.

Sharon set her own standard, her own goal. She decided that she would like to be a trained real estate agent and was committed to going to school to become one. This would give her a career she could rely upon if needed. Also, she could work at her own pace.

Aaron's actual statement was, "You never do what I want you to do. Why can't you just once do it my way?"

Her answer to Aaron's question was this: "Because you are toxic, Aaron. Even if I were to sacrifice my total identity to what you think I should, need, and ought to be, I would still not be enough. You would still be dissatisfied with me, and both of us would be miserable. I can't be responsible for your happiness or your unhappiness, Aaron. I'm trying really hard to be responsible for my own happiness. That's why I can't do it your way. I can only do what I can do."

I shared with Sharon the story found in the Gospels about a woman who knelt at Jesus' feet. She washed his feet with her tears and dried them with the hairs of her head. She had a very costly alabaster box of ointment. Judas Iscariot upbraided her for wasting this resource, worth more than a man's wages for three hundred days. The Savior rebuked Judas with the following words: "Let her alone; why trouble ye her? . . . *She hath done what she could*" (Mark 14:6, 8; John 12:1–4; italics added).

The Lord's standard of excellence is not perfection. It is to do what one can. I read these verses to Sharon, and she seemed to derive hope from them. This particular relationship improved because Sharon set her own standard. In doing so, she defined "enough" for herself and measured up to her own expectations of what a good person would do in her circumstances.

What Is the Loving Thing to Do?

Toxic people need love too, though they may not deserve our love based upon their conduct. That, again, is out of our control. Being a loving person is our choice to live life as a caring person, despite the other person's actions. We must evaluate the level of trust we can invest in each relationship. Remember, trust and love are two separate issues. Trust is the "fruit" of responsible behavior. Trust is a conditional investment. But loving is an unconditional investment. The loving thing to do with toxic people may be to stay as far away from them as we can. Being a loving person does not require us to be stupid or unguarded. It does not require us to trust those who have demonstrated that they are not worthy of our trust. Trust is about them. Loving is about what we choose to do.

Being a loving person and doing the "loving thing" will depend upon our ability to protect ourselves from toxic people. They are a dry well from which we cannot extract water. They are what they are. It does no good to become angry with them or to hate them. It will not change them. We must let go of the expectation we possess for them to be different than they are. Once we accept this reality, we can make a choice to love them. It is appropriate to mourn the loss of the relationship which "should have been." It is emotionally unhealthy to pretend the relationship is something it is not and may never be. Once we accept the way things are, have been, and will yet be, we have accepted the truth of our relationship with the toxic person. Let God be responsible to change the toxic heart.

A Way to Evaluate

Sometimes we are so close to the problem or so emotionally involved that we lose all sense of perspective. A helpful tool in evaluating what we should do when we don't know how to treat a toxic situation is to imagine that you are counseling your own child, who comes to you with the identical problem you face. Your child explains to you in precise detail the nature of his or her concerns. Next, your child asks, "What would you counsel me to do? I will not hold you accountable, because the decision is mine alone. I just want your honest opinion. Should I leave, or should I stay and work on it?"

Knowing what you know, how would you counsel your own child? My experience tells me that we will counsel our children with more objectivity than we will allow ourselves in the same situation. Sometimes we tolerate an intolerable situation that we would never ask one of our children to endure.

The toxic person we deal with may be our father or mother, our brother or sister, our son or daughter, our spouse, or an in-law. Some of these relationships are impossible to leave without completely withdrawing from the family. So we will have to devise a plan which will keep us emotionally safe during the interactions that normal living will thrust upon us. Consider this list as a part of your planning for dealing with toxic people.

CHECKLIST FOR PREPARING TO DEAL WITH TOXIC PERSONALITIES

- Affirm your desire to become your highest and best self.
- Let go of the expectation that the toxic person will give you what you want (acceptance, love, approval).
- Define your own standard of excellence.
- Define "enough" in specific terms.
- Ask yourself, "What would a good and loving person do?"
- Ask yourself, "How would I counsel my child in this exact circumstance?"
- Follow your own counsel.

The following story is about a woman, Sandy, who had to devise a plan to deal with her mother-in-law.

Sandy's Decision

Carol is a classic mother-in-law who feels that no one is good enough for her Jeff. She truly believes that Sandy seduced Jeff into marrying him and that Jeff married below his potential. Sandy has never felt accepted by Carol. They can make small talk with each other, but they both feel a cautious reserve. Carol is openly critical behind Sandy's back about her skills as a wife and mother. Sandy tolerates her mother-in-law but is deeply hurt by her statements, which find their way back to Sandy's ears via a sister-in-law and other family and mutual friends.

Jeff is aware of both his mother's disapproval and of Sandy's hostility because of it. He feels constantly torn between them. He feels that everything is a test of his loyalties as a son and a husband. He is always hearing his mother dropping hints about how he should insist that Sandy do a better job. Sandy is equally open in telling Jeff that his mother is critical, overbearing, and interfering. Sandy also expects Jeff to defend her by standing up to his mother and telling her to "butt out" of their lives.

Carol, the mother-in-law, is always buying gifts for Jeff and her grandchildren and her favorite daughters-in-law who bow to her wishes. Sandy feels that she can't compete and purposely discourages any relationship between Carol and her grandchildren as a form of punishment for Carol's inappropriate conduct.

What is the loving thing for Sandy to do with Carol, the toxic mother-in-law? First, Sandy has to be willing to commit to be her highest and best self in this situation. She needs to let go of the expectation that she will ever be enough for Carol. Next, Sandy needs to set her own standard of excellence and acceptance as a wife, mother, and daughter-in-law.

Sandy decided that she would invite Carol over for dinner once a month with the family. She felt it would be a good idea to organize, with the other daughters-in-law, a surprise birthday party for Carol. Sandy agreed to a number of things that were reasonable, not because Carol deserved it or because she was looking for any approval from Carol, but because Sandy was a good person. She imagined how she would counsel her own daughter in an identical situation and then followed her own counsel. But what else would be the loving thing to do?

I counseled Sandy to let Carol have her own "lousy" or "good" relationship with her son Jeff and with her grandchildren. I advised her to ignore Carol's critical comments by saying to herself and others, "That's Carol," and nothing more. The catty thing to do would have been to criticize her mother-in-law and speak ill of her to Jeff and others, constantly pointing out her flaws and shortcomings. The loving thing to do would be to ignore the mother-in-law's caustic comments and behavior and to encourage a healthy relationship with Jeff and the grandchildren.

I advised her further, "Sandy, do not force Jeff to choose between you and his mother. You would only be resented for doing so. Rise above ever speaking ill of Carol to Jeff. His mother will not change, and Jeff cannot change her. Don't expect Jeff to defend you or to stand up to his mother. Let him define for himself his relationship as a son."

Sandy also hated going over to Carol's home because Carol would spend the whole time doting on Jeff. She would wait on him hand and foot. No wonder Jeff enjoyed going over to his mother's. She did the same for the grandchildren but expected Sandy to work in the kitchen or join with her in waiting upon the rest of the family. Sandy would complain all the way there and back in the car, and while they were in Carol's home Sandy would bristle with quiet frustration. Jeff and the kids had a better time when Sandy did not go along.

I suggested that the loving thing for Sandy to do was to go and have a good attitude, but if she could not, then to stay home and do something she would like to do. "Send them off to Carol's with a smile and receive them back with gladness. Don't sulk or pout or play the role of a martyr. In this way, you remain in control of your life and avoid setting up unnecessary competition with Carol.

"Sandy, focus on being your own person and meeting your own standard of a good wife and mother and even a good daughter-in-law. This is the loving thing to do. All human relationships are composed of two people. You can only be one-half of any relationship to which you are a party. In a nontoxic relationship, you can enjoy emotional closeness and both give and receive loving behavior. In a toxic relationship, you can still be a loving person, but you must protect yourself by drawing boundaries with which you are comfortable.

"Define for yourself a one-sided program where you are willing to gift unconditional acts of kindness. Do this, not because Carol 'deserves' it, but because you are a loving person. To act in this manner fulfills the Lord's invitation."

Everyone wants to love and be loved. It has already been established that being loved by others is a wish—a worthwhile wish, but out of our control. Being a loving person is a goal within our grasp. Focusing on being a loving person can bring internal peace and the power of self-mastery. And perhaps more importantly, we will become more Christlike. Jesus taught:

> Ye have heard that it hath been said, Thou shalt *love* thy neighbour, and hate thine enemy. But I say unto you, *Love* your

enemies, bless them that curse you, do good to them that hate you, and pray for them which despitefully use you, and persecute you; that ye may be the children of your Father which is in heaven: for he maketh his sun to rise on the evil and on the good, and sendeth rain on the just and on the unjust. For if ye love them which love you, what reward have ye? Do not even the publicans the same? And if ye salute your brethren only, what do ye more than others? Do not even the publicans so? Be ye therefore perfect, even as your Father which is in heaven is perfect. (Matt. 5:43–48; italics added)

This particular scripture requires the disciple of Christ to live a higher law. It is the law of love. It is consistent with "the greatest revelation that God has ever given to man." Toxic people are wonderful guinea pigs upon which the Christian ideal can be practiced. They *are* "your enemy." They do "curse you," "hate you," and "despitefully use you." This wonderful scripture concludes by saying, "Be ye therefore perfect, even as your Father which is in heaven is perfect."

In this context, being perfect is not about being obedient. It is about being loving. These verses talk about becoming a loving person. The intent of the scripture is to say, "Be ye therefore perfect [in loving], even as your Father which is in heaven is perfect [in loving]." This brings the discussion about giving and receiving criticism in the Lord's own way full circle. It is not about finding fault. It is about loving! It is about surviving as a disciple of Christ in a telestial world. It's about living in the world, but not being a part of the world. It is not an "eye for an eye" and a "tooth for a tooth," for very soon we would all be blind and toothless. It's about living in the real world and applying the principles of righteousness. It's about calling upon the powers of heaven. It's finding out that there is power in living the gospel of Jesus Christ.

Assignment for Chapter 12

1. You will find toxic people at home, at work, and at play. These are people who are critical of you, and no matter how hard you try to please them, they will still be critical of you. By definition, a toxic individual is one that will not give you the unconditional love, acceptance, affection, approval, and recognition that you feel you deserve. Therefore, your assignment is to define for yourself how much you are willing to do for the toxic person. If you let him or her define the standards of your performance, you will find that it is never enough. Therefore, you must define "enough." For example, how many times in a week are you going to call or see this person, and what part of his or her criticism are you willing to act upon?

CHAPTER 13

A NEW BEGINNING

Frequently, when people learn of the art of giving and receiving criticism, they will ask, "Where was this information when I needed it thirty years ago?"

My answer is, "It's never too late for a new beginning." Jesus Christ demonstrated the power of loving words. There are children and grandchildren, friends and neighbors who are starving for the want of kind words.

Jesus Christ demonstrated the power of loving words and warned of the danger of words that defile. He reminded us that "those things which proceed out of the mouth come forth from the heart; and they defile the man" (Matt. 15:18). Jesus instructed the Prophet Joseph, that "that which doth not edify is not of God, and is darkness" (D&C 50:23). Paul urged disciples in all ages, "Let no corrupt communication proceed out of your mouth, but that which is good to the use of edifying" (Eph. 4:29).

Modern-day prophets reiterate the timeless message of the need for loving words. President Thomas S. Monson has repeatedly borne a fervent testimony to the importance of giving loving words and of speaking kindly one to another. He has lived his life and walked the Savior's path with this mantra: "Our opportunities to give of ourselves are indeed limitless but they are also perishable. There are hearts to gladden. There are kind words to say" (*Ensign,* December 2003, 2).

So passionately does this prophet of God feel about the importance of "kind words" that he quoted the entire hymn "Let Us Oft Speak Kind Words."

Let us oft speak kind words to each to other
At home or where'er we may be;
Like the warblings of birds on the heather,
The tones will be welcome and free.

They'll gladden the heart that's repining,
Give courage and hope from above,
And where the dark clouds hide the shining,
Let in the bright sunlight of love.

Like the sunbeams of morn on the mountains,
The soul they awake to good cheer;
Like the murmur of cool, pleasant fountains,
They fall in sweet cadences near.

Let's oft, then, in kindly toned voices,
Our mutual friendship renew,
Till heart meets with heart and rejoices
In friendship that ever is true.

Oh, the kind words we give shall in memory live
And sunshine forever impart.
Let us oft speak kind words to each other;
Kind words are sweet tones of the heart.
(*Hymns,* no. 232)

On another occasion President Monson admonished, "Let us take heed of his [Paul's] wise counsel, 'Be thou an example of the believers, in word, in conversation' (1 Tim. 4:12)," making reference to the Lord's counsel, "Cease to contend one with another; cease to speak evil one of another. . . . And let your words tend to edifying one another" (D&C 136:23–24).

President Monson went on to say, "Consider the observation of Mary Boyson Wall, who celebrated her 105th birthday a few years ago. She married Don Harvey Wall in the Salt Lake Temple in 1913. They celebrated their 81st wedding anniversary shortly before Don died at age 103. In a *Church News* article she attributed longevity in life and in their marriage to speaking kind words. She said, 'I think that helped us through because we tried to help each other and not say unkind words to each other'" (*Ensign,* May 2000, 52).

Neither you nor I will pass through this life without tribulation. There will be those who will love you and those who will take advantage of you. Sometimes the same person will do both. We are here upon this earth to gain experience. We are also here to give love and encouragement to others. How much we could help and lift each other if we would only learn to love one another! It would make this life easier and more fulfilling and bring us all closer to living with God in the next.

God's work is to help us become our highest and best selves. Joseph Smith taught, "It is not all to be comprehended in this world; it will be a great work to learn our salvation and exaltation even beyond the grave" (*Teachings of the Prophet Joseph Smith,* 348). There are only two choices for man: to act and to react. We can choose to be like our Heavenly Father and help others become better, or we can choose to react to undesirable behavior by tearing others down through improper criticism. Because we can choose how we act, it is easier to act like a Christian than to react like one. Our reactions are our responses to how others treat us. If we are to act and react as Jesus, who marked the path and led the way, we will learn the art of giving and receiving criticism in the Lord's own way. The result will be a better, stronger, and more loving you. You will be empowered to love as Jesus loved, fulfilling His command: "What manner of men [and women] ought ye to be? Verily I say unto you, even as I am" (3 Ne. 27:27).

Dr. John Lewis Lund is a native of Olympia, Washington. After graduating from high school, he enrolled at Brigham Young University and began studying sociology. Shortly after that he left for two years to serve a mission to Mexico. He returned to BYU to complete a bachelor's degree in sociology and a master's degree in education. He pursued a second master's degree at the University of Washington in Seattle. It was there that he determined to study interpersonal relationships. His doctoral work at the University of Washington in interaction analysis produced a book entitled *Avoiding Emotional Divorce.* In 1972, Brigham Young University awarded him a doctorate degree in education.

Brother Lund has been employed as an educator for the Church Educational System since 1965. His assignments have taken him on a nearly forty-year journey throughout Washington, Idaho, California, and Utah. He has served as an institute of religion director adjacent to Utah State University, the University of Idaho, and the University of Washington. His last assignment was as an instructor at the institute of religion adjacent to the University of Utah.

Because of his expertise in interaction analysis and transactional analysis, he is a much sought after mediator in marriage and family relations. He served for five years in the state of Washington as a family court commissioner. Dr. Lund does not work as a mental health therapist in Utah, but he holds three certifications in Utah as an arbitrator, a mediator, and a negotiator working with the courts in domestic relations. He functions as a marriage educator and helps people to resolve conflicts in healthy ways. For the past three years, Dr. Lund has served at the request of both Governor Leavitt and Governor Walker as a commissioner on the Governor's Initiative for Marriage.

His Church service includes being a bishop in Olympia, Washington, a bishop in Moscow, Idaho, and a member of a stake presidency in Logan, Utah. He has served on several high councils, and he presently teaches a Sunday School class in Murray, Utah.

Brother Lund and his wife, Bonnie Gertsch, of Midway, Utah, are the parents of eight children: John Jay Lund, Robert Earl Lund, Heidi Savage, Kaari Smith, David Eric Lund, Kristi Lund, Chariti Carman, and Joseph Ammon Lund. They are the proud grandparents of sixteen grandchildren.